Day of Your Birth

by
Bernice Prill Grebner

Published by Grebner Books, Publisher
5137 North Montclair Ave. Peoria Heights, IL 61614

Graphics — Coventry Creative Graphics, Peoria, Illinois

Cover Design by Marjorie Grebner Welsch
Executed by M&D Printing, Henry, Illinois

Copyright by Bernice Prill Grebner — Grebner Books - 1990
No part of this book can be reproduced except by permission of the copyright owner.

Second Printing 1992

CONTENTS

	PAGE
Introduction	1
Prologue	2

Day of Your Birth

Aries	3
Taurus	18
Gemini	32
Cancer	46
Leo	61
Virgo	76
Libra	93
Scorpio	108
Sagittarius	124
Capricorn	140
Aquarius	154
Pisces	170

Year of Your Birth	187
Twenty-First Century Predictions	217, 218
Centuries	218
Conclusion (human interest stories)	220
Epilogue	223

Dedicated to

JEFFREY WILKEN SHAW
(the golden knight)

The Day of Your Birth

INTRODUCTION

Each day of the year has its own vibration and its own destiny in time. Even though each individual born on a given day in a given year has his or her own unique pattern of personality and character, there exists an overall destiny for all born on the same day, regardless of the year.

> Fades the light,
> And afar
> Goeth day, cometh night;
> And a star
> Leadeth all,
> Speedeth all
> To their rest.
>
> by Bret Harte

> The patient stars
> Lean from their lattices, content to wait.
> All is illusion till the morning bars
> Slip from the levels of the Eastern gate.
> Night is too young, O friend! day is too near;
> Wait for the day that maketh all things clear.
>
> by Bret Harte

Bret Harte lived from 1839 until 1902, was born on August 25th in Albany, N.Y. He was known for his very observant eye. His Sun and Mercury were both in Virgo, South Node in Pisces.

As we enter each Sun sign, the over-all tendency is the same, but each day during that sign's tenure is different. In other words, each day has its variances. I am not speaking of arising each day at 7 a.m. or having lunch each day at the same time; I'm talking about the varied experiences that happen differently each day, even though broadly speaking we may handle them in a particular sun sign fashion.

Bernice Prill Grebner
March, 1990

Prologue

Achievement Day by Day, by Day

With each setting of the sun, I review my day.

When I am satisfied I have done all things in that day to the best of my ability and with the fullest of my effort, I feel at peace and in control of my life and destiny.

The greatest things in life seem to begin with a subtle hunch, that if followed turns into a major achievement. The best opportunities in life usually are those which do not hit us over the head but those that come like whispers. We need to be in constant awareness of these ideas that come softly because we are not always going to get them loud and clear.

Life Begins With A Day!

Jeffrey Wilken Shaw						February, 1990

The Day of Your Birth

ARIES
MARCH 21-APRIL 19

Aries means I AM. It denotes action, courage, arrogance. Aries people can be self-centered, easily bored, fearless and impulsive. It is a positive and masculine sign. Positive and masculine means electric, going after what is desired rather than waiting. It indicates the pioneer, the fighter. Aries is cardinal which means action and leadership. It is fire which stands for exuberance, moving forward and not standing still. Aries is ruled by Mars and is associated with the first house of the horoscope, the first house representing the physical body and the personality others initially see. Aries do not easily put themselves in others' shoes. Aries rules the head of the physical body. The zodiacal symbol is the Ram. The birthstone and the jewel is the diamond. Aries people love challenges, movement, action. They begin things but may not finish them, for they are leaders not followers. The flowers are the daisy or the sweetpea. The metal is iron.

Aries is symbolic of the sprouting seed shooting up out of the earth and synonymous with self.

Aries rules any sparkling, fiery substances. The tree for Aries is any tree that is thorny and filled with briars.

March 21

You who are born on this day will take on much of the Pisces influence which will give great compassion and sympathy making you a very unique Aries. It also gives aggressiveness and leadership qualities. Whatever trait is dominant all depends upon who is dealing with you at a given moment in time. Professional associates may see you as less considerate, more forceful than close personal relationships see you. This makes you a very complex personality. You have a tendency to want things to move along very quickly. Most of the time you see things in a big way, for it is not easy for you to deal with the small ideas or the insignificant. You can lose your patience and temper at one moment and at the next moment be very considerate. But you do not only lose your temper with others, you also berate yourself in bursts of temper.

Florenz Ziegfeld (1869)

_____

_____

March 22

You are very intuitive and have very special connections with the intangible forces around you. This position gives the ability to work very hard toward a goal no matter how much effort it takes. This is a master number and makes you a master builder so that it is very probable that you can achieve and execute some brilliant plan in your lifetime. This date gives the bearer the ability to make a dream concrete reality. You are a lover who knows how to love spiritually as well as physically thereby maintaining a balance between the two. This influence gives you high minded goals and objectives, career-wise and personal relationships. Above all a unique MASTER project will no doubt be achieved in your lifetime. You may be one of the few Aries who starts things but also finishes them.

Karl Malden (1914)

March 23

This position can bring you business success in life. There is a talent for vivid expression that brings great appeal to the masses. This talent for communication results in your being able to talk others into almost anything. It also gives a talent for broad and positive ideas that produces profit in a financial way or gives a leadership image. Even though you may be good with words and understand on an intellectual basis, there is also an underlying sympathetic nature that shows up when necessary. Another excellent part of this influence is the ability to organize in addition to bringing out the best of ideas and insights of others. Whatever is at hand you will be able to deal with it in most cases for this influence gives the ability to stick to something until positive success is achieved. You have a natural flair in understanding people which insures you choosing the right mate. You have instinctive talent where shopping is concerned for you know the value of items and know when and when not to buy. Overall you will more than likely have financial well being; not necessarily in the millionaire class but always adequate.

Joan Crawford (1908)

March 24

This position makes you very artistic and very good with the art of loving. If not an artist you have an appreciation of the arts. You are a natural born humanitarian and very active in that direction at some time in your life. The image you show the world is entirely different than the one you show your mate. The daring and positive leadership you show humanity is well able to accomplish much on a public basis. To a mate you love, there will be sensitive, loving, gentle caring. One of your real values in life is the art of being a loyal friend. You are charming and very diplomatic to the world outside and loyal to a loving mate. However, when someone fools you or hurts you in some way, you can show a very hard streak that surprises people.

Steve McQueen (1930)

March 25

You are very intuitive and psychic. Tolerance is second nature to you and you find no reason to hold grudges. Mostly you are a very happy and peaceful person. This day gives you the ability to be a leader for others come to you for advice. Your natural instinct with people, how they feel, what makes them tick can result in your being a counselor or diplomat. Somehow you know the key, the formula that can bring many opportunities to people others are not able to do. You are best when following your own instincts and listening to your own higher intuition. When you go against your own logic for yourself (and others) you get into trouble. You may have a talent for music, poetry, or anything where you are picking up that which seems too intangible to others. You can become a great spiritual leader, not only in the sense of your own correct instincts but helping others because they listen to you.

Elton John (1947)

March 26

You are impressed with music, poetry and the spiritual world. At one point you may feel the intense connection with the cosmic world and be satisfied being alone with your own thoughts and inspirations and at another time you allow loved ones to take advantage of you. You are a dual character which results in a complex combination of being aggressive and submissive. The times when you are submissive others will impose on you selfishly. The times when you are aggressive you will go after getting what you want. If you balance these two qualities and use them at the right times and places, your success in all areas of your life will be much more assured and permanent. You have a fine business talent especially when you follow your own instincts. Despite your sensitive feelings for others at times, you seek the perfect mate which can delay or deny a real romantic relationship. There is a quality of Neptune and Saturn on this day which can either result in making dreams concrete reality or the dreams will wipe out the realities or the realities will wipe out the dreams. It is up to you which way you want to use your fantastic instincts.

Duncan Hines (1880)

March 27

You can become an excellent leader or one who does his or her thing. There is an exuberance to your nature which makes you very acceptable in social circles. You have the ability to be humorous which is good therapy for yourself and well as others around you. Optimism is also part of your nature. Nothing is too large for you to tackle for you have a tendency to gamble with life. There is an adventurous streak to your nature. You can be very active and energetic and more than likely get things done quickly. When it comes to your vocation you should not work where limitations or restrictions are put on you for it is your nature to expand and broaden your interests. You can have much passion to your nature whether it is used for work or play. You have an objectivity that gives you the ability to step back for a broader look at something. It seemed assured that you can be most objective in a matter when you need be.

Sarah Vaughan (1924)

March 28

This influence makes you rather independent and very determined as to what you have to do. You have your own way of doing things and have a reputation for getting things done without delay. It may seem like you jump into things too quickly but in reality you think quickly and have actions all planned out beforehand. You are definitely not a carbon copy of anyone else and expect everyone else to be just as individualistic. Even though you may not be the world's greatest diplomat you do try to be fair in your own way. You may not always show it but you have areas of your life where you can be very emotional. You are ambitious, responsible, and can get ahead in the business world. This gives you the drive to start a business with innovative ideas which you couple with hard work.

Paul Whiteman (1891)

March 29

You possess a changeable nature much to the distress of those close to you. This influence gives you the ability to express yourself well for it is important to you to make your feelings known. You possess a drive to experience a variety of things for your nature is curious. Overall though you can adapt to any situation you find yourself. Your talents could lead to writing or any kind of communication work. You have psychic talent and the means to express your psychic impressions. You have a talent for tuning in on situations quickly. There is also a tendency to criticize but since you also criticize yourself at times, others go along with it. A talent for poetic, musical or dance expression is also innate to your nature. Impatience with others has to be overcome. Your adaptation to people and your immediate environment is so great that you become restless with those who cannot. You seek new worlds to conquer continually.

Eugene McCarthy (1916)

March 30

You appreciate beautiful surroundings, attractive people, art objects and you need these things around you to be at your best. You have a loving nature and can be very diplomatic for life has taught you when to speak and when to keep quiet. Your understanding of others attracts people to you. There is an expansiveness to your nature that keeps you from becoming discouraged. You can be very objective in your thinking that keeps you from going off the path of your destiny or from listening to the adverse advice of others. Your natural flair for philosophy shows in almost everything you do. You have a disdain for negative thinking and expressions.

You help others overcome negativity by a friendly, cheerful attitude so that you change them by example. Part of the destiny of this day is to make conditions around you more harmonious.

Warren Beatty (1937)

March 31

The important thing to you in life is more than material well being for you have some little voice deep inside of you that knows money just does not bring happiness that spiritual development does. There is somewhat of the mysterious in you for you can be very secretive. Even though money is not your main aim in life you seem to attract all that you need. This is the spiritual law to those that believe, that they have enough of life's substance to protect and provide. Others seem to come to you for assurance and wisdom. Wisdom comes from your mouth with the right words although at times you do not know where the words come from. It is as if you are a vehicle for a higher spiritual source. Above all else you remain an optimistic person. There may be a time when a special sacrifice is expected of you but you will be capable of meeting it. This position can also lead to a leadership position with some religious or spiritual group.

Johann Sebastian Bach (1685)

April 1

This influence represents leadership and initiative. Born on this day makes you very adaptable and flexible to life's new experiences. You have a talent for communication with others that your natal Aries Sun position may not give you all by itself. There is a tendency for you to want to be alone at times and this is as it should be as long as it isn't carried too far. However, your need to communicate will bring you back quite naturally to the area of people. Your talents can also make you a leader of ideas in a group or bring involvement in any innovative constructive projects or causes. This position gives you a great deal of creative talent in most areas of your life. You face your obligations even though your tendency, at times, may be to stop in mid-stream. You usually do not succumb to the temptation to leave something before its completion. You know when to enjoy yourself and when you need to dedicate yourself to the job at hand. You also have the innate ability to choose work that you enjoy; therefore, this couples the combination of pleasure and vocation in a very successful teaming.

Debbie Reynolds (1932)

April 2

Love is most important to you and as a result it brings you into a special closeness with those you love. With those loved ones you give a quiet kind of understanding as well as special spoken expressions when necessary. You possess a genuine caring for those you come in contact and coupled with your ability to share and be generous makes you a well liked person in your group of associates, personal as well as business. You will always be happy because it is your nature to be so. You have a certain sensitivity where other people's emotional needs are concerned. Learning early in your life the value of cooperation, you remain ahead of most others in pursuance of your perfection. This sense of cooperation gives the ability to make inferiors feel superior, dealing with all people with diplomacy and grace. You may also be able to do two things at once which will result in your greater accomplishments in life than the average person can attain. Your need of a congenial companion in life is paramount to your greater feeling of joy and well being.

Alec Guinness (1914)

April 3

You have poetic imagination. By that I do not necessarily mean you are a poet who writes verse but someone who has imagination, dreams, visions and musical or artistic attunement. Because there is a certain streak of reality to your nature, you can go far in one of the creative arts, the practical idealist. You have a talent of foresight (looking into the future) and a certain optimism that will always make you ultimately successful. Psychic ability can also be your forte if you develop its expression. It seems very important that you should develop your intuitive and predictive talents for you could be very successful with it. There is also a certain nobility to your nature. However, your foresighted talent can make you easily bored with daily mundane existence so that once in a while you go off on an adventurous escapade. In many other ways this makes you mysterious for people will think they really know you, but soon most discover there is much more about you that will always remain hidden. You need a certain detachment to be at your best, a freedom to do your thing and follow your own star.

Marlon Brando (1924)

April 4

As with all the days under the Sun sign Aries, there is leadership with original ideas. This particular day gives a talent for organizing. It gives ambition, the vision, the right procedure of carrying things out, and the foresight to see the finished product. You born on this day are so sure of this vision and your methods that you will not let anyone stir you from your destined path whether their opinions go along with yours or not. You can be idealistic in regard to a mate and will not settle for less so it may take you a little longer to acquire the proper relationship. Along with these other attributes is the ability to attract money, simply because you always have the idea that will do it. Your ideas are very unique but also very workable. Eventually you can attract power with your ideas and the money at your disposal. In many instances even though you are seemingly very practical and realistic you are also somewhat of a maverick.

Arthur Murray (1895)

April 5

You have a great understanding of a multitude of intellectual subjects which you can give a discourse on at a moment's notice. However, you must not get so impatient with those who do not have your intellectual understanding, which you sometimes do. You have a certain impatience with delays and detours. Nothing seems to go forward as fast as you would like. You, also have a talent for enjoying your friends but you must watch so that fun, games and laughter do not take away energy and concentration and time from your ultimate destiny with humanitarian causes. You attract people to you because they view you as being strong, alert and very alive to life. Because of your strength and enthusiasm with things is the reason your power can accomplish so much for the whole of mankind especially if you gear yourself to more selfless expression and action. You have so much energy that if directed towards whatever you want to attain, nothing is impossible to you. Above all, there exists in you a powerful talent for expression in writing or any other form of communication. You may have a voice and much activity in community affairs where you can be a power of great influence.

Bette Davis (1908)

April 6

This position gives you the ability to see both sides of a question which will ultimately make you realize that you have a fine balance between energy and ideas. This influence gives you a fearless drive to start new things, put them into action, get them going and then let others take over what you have initiated leaving you free to go on to other things. You have a very creative mind and usually attract companions of like qualities. Your efforts to criticize others usually falls on willing ears because your approach is one that accents the positive qualities along with finding faults; thereby through this very special talent you do make them think. You could make an excellent leader in educational fields. Though not necessarily adventurous you can take off on a little adventure now and again. However, you are mostly geared for the comforts of a well endowed home which has to be a place of harmony and beauty. You have a talent for artistic expression and should activate this artistic talent into a form of some kind even if only for your own amusement and therapy.

Harry Houdini (1874)

April 7

This position helps you to respond to a more cosmic and universal set of values. There exists within you a talent for the mystical which causes the need for isolated meditation at times. You are probably a mystery to your friends and close associates, which makes them stand in awe at times. There is a very spiritual side to your nature and you seem to have some kind of higher spiritual contact which gives you an overall peace to your daily life. You have a great deal of tolerance for an Aries and you need to watch the tendency for self sacrifice where others are concerned. In this regard you may deny your own wishes and pleasures to please others. Follow your OWN spiritual directions for you have great insight and would do well in a leadership position in the spiritual field either as an instructor or directly in the ministerial side of it. Never get into the mood of self pity but instead do something creative like writing poetry, music, or the perfection of your occult or psychic skills. In other words, get into something bigger than yourself, inspiring others who have greater problems than you do. Find someone with a greater difficulty and get involved with it but naturally not to the point of becoming a crutch. It will be a lesson for you as well as the one you help. The artistic expression of some kind can be used for relaxation and rejuvenation for yourself when you get hyped up or pushed down. Both helping someone else and artistic expression can get you out of any self pitying mood or depression you may get into at times, as we all do.

James Garner (1928)

April 8

With this influence you are very explosive in many ways having a temper, but this same influence used wisely can give you great enthusiasms with what you do. However, just as often your exuberance works in positive ways for you can talk others in or out of anything. One way or another you will have your way because you do have a winning personality. You will first try to influence others through smiles and charm but if that doesn't work then the temper will make its appearance, or you may just walk away in boredom. Those close to you never know. Taken on a higher level this influence can give you an innate talent for philosophy and abstract thinking. You can become interested in organizing not only business ventures but helping neighbors, brothers, sisters or friends organizing their affairs. You do not intrude on their affairs but help them on their level. If you can stick to something long enough without getting bored, this talent of yours can bring financial as well as vocational success and a measure of fame. It is all up to you. In many ways you have foresight; thereby leading to success quite naturally without much effort. As a child you can have wisdom beyond your years.

Sonja Henie (1912)

The Day of Your Birth

April 9

You have a great deal of practicality but underneath this practical nature lies a personality that desires to be a maverick. At various times in your life you may shock those around you with some unexpected actions. All in all you are able to enjoy the little things in life to the fullest. There is a great deal of understanding to your nature and somewhat of the counselor comes out with your friends and immediate associates. You are solid, refined, and gentle so in the end you should be compensated for your fine nature with much happiness. You may tend to finish what other people start which makes you a very unique Aries indeed. You possess a great deal of global knowledge that you share with others easily if they show any signs of interest in world affairs. Even though you are very interested in world affairs, you do stay close to your own domestic base.

Paul Robeson (1898)

_____

_____

April 10

You are very adaptable to any situation that comes up in your life whether positive or negative. This influence of this day gives you the ability to communicate and be at one with your friends, neighbors or with whomever you come into daily contact. It does not matter anyone's social position, up or down, everyone to you is human and deserves equal consideration. However, underneath all this affability there is a stubborn streak in you that leads to your getting exactly what you want from life. Any obstacle that may stand in your way, to you, is only a temporary delay and only makes you more determined than ever. Life is a challenge to you and achievements are most important. You have the ability to use your words and expressions to such advantage that you can make everyone believe exactly what you want them to believe when necessary for your greater good as well as theirs. Above all, you make others feel comfortable in your presence. You can become a leader in community affairs or within any organization for humanitarian causes initiating many of your own ideas for the common good. This is true when you are at your best.

Omar Sharif (1932)

_____

_____

April 11

You have a cosmic connection and many times you may seem to be listening to the beat of a different drummer. This influence gives you a psychic sense that if used and developed could make you very successful in the spiritual field not only in popularity but in the humanitarian sense of contributing something of value even for future generations. There is a refinement to your nature and a strong sense of social grace. Because of this even though you may be a little different, you are probably very popular in your social world. You have a great deal of diplomacy and for this reason can do well in the business world. You have a fine taste for fashionable and beautiful clothing and could use this talent for designing or decorating. However, you must watch the tendency to spend too freely on valuable and expensive beautiful things; that is, unless you have the money to do so. If you balance your spending with saving and investing, you will be well set not only for present status but with your future.

Oleg Cassini (1913)

April 12

There is a sense of mystery about you. Most people may think they know you but they may not. However, you can be gregarious when you want to be. You are sensitive, artistic, idealistic and very perceptive to the moods and feelings of others. Yours is an understanding and sympathetic heart. There is great enthusiasm to your nature and once you accept something you can go through any sacrifice necessary. You can be intuitive where your mate's needs are concerned. There is a certain cosmic attunement this position gives which makes you seem to be way off somewhere in the clouds at times. When you examine a project or pick up on a person, you get to the center for you have the ability to understand more than just surface appearances. This can make you a valuable asset for any large or small corporation.

Henry Clay (1777)

April 13

You use a lot of energy and drive for achievements in the vocational world. You go for this desired ambition regardless of what you have to do to get it. At the same time, however, you generally get along well with the people around you in this drive for achievements which is no small task. You are blunt at times which surprises those close to you personally. You know what you are doing at every minute even though those around you may be dismayed. There ia a part of you that can be rather stingy with your finances and this tendency to be tight will be challenged at some point in your life uncovering a streak of generosity to your nature. Those around you will never really know whether you are going to be generous or stingy. You are an idea person and once your ideas are executed can bring very excellent results. Those you take into your personal world will be those who you enjoy very much and with whom you can be yourself in every way. However, they are going to be a very select few perhaps tested by you first. Dedication to a career and generosity are the special characteristic you MUST ENDEAVOR TO PERFECT.

Thomas Jefferson (1743)

April 14

You possess an enthusiastic view of life and are optimistic when others cannot see a reason for optimism. This gives you great magnetism with people most of the time, but at other times your great adventurous spirit repels people. You do have a serious side to your nature, a side most others do not see. There is also a very sensitive feeling nature in you where and when you can be hurt. Even though you can be disappointed at times through delays or neglects from others you do not let on to those around you. You have a talent for entertaining and the dramatic arts. It would be excellent for you to get into one of these arts even if just for your own benefit as you need some kind of self expressive project to catch the overflow of your exuberant nature. You have a strong need for some kind of self expression and/or a cause that is bigger than you are, a cause where most of your energy and natural flare can extend itself. When you rise to achievements for humanity in general you can become great.

Loretta Lynn (1932)

April 15

You can be a leader or an executive of some kind if you so choose to develop yourself in this area. You are an idea person and are usually the one who starts things for others to take up and finish. You are more than likely interested in material things or those things that relate to the physical world including sex. Spiritual and inspirational things do not interest you as much unless other aspects in your astrological or numerological chart say otherwise. This doesn't mean you are not spiritual; it simply means it does not take priority in your life at least not early in your life. People like you for you can be very amiable but they may not be sure how long your exuberance and friendly attitude will last. Love for a mate means a lot to you and when you find such a mate he or she can be the inspiration you need to fulfill the promise of your destiny. Yours seems to be the destiny of starting with an idea, putting it into practice and then letting others take the ball. You can express yourself well when the enthusiasm is nigh; but when the enthusiasm is low you may not say a word.

Elizabeth Montgomery (1933)

April 16

Universal concepts mean a lot to you and you have strong original traits to your nature that causes you to stand out in a group. Because you have positive mental concepts, you will be able to succeed at almost anything you try. You are very spiritual and somewhat mysterious to others. Others may think they know you because of your great versatility and charm but most of them will not really know you. You are capable of being a leader or one of the sheep depending upon how you size up the possibilities in the very beginning of the situation. You seem to be a natural philosopher and usually know just how to play the game. In the beginning you instinctively know the odds of a given situation and in the end it is proven to you as well as others your odds were correct. You have a talent for the psychic, music, dancing, or any of the other poetic arts. You seem to be in touch with the intangibles of life but in a more realistic and balanced way which shows up more and more the older you get. This makes you quite an integrated person. You will be attracted to a strong spiritual love, but a love that also can exist exceptionally well in the daily mundane world.

Charlie Chaplin (1889)

The Day of Your Birth

April 17

This position enables you to form very objective conclusions which results in a very balanced nature on your part. You deal with the outer world as efficiently as your inner personal world. You have a great deal of integrity in dealing with your career which when coupled with your talent of not letting others lean on you can bring great achievement. When it comes to your spiritual values you have a broader view than mere convention. Philosophy on a larger scale comes naturally to you. You see yourself and those around you in a more holistic manner. You have a more complete nature, giving each part of you its due. There is a generosity to your personality so you give love as well as material things. Your requirement is for honesty in love and when you receive that as well as being able to give it, your happiness is assured. Whenever the chips are down in your life you always have the ability to step back, take an objective look and act upon that objective decision. Difficulties only pivot you to another level of advancement.

William Holden (1918)

April 18

This influence makes you home oriented. You may also have great sensitivity toward your family members. You love your family and are interested in your heritage and family tree. You have a talent for dealing with people in the sense that you pick up on their needs; therefore, you usually attain business success for you know what to provide and what will go over. You have a deep understanding of the human condition and would do well in another field of helping those limited and suffering in some way. You are not necessarily gregarious or caught up in crowds but prefer to do your own thing and perhaps, need to be alone at times, meditating, regenerating yourself to the higher cosmic force. You need a harmonious marriage or your health suffers. Most of your life you will have a steady income that will provide comfort and protection. You may not necessarily be a millionaire because deep down you may not want the responsibility of that much money.

Leopold Stokowski (1882)   Clarence Elmer Prill (my brother)

April 19

You are very expressive and curious. Intellectual pursuits may be your forte and because of this you can reach great achievement in any field. The doors are always open to you because of your KNOW HOW with words. You know how to express yourself with business and romance. You are a multiple personality, having just what it takes to deal with any kind of situation that crosses your path. You are aggressive when you have to be, tolerant when you have to be and so on through life's varied experiences. This influence also makes you self confident for you know just what to do at the right time. Be sure you acquire a mate who has your same kind of know how or one who is just as worthy in most areas as you are; otherwise you will be most unhappy and uninspired. You need a mate with whom you can express yourself and visa versa. This is a day that combines Aries and Taurus which makes you a more complex but integrated person.

Dudley Moore (1935)

_____

_____

TAURUS
April 20 to May 20

Taurus means I HAVE. It is stability, stubborn determination, reliability. Taurus people are steadfast, practical, patient and enduring above and beyond average. They are money conscious and sometimes lazy. Taurus are slow (unlike Aries who are fast) but finish what they start. They love the good life, food, luxuries, drink, etc. However, they are the builders and can accumulate a lot of the world's resources. Taurus have fixed opinions and are unchangeable with their habits. The symbol of Taurus is The Bull. Their ruling planet is Venus. It is feminine, magnetic, fixed, and the earth element. Their birthstone is the sapphire. The flowers are the hawthorn, or Lilly of the Valley. The metal for Taurus is copper.

Taurus rules all substances that reflect and show high polish. The tree for Taurus is any tree that is a fruit tree.

Author's Note: The additional quotations on the next page are in honor of my grandfather, the 1st generation astrologer. I hail you wherever you are grandfather and thank you. Grandfather is in another world now since he passed from this life many years ago but he is long remembered for his foresight.

The Day of Your Birth

"For the errors of others a wise man corrects his own.."
—Publius Syrus

"Nothing is so infectious as example."
—Charles Kingsley

And because TAURUS is so sensuous this lovingly fits them.

When one finally sees, hears, and takes into one's heart the image of the beloved, he is at peace in love and has it forever.

The following quotation from the Bible also fits Taurus—

"Let us hold fast the confession of our hope without wavering."
-Heb. 10:23

"And run with patience to the fight set before us."
—Heb. 12:01

April 20

You have a very loving nature with a very strong consciousness of responsibility and loyalty towards loved ones. Some people enjoy having loved ones do things for them, but you enjoy thoroughly doing for and giving to loved ones. Activity in your home with those you love, whether family or friends, give you much pleasure. You can have artistic talent, singing, painting pictures, or designing. You, no doubt, have a fine command of the artistic world whether with performance or historical and current facts about the artistic and creative world. Once you accept a project you finish it no matter how much effort it takes on your part. You will give a lot of love and never count the cost. Your ability to love others survives anything they may do which can be your noblest characteristic of all.

Ryan O'Neal (1941)

_____

_____

April 21

You are interested in the world around you and have an intellectual grasp of the world at large. There is somewhat of the poet in your nature which can give you an interest in all the arts. You have great foresight and even though, at times, you get moody, it doesn't last long for your exuberant spirit gets you out of it quickly with your great sense of humor. If you desire something you can make long range planning in order to get it and you are capable of making any sacrifice necessary in your steps to achieve it. At the same time you have a poetic nature you can also possess great optimism and humor. This combination is unbeatable; especially coupled with your Taurus durability. Enthusiasm, wide interests, idealism and mystery surround you. There is a great spirituality to your nature that could take you into the religious field or some similar spiritual area.

Queen Elizabeth II of England (1926)

April 22

You have a strong sense of the universal to your nature. However, while you are practical and realistic in a business sense, your drive and ideas seem to be very creative. This makes you capable of leadership positions in whatever you do. You are not easily fooled in any situation whether business or personal. You seem to realize that a higher power takes care of the final justice with us humans so that if you do favors and little acts of kindness, you seem to know instinctively that a higher power will give you just rewards. You also realize that this reward doesn't have to come from the person for which you do the favor. Business or some public endeavor is your forte. If friends and associates do right by you, your appreciation is above average. Above and beyond all your kindness is a very strong individuality resulting in your being a leader, not a follower.

Glen Campbell (1938)

April 23

You have a touch of the humanitarian in your nature. You can communicate with others giving true understanding which makes you welcome in any family circle or social group. You can be a little impatient at times but in your overall attitude you accept what is and do the best you can at the moment. You can be very active and are most apt to act upon ideas and follow through on what you tell others you will do. Your intellect is very high and you continue to improve your knowledge of things as you progress through life. You could be a writer or one who can teach others.

The Day of Your Birth

One thing you may have to learn is to adjust your moods so you are not so unpredictable to those close to you.

Shirley Temple Black (1928)

April 24

You are someone with whom others like to associate. You are pleasant, sociable and considerate. People seem to like you instantly for there is a warmth and harmony about you that comes across easily. You may have artistic talent of some kind for you like to create that which is beautiful. You can be emotional but not to the extent you forget to be practical. You have a well balanced nature and seem to know the right values with life. You are a good organizer, especially with your finances and your time. There is something about you that causes others to cooperate with you without effort on your part for they seem to instinctively know you are very capable even before they know anything about you.

Shirley MacLaine (1934)

April 25

The influence this day brings is to make you either very emotional and high strung or it can give great psychic ability. There should be a tendency developed where you rise above little non-essential things that arouse your emotions and concentrate on using your emotional difficulties as pivots to a higher level of thinking and feeling. There is much hidden potential within you. You can at other times be described as an iceberg, only a small portion of yourself showing. This results in making you a very complex person to say the least. There is nothing you can't do once you set your mind to it. This influence can either make you a great builder or very destructive. It's up to you. You are a natural born psychologist and also have a very persuasive quality to your powers of communication. This position can be emotional or can give you great strength of endurance and unlimited talent amounting to heroism. As I said before you are a complex person.

Al Pacino (1940)

April 26

You have a jovial nature which attracts a large group of friends and acquaintances. You usually have a good time with whatever you do. When you have a good time, you see to it others have a good time also. But when work and responsibility calls, you can get just as involved. This combination of fun and duty in balance makes for a successful teaming of talent and a well balanced and happy existence in life. Another side of you just as easily can pursue the intellectual path, take a walk alone, go to the theater all by yourself. I would say this makes you a well balanced person. This position gives you a lot of noble bearing and a great drive for being the best you can be. You also have talent if you desire to be an executive in the business world.

Carol Burnett (1934)

April 27

This influence lends itself to the material world; and because of this great effort should be made to balance it with meditation, prayer and spiritual development. In some ways this makes for conflicts but not to the point you lose your stability. You also possess a certain stubborn quality which means you must make an effort to let others have their way of thinking even if it disagrees with yours. You are clever as well as strong so in dealing with others use your clever mind instead of trying to over power others with your strength of will. Use your power in a more subtle manner. You may have a tendency to brood over a hurt making of yourself at times a self styled martyr. Learn to put yourself in the other person's shoes.

Ulysses S. Grant (1822)

April 28

You have a way of expressing yourself that is very convincing and because you are able to influence others in such an easy manner you achieve your goals much faster than most others. There is a certain exuberance to your personality and an exciting childlike quality that endears you to those who come in contact with you. There is an artistic flair to your personality whereby you find beauty wherever you go. There is a sense of drama to

The Day of Your Birth

your lifestyle which makes you colorful and responsive. You can be a pioneer or some type of self styled leader. Others appreciate your ability to give them advise on financial matters or vocational matters. You should get involved with the dramatic arts, if not for a vocation for a hobby.

Ann Margaret (1941)

April 29

There is a cosmic influence to this number and as a result you seem to listen to the beat of a different drummer than most people. You have a great command of wisdom coupled with great psychic talent. Your talent for philosphy and wisdom makes you capable of perceiving the truth in most things. Love is one of every human being's greatest needs but especially yours, giving and receiving in balance. However, do not read things into the statements and actions of lovers that may not have been intended. You will usually attract understanding mates. You also possess a measure of peace that takes you a long way in life.

William Randolph Hearst (1863)

April 30

You are rather idealistic and at times poetic. There is also a certain mystery to your nature which makes you not easily understood or known. The influence with this day makes you interested in philosophy and the finer developments like music, books, classic and current theater. You possess a well rounded interest in life so that sports and physical exercise of all kinds also interest you. Sometimes, you have a tendency to overdo. You have the ability to sacrifice if need be and tend to become very spiritual as you progress through life. Don't procrastinate by putting off until tomorrow what you can do today. But all in all you have a tendency to be well balanced with work and play once you set up a schedule of timing with your daily, weekly and monthly events and responsibilities.

Cloris Leachman (1930)

May 1

You are more of a lover than a fighter. You know how to get along with others whatever the relationship. You should have a creative hobby; such as painting, music, poetry, or whatever helps release this excessive love you feel. Sometimes it can make you a little moody or dreamy, but if you have a creative release, which can also be some sport, it takes a more positive avenue of expression. Because you need so much love and affection you may overdo in your attendance and service to a loved one. This position can make you excel in the art of communication and, perhaps, to the point where you could be a writer. Most of the time you are optimistic and vibrant. You will keep on an even keel when you incorporate into your life many outside interests.

Pierre Teilhard de Chardin (1881)

May 2

The influence born on this day makes you very intuitive and wise. You seem to be able to tune into space itself and come up with very prophetic visions. However, on a personal level it makes you very secretive and private about your deep relationships. The good thing about you is you have patience and persistence which gives you the talent of being able to wait for something or to get through a difficult period with a minimum of discomfort. At certain times you may need to get off by yourself and meditate and contemplate. There is a calmness about you that is very therapeutic to others. Yours is an excellent talent for listening to people with whom you give an interchange of inspiration and hope. Whatever responsibility you have in your regular routine of life you can do so with a great deal of sacrifice, if necessary. You, also, may have an ability where music and poetry is concerned even if just in the appreciation of it.

Bing Crosby (1904)

May 3

You are a busy person who gets a lot accomplished. There is a strong talent for business with executive proficiency. You have a cleverness about you; whereby you can always figure out a way of doing something a better way that takes less time but also a way that can be more profitable financially.

The Day of Your Birth

This position also gives you a positive optimistic attitude with life. There is a sense of humor to your nature and coupled with your organizational ability causes you to go far with whatever you desire to accomplish. The self confidence with this influence quite naturally leads to leadership at some point in your life. You have a flair for philosophy which could result in some type of lecturing or writing on the subject. You possess an innate ability to be foresighted which could also extend itself to predictive tendencies.

Engelbert Humperdinck (singer) (1937)

May 4

Being able to understand others and identifying with others can make you somewhat of a humanitarian. There is a certain nobility and generosity of spirit about you that endears you to others. With all your objective understanding you have a practical side, too. If you are to be aware of something you need to watch about yourself it is not to allow yourself to become a crutch for others. Always keep the balance between your realistic, practical nature and your exuberance in helping others. There is great spirituality with this day's influence and a magnificent understanding of all objective and abstract truths. If you take this innate understanding of abstract knowledge to its full potential you could become successful in the writing or teaching fields. Don't allow yourself to get into a rut with people for your noble spirit may want to take on heavier burdens than is good for your own growth and freedom.

Francis Spellman (clergyman) (1889)

May 5

You are restless and may want to be on the move most of the time. There is a strong curious trend to your nature. You are very flexible for a Taurus and extremely magnetic. You project a vibration of enthusiasm and are definitely not boring. Moving fast makes you unusual for a Taurus and you no doubt get very impatient with slow moving people. You stay curious and interested in all that goes on around you no matter how old you get so in a way you may age physically but mentally you remain young. You have a talent for attracting people because of your entertaining ways. This position may give you a talent for communication in writing or speaking and as such you may end up in a leadership position in your community's affairs. You may also have an excellent singing voice.

Karl Marx (1818)

May 6

You have great intuition and a concept for the truth of our cosmic connections that is beyond average. There is a spiritual and religious trait within you that makes you somewhat fearless with your actions and quality of life. You have compassion, tolerance and a certain humility that attracts others to you. There is an artistic talent either dormant or active that is part of your nature. This position gives a strong tendency to favor your family and home life which gives you a great deal of happiness. One word that can describe you above all others is your great ability to show and give LOVE.

Sigmund Freud (1856) Rudolph Valentino (1895)

May 7

You possess an inner spirituality in addition to a seriousness that isn't apparent because your outer nature is exuberant, humorous and optimistic. You are philosophical and foresighted. This influence also gives you a generous spirit and no matter the background of your formative years, it gives a refinement with good manners and a certain social flair. Your greatest talent is your ability to understand and sympathize with others. Coupled with your social grace is your ability also to be satisfied with yourself and go off alone and meditate, rejuvenating yourself in communion with the spiritual force either through study or walking among nature.

Peter Ilyich Tchaikovsky (1840) Gary Cooper (1901)

May 8

If you use your creative ideas and talent and build something permanent and worthwhile as a foundation for others as well as yourself this can be a very potent position for success. If there is a difficulty in achieving this success it is your tendency to talk too much instead of taking action. This position means discipline with time and sometimes you do not face your duty when you waste time. Organize, break free to be your individual unique self instead of worrying about what others might think which can be only useless gossip on their part. You can work very hard once you set your mind to it. You can become a great asset to your community especially when you use your own creative ideas.

Harry S. Truman (1884)

May 9

You are a communicator and curious about almost everything. There is a variability to your nature that is exciting and interesting to others but you must watch the tendency to scatter yourself too thin. Also, you should not spend so much energy on matters of little or no importance. You may, at the time, think these matters are important but when you use the natural good objectivity with which you were born, you will realize the trivia of these little emotional sidetracks. Use your innate talent for objective judgment instead of exaggerations. A good field of endeavor for you could be writing, publishing, or any part of the field of communication. With this influence you can be balanced between the subjective and objective approach to life giving you a very integrated personality.

Albert Finney (actor) (1936)

May 10

Love is your forte. However, coupled with your ability to attract love is the ability to attract material comfort adding to your well being. You truly enjoy a full life, physical and spiritual. You have artistic talent like singing, painting, dancing. You have the ability for leadership because your methods are unique and original and easily followed and imitated by others. You are the one copied; not the copier. You have great talent for ideas, starting a project, but also carrying it through which gives you much satisfaction and many successes in life. A great talent of yours is your ability to see how a project will work out in the future. You love deeply and usually attract deep love in return. Another special talent is the dramatic arts for you can express yourself well and understand drama in all its aspects.

Fred Astaire (1899)

May 11

This influence makes you rather mysterious in many ways and somewhat of a spiritual mystic. You have a certain feel for things and you usually turn out to be right in the end. You are a person who is able to tune in on the secrets of life and the universe itself and for that reason you will seem to be able to hold a certain subtle control over people and experiences of life. This influence gives you the ability to get to the bottom and the center of things and people; whereby you can uncover motives, reasons others cannot seem to do. Compassion and a certain quiet tolerance is another part of your nature. This also gives you the ability to control your emotions and raise yourself up from any emotional problem or limitation.

Irving Berlin (1888)

May 12

You have executive ability and a social friendliness that insures popularity and success in whatever you choose to do. Mostly you are positive with life and exert an enthusiastic influence on the others around you. If you have a negative influence that appears at times it is a kind of "control over others" kind of situation. This position also gives you an objective view of life that makes you able to be quite happy with most things you do. You may not like to do some of the things you have to do, but regardless you will do these things because you have a fine sense of responsibility and discipline. You have a rather complex nature being able to successfully combine optimism, exuberance, nobility with this disciplined and responsible nature. You are also one of those rare people who can be a delight in a group but also have enough joy of life to be completely happy by yourself when the need arises.

Florence Nightingale (1820)

May 13

You are a "people person" with a lively interest in most all things. This position can make you a genuine humanitarian who not only espouses unity of all mankind but acts upon these beliefs. Needless to say you are good with friendships, always willing to help. There is a certain nobility about you and coupled with your ability to respond to your duty, you attract friends and associates in all walks of life and on every level who respect you to the fullest degree. You understand people and can always tune in on their real motives. You may allow your generosity to get the best of you sometimes which could end up in your having extravagant streaks. Above all, this number thirteen day can give you a real cosmic connection and real universal values.

Joe Louis (1914)   Stevie Wonder (1950)

May 14

You are rather head strong at times. You are very individualistic and start things you may not always finish. You may express yourself very well and have quite an influence over others in a leadership sense. You are a pioneer always ready to introduce that which is new and progressive. There is a spirit of adventure in your soul and because of this you do attract much in the area of romance. Yours can be determination in getting what you want from life or you can exhibit many stubborn qualities, stubborn qualities that may frustrate those around you. This day's influence gives you a talent for writing and speaking or any form of communication.

Bobby Darin (1936)

May 15

You are very cosmic and universal in your thinking and possess a very positive nature. You follow the beat of your own higher drummer rather than other people around you. There is no in the middle where you are concerned. It is either all or nothing. You have strong likes and dislikes. There is a quality of the intuitive and psychic in your nature. This position can make you generous and very objective in your outlook on life.

second nature to you and you may also have a poetic or musical inclination. Social affairs and entertaining others is all important to you.

James Mason (1909) Eddy Arnold (1918)

May 16

What exuberance you have. You are optimistic and very good at listening to others with complete understanding. You are a very strong and stable person. But even with your strength of character you are very human so that you have your rainy days like everyone else. The difference lies in your ability to rise above your problems and being able to look at them objectively. You are very intellectual and have a refined sense of what pleases you, not only with your personal relationships but with what entertains you in your leisure time. You no doubt much prefer the kind of entertainment that has a sense of class to it. With this day's influence you should possess a rare kind of foresight.

Liberace (1920)

May 17

You are very realistic and practical in your approach to life. There is strong determination in your nature and nothing stumps you for very long. In many ways you are a trouble shooter being able to solve any problem that comes your way. You have the ability to achieve great success since you have a strength that separates you from the weaklings of society. That which makes you unique is the strange combination of practicality and individualism. You believe in the right of each individual to be him or herself and will fight for that right whenever the situation confronts you. Because in most cases you are doing what you yourself feel compelled to do, you retain an optimistic and uncomplicated attitude with life. If you do get into a difficult and complex situation in life, you are realistic enough to get out of it or solve it for you fully understand that you yourself got into it in the first place and that you are the one to get out of it by rowing your own boat.

Archibald Cox (Lawyer) (1912)

The Day of Your Birth

May 18

Born on this day gives an influence that makes you good in the art of communication. Life works better for you if you get into some kind of communication field as a vocation where you can use some of this excessive verbal energy into something productive rather than idle chatter. You have a certain curiosity to your nature that makes you appealing to others for you show interest. You understand people well; especially when you are not caught up at the moment with self pity. The best thing you can do is to use your talent of perception to help others for you have a lot of natural insight. Also get into some sport where exercise can keep you fit in addition to balancing too much mental energy.

Margot Fonteyn (ballet dancer) (1919)

_____

_____

May 19

You are a lover; not a fighter. To be with a person you love in an intimate place where it is comfortable and peaceful is a gift from the heavens as far as you are concerned. You have artistic talent and it would be well for you to get into home decorating or fashion designing. You could be a leader in community affairs or have success in some business venture. People gravitate to you because you seem to have an understanding they need. You instinctively know how to bring out the best in people, but you realize everyone has human foibles. You can be a very strong person and one who would not easily be told what to do but because you are so diplomatic others may have to find this out the hard way.

Mike Wallace (1918)

_____

_____

May 20

You have a Taurus nature and somewhat of the Gemini for this influence is a dividing day known as the cusp. You have a very spiritual nature and while you may be talkative you do not reveal much of your personal life. If you do reveal intimate personal things it is to someone very close and someone you trust very much. This day's influence gives you a fine connection with the invisible forces whether this is poetry, music, dancing, or psychic talent. In this case we might say that the invisible forces are the muses. You can be tolerant and sympathetic for you feel a closeness to all living things and because of this you seem to get a greater spiritual satisfaction with life than most others do. Being able to love someone spiritually is another great part of your nature. Above all you should have some kind of poetic or musical expression even if it is just for your own amusement and satisfaction. You can be very mystical for you are in tune with the powers that be.

James Stewart (1908)   Cher (1946)

GEMINI
May 21 through June 21

The symbol for Gemini is The Twins. It is a dual sign and the ruling planet is Mercury. Gemini is a masculine sign and is positive and electric. It is Mutable Air. The key words for Gemini is I think. Gemini people are communicative, nervous, curious, and eager for life. They deal very effectively with their immediate environment and seem to prefer it over the FAR AWAY. They are subjective in their dealings with life. They know a little bit about a lot of things. They have the ability to have more than one thing going at the same time. In many ways they seem to retain a youthful outlook on life even into old age. This may be because they easily keep up with current fashion and musical and artistic trends. Gemini rules the lungs, arms, shoulders and nervous system. They have great versatility with the ability to see other people's point of view. They are adaptable and flexible. Gemini people have a fascination for romance, especially in the wordful expressions of it.

The jewel for Gemini is the Emerald and the aquamarine. Marble is also Gemini ruled. Gemini's flower is the rose and the honeysuckle. The metal is quicksilver or any flowing and veined substances. Gemini rules blues, violets, soft browns, and mixed colors.

The tree for Gemini is any kind of nut tree like walnut, filbert, or hazel.

May 21

One of your best traits is your desire for leadership in business and the ambition necessary to attain it. This position gives you the ability to organize and solve problems, any kind of problems. You get down to the basics of a situation and can master what you set out to do. You have original ideas and a sense of courage and fearlessness that automatically gets you before the public in some way. Learn to be diplomatic and cooperative for you may have the tendency to see only your own way. The financial side of your life should bring success and a sense of well being and satisfaction. You possess a great deal of instinctive knowledge even without cracking a book on any given subject.

Henri Rousseau (painter) (1844)   Raymond Burr (1917)

May 22

There is a cosmic vibration on your day. This influence gives you the tendency to follow the beat of a different drummer at times even though your spirit of cooperation with others is way above average. This can make you one of a kind person. You have a great deal of tolerance and compassion in your nature. In some ways you are very poetic and musical for your imagination and creative talent expresses itself well. When you love you have the ability to be sacrificial and very demonstrative. If there is a weakness it is your inclination to let others lead you; especially is this true when you care for them. Follow the more individualistic and creative part of your nature which is universally inspired. When you love, it is as natural to you as breathing to express it. However, sometimes you get into trouble with this tendency since most others are not as outgoing with their expressions of affection as you are. Do not change your nature to please others for we need people like you around to help the world show their proper feelings and affection.

Laurence Olivier (1907)

May 23

This influence gives you charm and warmth and coupled with your talent for exuberant expression leads to great popularity. You touch many people and because of your instant rapport most people call you friend although to you most of them may be merely acquaintances. This influence gives you the power to express humor mixed with those times when you are very serious. You possess a multitude of talents and it is important for you to realize that you must find a single direction for your talents in order to develop expertise in one direction. This does not mean that you must drop the other things, it simply means you must discipline yourself in your tendency to scatter. The tendency to scatter your interests simply results from your drive to experience all things. You could be successful in the writing field or some area where you are communicating with the public. In this way you can productively use your imaginative talent. You can be an expert in vocal expressions and unless you have other planetary influences in Sagittarius you must exert an effort to listen. Listening may not come as naturally to you as talking.

Joan Collins (1933)   Bernice Prill Grebner

May 24

Born on this day you possess a cosmic connection with the universal force. By this I mean you will follow the beat of a different drummer than the average person. You do your own thing most of the time. You are artistic and have a loving personality. You are psychic and intuitive. At times, even though you have a very spiritually attuned nature you may go off in emotional upsets that surprises the people around you since you will normally be very sensible. You can work very hard and can be counted on to do what you say you are going to do. Once you have set your mind to something, you usually attain it for you have more of a drive than most people realize. You will constantly pull little surprises during your lifetime that will keep things exciting. You will be a leader, even though at times it may not appear that you are a leader. You will learn how to be cooperative and because of this others will be taken off guard not seeing your inner independence.

Queen Victoria of England (1819)   Ludwig Duhs (author's grandfather)

May 25

You have a way of being outspoken and very good at expressing yourself in a very glib way. It is important that you do not hurt people with your truthful manner of saying it like it is. You also have the ability in the

The Day of Your Birth

opposite sense to express what people want to hear being able to captivate your audience easily with the sway of your words. You must try to achieve a happy balance between these two attributes. Use your talent in some type of writing or higher form of communication with the public as a whole rather than just one or two close friends. You love to travel and see the world and have the ability to relate to all manner of people. The thing to avoid is exhibiting your distaste for people who are not as fast with their intellect and expression as you are.

Beverly Sills (opera Singer) (1929)   Leslie Uggam's (1943)

May 26

You have the ability to form firm and sound foundations in everything you do. You have very high values with what you want from life. You have an instinctive knowledge where love is concerned and realize that you must get as much love as you give in order to experience full happiness. When you love someone you are very generous to them. Your family life means a great deal to you. One of the greatest of your talents is your ability to begin projects on a firm foundation. You, also, learn your lessons well from life and therefore move along the road of development much faster than others.

John Wayne (1907)

May 27

There is a restlessness to your nature at times that hides a very serious personality. All that is mysterious appeals to you from the mystic to the beauty of nature. Because of your very broad, but perhaps complex nature few really get to know the real you. You understand life in all its facets and also realize that everyone has a facade of some kind covering their true nature. In addition to your talent for the mystical things of life, the intangibles, you have the ability to express these insights into words or music. Ultimately you could develop a career as a great humanitarian.

Dashiell Hammett (writer) (1894)

May 28

You are a joyful person, always trying to spread happiness to those around you. There is some of the artist in you and what with your ability to organize and plan, could bring you great success. This influence makes you seek harmony around you and you do this by making others feel harmonious and at peace first and foremost. You could have a career in dealing with fashion, jewelry, home decorating and all things that require an artistic outlook. Another field of endeavor could be the counseling field where you can easily help others see and find themselves.

Ian Fleming (1908)

May 29

You are by nature peaceful and exude a calmness that attracts people to you. People instinctively know you will understand. You have artistic talent for you are very creative and imaginative. Your interest covers a lot of ground from gardening to classical music and you do everything exceptionally well. You are tolerant, compassionate and have a certain idealistic tendency. Because you are so idealistic, you are likely to have disappointments in life. Your nature is forgiving so you continue to move forward without remorse nor do you hold any grudge because you turn the other cheek in the true Christ spirit. In the end you win out over any adversary.

Bob Hope (1904)   John F. Kennedy (1917)
Marjorie Grebner Welsch

May 30

You are the executive type and can be a leader in the financial world. If you develop your leadership talent in this life, and because you are also honorable and honest, you can attract a large following. This position give you considerable talent for ideas in how to make money. You represent the achiever in your community; someone who gets things accomplished. Because you have the ability to get things done, others may take advantage of your exuberant and understanding nature and try to get you to do things for them. This can be carried too far to your disadvantage but also to the disadvantage of others simply because they may need to learn to do things for themselves. We do not really help others if we allow ourselves to become a crutch; thereby stunting their growth.

Howard Hawks (1896)

May 31

You like to do things in a large way. You are very understanding of the human condition. You like all things connected with the cultural aspects of life. In other words you have class. Because you have such broad and vast vision you may become a little intolerant of those who do not at times understand. Sometimes, it is like you have your foot on the gas peddle, raring to go but the car is not in drive yet. This influence makes you become impatient with time because you seem to instinctively feel you have so much to do. You could be a good writer or a communicator or teacher of philosophy, science, or any of the abstract studies. Fascination for distant places also has its appeal.

Joe Namath (1943)

June 1

This position can make you very psychic with a great tolerance and compassion for others. You have a quiet way of doing what you have to do each day and if that day calls for you having to make a sacrifice you do so without any hesitation or complaints. You are somewhat secretive and inclined to view the mystical life as an ideal you strive toward. This gives a potential for the ministry of some kind for you understand spiritual philosophies exceedingly well and are no doubt in touch with the cosmic force. If you follow your own intuition you are going to do all right with your world. Loved ones are important to you for they come first beyond anything else you deal with in life.

Andy Griffith (1926)   Marilyn Monroe (1926)

June 2

You have executive qualities which can make you successful in some kind of business that deals with fashion, jewelry, cosmetics, or hair styling. You can be emotional where loved ones are concerned but always have the ability to express your feelings with loved ones. This influence also makes you very perceptive where financial dealings are concerned. You just have a feel for the right thing to do in financial transactions. You are also very perceptive about people and seem to know instinctively when and if they are trying to deceive you. Therefore you most always have the advantage in a given relationship or major decision in your life. You love deeply but your love while deep and sure allows freedom for your loved ones to grow in their own right. You are not possessive. You generally refuse to allow anyone, including loved ones to use you wrongly. You always have the tendency to set the score straight.

Marquis de Sade (1740)   Johnny Weissmuller (1907)

June 3

This position gives you the drive to be a humanitarian in one way or another. It motivates you to do something about the suffering of others. Just be sure you do not let it encompass you to the point of allowing others to take advantage of you. You are a very active person and very sociable so that you are no doubt invited to many functions. It is best you work for yourself and get into some creative art projects. Literature, music and all higher mind subjects attract you. You are well read and have the ability to project yourself as a person of worth and fine breeding. Most of the time you are optimistic and humorous, but temper pops up occasionally that usually surprises people.

Tony Curtis (1925)

June 4

You are a person who starts things for others to finish. It seems to be your role in life to initiate the action others never get around to doing. In many ways, you have a fearless nature. In another sense, however, you are very durable, practical and determined. You get involved in a problem and have no rest until you solve it; however, once it is solved, you leave it to others

The Day of Your Birth

to take over for your enjoyment and satisfaction comes in the initial act of discovery or challenge. You have a great appreciation of Good Old Mother Earth and like nothing more than to plant flowers, a garden or be among all nature's creatures in the woods or forest.

Dennis Weaver (1924)

June 5

You possess an instinct for helping and directing others. There is a great amount of compassion to your nature, but not so much that you allow others to make of you a crutch. You seem to be in tune with the higher cosmic force and instinctively have the answers other people do not have. Many people, as a result, turn to you for an uplift for another one of your greatest talents is your ability to be entertaining, planning parties, games, etc. You seem to have a knack for helping people laugh. There is an uncanny strength about you that you seem to get from a higher spiritual source. You do a good job in whatever you do, fulfilling each day's work to the fullest so that at the end of the day work well done is your greatest compensation and satisfaction.

Jean-Paul Sartre (1905)

June 6

You are a most understanding person. Artistic talent can by your special forte. There is a tendency for you to scatter your efforts in too many directions and therefore you limit yourself. You possess a great intellect and it would be wise for you to direct this great intellect in one direction becoming a great authority in whatever field you direct it. Integrity, nobility and generosity is uppermost in your character. Your need to cooperate and have harmonious conditions around you may cause you not to speak your mind. However, in the end the over-all development of your efforts will be communication, give and take on an equal basis, saying it like it is but with ease and diplomacy.

Nathan Hale (1755)

June 7

This influence makes you capable of being a practical idealist. In other words, you possess the ability to dream and scheme and at the same time you seem to find a way of making the dreams a living reality. You are electric which comes across as a very magnetic electricity if that is possible. Perhaps, a better way of saying it is you seem to have the best of both qualities positive thrusts forward and a strong magnetism to pull to you. It does not take you long to become acquainted with strangers because you sense immediately the atmosphere of those around you and seem to know exactly what to say and do to attract them. You can be very perceptive leaning to the psychic world and the occult; however, most people may not know this side of your nature at first. You have power to communicate with nature and animals and all that is not apparent to most others. There is a tender compassionate side to your nature which helps you to understand suffering of others but with all this you are optimistic and bright with your outer personality. If you follow your instincts and couple them with your warm personality you should be able to reach any success you want from life.

Tom Jones (1940)

June 8

You are very talented in the art of conversation. This is quite a combination of practical business sense and the ability to communicate to all manner of people. You recognize an opportunity, seize it, and are not afraid to make spoken or written contact in order to begin action on it. You tackle what attracts you and because you are not afraid of looking like a fool, you tread where others fear to walk and end up in the front row of success. You are curious, continue to learn about all things that cross your path. There is a strong likelihood that you will not get into any vocation you do not like for you are most apt to get pleasure out of what you do; thereby compensating you not only financially but in every other way. This influence gives you a talent for mixing reality with your ideal, the practical idealist. This position can also give a talent for expression in one of the fine arts.

Frank Lloyd Wright (1869)

June 9

You love to be surrounded by things of beauty. You can be a person of refinement and culture. This is an excellent position for a person who can become a leader in cultural movement within the community. It gives an innate understanding of artistic accomplishments thereby making you capable of being a fine critic. Your whole dedication to life is love and beauty. You are innately a very happy person and can spread happiness to others just by being around them. You also have an instinct for diplomacy and the ability to counsel and direct others. As you get older you acquire more and more wisdom. Eventually you get quite a reputation in your community as the one others can turn to for good advise and understanding.

Czar Peter the Great of Prussia (1682)

June 10

You are mystical and have a fine sense of the occult and the intangible things of life. There is great idealism to your nature and at certain times in your life there may be struggles to combine the ideal with the practical realities of the twenty four hour a day life. The best possible way this can work is to be a practical idealist, working to make dreams and visions come true in the real world. At times you are aggressive and step out in front of others and fulfill a leadership position in society. You are a mystery to most people because there seems to be two natures within you and it is not always predictable which will take prominence. Take the advise of your spiritual nature and don't resist making the struggle for development of your higher self. Above all you are an idea person and cannot seem to control expressing your ideas or espousing a great cause.

Judy Garland (1922)   Prince Phillip (1921)

June 11

This position makes you capable of being an executive. It is possible that you can attract great success in the business world and thereby amass a lot of money. You possess a personal magnetism that seems to attract successful people who aid you in your personal achievements. All it takes on your part to meet these achievements is some effort and/or acceptance. This position seems to indicate the spiritual force is on your side so much that all you need do is turn the button to ON. If there is a negative side it can be success going to your head; thereby making you somewhat dominating. However, if you develop the spiritual side of your nature equally with the business and vocational side, success will be yours in most every area of your life without any problems. Above all, use your instincts for they are probably going to be correct for you. Lastly, it is important that you keep the physical, mental and spiritual sides of your nature in balance with each other.

Richard Strauss (composer) (1864)   Chad Everett (1936)

June 12

You can be a true humanitarian for you deeply understand the sorrows and difficulties others have. You are always ready to give a helping hand. It seems to be a big part of your road in life to play the role of the Great Knight or Great Lady but you also have a lighter side to your nature being able to enjoy life at a party, a sports event or whatever. You have the uncanny ability to enjoy what you are experiencing at the moment. You are well able to understand experiences and events as they really are and relate to them in a thoroughly correct way most of the time. You are truly of God for your greatest satisfaction comes in realizing that you are a big part of God's plan not only for yourself but others.

George Bush (vice president) (1924) (President)

June 13

Most teachers of cosmic knowledge interpret the 13th as a lucky day to be born. It is a vibration strangely connected to the cosmos. You people seem to be able to feel a higher vibration than most other mortals. This influence can make you a capable executive or leader of new movements. In many ways when you get involved in community affairs, whether social or business you are considered a miracle worker. You initiate ideas, get things rolling in expert fashion. You love family and friends alike and have an understanding not only of your own needs but the needs of those close to you. In many ways you have subjective objectivity or call it objective subjectivity (if there is such a thing). In other words you can deal with the things at hand, but at the same time see future events casting their shadows. This gives the unique ability to act in the present in a productive manner that insures the future.

Richard Thomas (actor) (1951)

June 14

You have many facets to your nature. One represents a practical, sensible image; and the other is humorous and cheerful especially when you take someone into your inner sanctum. There is no experience or situation in your life where you cannot call upon some hidden part of your nature to provide adequate action and understanding. You are aggressive when you have to be and as the modern expression goes, laid back if you have to be. You are expression itself, perhaps good at writing or any other kind of communication work. There is a spiritual side of your nature that gives faith as an underlying strength.

Harriet Beecher Stowe (1811)

June 15

You are naturally optimistic and exuberant. Naturally this makes you sought after as a companion. If anyone can withstand the hardships of life you can because you fully realize that in a manner of hours, or days things will turn around again. You inspire everyone you meet and generate an aura of exuberance that makes everyone you touch feel good. You have a well balanced nature that makes you sensible in every situation so that as a result others come to you for advise and counsel. There is also an artistic streak to your nature that if developed could bring you before the public in a very successful manner of expression. In other words you come across.

Edward Grieg (composer) (1843)

June 16

You are serious and practical most of the time. You face your responsibilities and duties in a dedicated manner. A certain sense of satisfaction comes when you do things well, as you usually do. If there is a difficulty with this position it can be not being able to delegate authority to others; thereby creating a situation of doing things others should be forced to do. Your home means a great deal to you and you no doubt spend a lot of time doing things in it. You have a mystical and psychic talent and if you follow your own perceptions you won't be wrong. In many ways you can be secretive; especially about the things that are important to you.

Stan Laurel (1895)   Erich Segal (writer) (1937)

June 17

This influence makes you quite a talkative person but this does not mean you cannot listen or be quiet when you want to be for you can. You are quite a talented person in the art of communication and quite astute at being able to act upon the mood of the moment. You love to see new places and learn new things so as a result your life will be variable and interesting. All about you one can sense a connection with the universe or cosmic force for you are different and unique. When you are quiet you seem to be tuning in with this force and renewing your energy, not only physical but mental and spiritual and when you are talkative a little of the universal values comes out on occasion. At least this is the finest of your talents.

Igor Stravinsky (1882)

June 18

You are a lover, not a fighter. This position gives you a talent for home decorating or any kind of beautification work. In many ways you are a humanitarian, always ready to help someone improve themselves or their situation in life. Above all, you adore trying to make others happy. There is a certain refinement to your nature that endears you to everyone who crosses your path, and as a result you inspire many people in your walk through life. Somehow, you get by with things many others are condemned for because your charm and magnetism has a way of attracting the good things in life including gifts and opportunities. If anyone is a fashion place, you are for this gives the potential for knowing just how to dress for every situation. But as I said before, you have a talent for love that supersedes everything else in your life.

Paul McCartney (1942)

June 19

This brings out a mystical influence to your nature. You have an innate way of understanding the occult and the nebulous. You are tolerant and compassionate above all. It is important to you to understand yourself and by understanding yourself you thoroughly understand others. Possessing great insight into people and outer events is one of your most precious talents. Either the appreciation or the performance of music can be another one of your finer talents. This gives the inclination to gamble with life at times for you seem to sense just the right chance to take at the correct point in time. If you have a problem in life it doesn't remain long for you have an uncanny ability to solve problems in the surest and quickest possible way.

Lou Gehrig (1903)   Duchess of Windsor (1896)

June 20

You have a business head on your shoulders and have a sense of what the public needs and desires are; therefore you can capitalize on this talent if you so choose. You are really organized and coupled with your vitality and energy get things done in fast gear. A lot of change and variety is necessary to you in order to keep the enthusiasm and exuberance alive. Activity excites you and seems to give you even more energy instead of depleting it. You are like an electric current for there is always more where that comes from. A leadership quality is one of your greatest talents, but even though leadership is an essential part of your nature, you can move over and let other lead when they have a good idea or two. In many ways you inspire others with your ability for self improvement but in other ways you can come across to others with too much self interest. You can argue for a point you believe in and have a frank and open way of expressing yourself.

Errol Flynn (1909)   Chet Atkins (1924)

June 21

This is a cusp day where the influence of Gemini and Cancer are in combination which makes for a complexity. There is a spirit of adventure in your nature. You are always ready to go anywhere, do anything in a split second of time. The big and broad view of life appeals to you and your imagination. Vivid ideas set you apart from others around you. Because of this, there is a certain detachment with others. In one sense you can represent a person who understands others and is always ready to play the humanitarian role, but in another sense you only let others get so close and no closer. In the long run you may only have one or two deep friendships who have stood the test of time. If you have difficulty it is that you have a tendency to procrastinate at times. While at other times you do things quickly. This again shows your complex nature; at times difficult to understand. At your best you can be a natural born philosopher if you work on it.

Martha Washington (1731)   Maureen Stapleton (1925)

CANCER
June 22 through July 22

The key phrase for Cancer is I feel. They can be sympathetic, moody, sensitive and touchy. They are interested in security, and family. They have a talent for being protective of those they love but are also easily hurt by loved ones. Outside of family and home life, they would do well in an occupation dealing with foods or some other profession that deals in home life staples. If they have a problem with their health, it could be the stomach. Other attributes are imagination and a certain tenacious quality.

Cancer is a feminine sign and this means magnetic, drawing situations and experiences to them rather than having to go out and beat the bushes down. They can also be very shy and sometimes very introverted and withdrawn.

The jewel for Cancer is the pearl or moonstone. Their flower is the larkspur or water lily. The metal for Cancer is silver. Cancer also rules soft, smooth substances. It is also interesting to note that Cancer rules palm trees.

Cancer is the sign of the home and the mother or any situation in life where nurturing of some kind is necessary.

The crab is a symbol for Cancer which means Cancer people hold on.

June 22

You are a person who has the best of two worlds at your fingertips. One side of your character is very solid, stable with family life and the other side of your character is progressive, creative, and a leader with ideas and innovative methods. You possess creative intelligence but at the same time are very compassionate and sympathetic. This is quite a combination and results in your being a very unique character to say the least. There is a possibility you possess great cosmic insight with the desire and ability to share and teach this knowledge and truth.

Kris Kristofferson (1936)

June 23

You can be talkative, expressive, and fun loving. However, there exists a restless part to your nature that may not be disciplined and directed until after you reach the age of thirty. You may have a talent for writing, either prose or poetry. You also have an instinct for the psychic, music and dancing. In many ways this indicates you following your own philosophies of life and trusting in your own judgment with continuing experiences proving you to be right. Once you direct your life to a definite purpose you can have remarkable success. This is true because you have a joyful spirit that makes you know how to laugh and have fun but it is also a spirit that can direct you into serious dedication to success if you work at it.

Duke of Windsor (1894)

June 24

You love life and people. You should direct some of your great consciousness of beauty into some artistic endeavor even if only for your own satisfaction and enjoyment. This sense of loving and appreciation sometimes covers up dissatisfaction and hurt you may suffer from others. You have a belief that accenting the positive will make it all right but that is not necessarily the case. You can suffer hurt but prefer not to burden others which isn't always wise since then you bottle it all inside. This isn't good for eventually it can affect your health. You are loyal to your family and home and work very hard to make the domestic scene the best it can be. There is generosity to your nature and an unyielding optimism which never lets you down. Unlike June 23 people, you are not likely to waste your time on trivial experiences or experiences just for the sake of pleasure. You are probably more selective in your choice of friendships than most others in your Cancer sign group.

Jack Dempsey (1895)

June 25

You have a practical nature,and are very conscientious of your responsibilities and duties in life. Your great satisfaction and joy comes in fulfilling your daily obligations with a job well done. In comparison with most others around you, you can accomplish much in a given period of time. It is the story of the tortoise and the hare for with steady progress, without delays or pauses, you seem to get there first. Others may seem to go faster at times, but in the end that is just an illusion. You are able to express your solid views and are always able to constructively advise those in trouble. You possess great feelings of responsibility for your relatives and would do anything to help them when they are in need of your assistance.

Carly Simon (1945)

June 26

You like to move about and cover a lot of ground with your curious nature. You can talk about any subject under the sun. Organizing people and projects is one of your special talents. Getting rather vocal about things

The Day of Your Birth

you believe in is another one of your attributes. Along with this ability to communicate with people is a strong business head which assures success. You could make quite a speaker who projects him or herself well with original ideas that would automatically attract a following. You enjoy people and know no strangers, and as a result no doubt accumulate quite a group of friends and acquaintances. This position can also make you successful in business because you possess an instinct with what people want in whatever field of life. People take to you right away, thus you get your point across without too much effort on your part.

Pearl S. Buck (1892) (writer & explorer)

June 27

Love is your world. You adore the artistic, the refined things that life can give you. You need to live in a beautiful and harmonious surrounding. You have a potential talent for home decorating. A combination of what is beautiful but still practicality is a strong instinct with you. You want to be beautiful and good to look at yourself but also prefer to have a mate who is also easy on the eyes. However, what you are and what you do is not just a china vase, there has to be a utilitarian value. You would do well to have an artistic outlet such as art, music, or any one of the finer arts. This kind of artistic hobby is an excellent release for your sensitive appreciative nature.

Hellen Keller (1880)   Captain Kangaroo (1927)

June 28

You are sensitive and perceptive. This influence makes you tolerant but you must be careful not to let your tolerant nature allow others to impose on you. You have a tendency to sacrifice yourself and your own feelings for others. Be sure you do not carry this concern for others too far. You have a talent for music whether it is performance of it or just appreciation. Music should be a part of each day. Music can calm you or it can excite you. The sensitivity that comes with the influence of this day can be either positive or negative depending upon how you set yourself to react. Therefore, your experiences can be as happy and as exuberant as you yourself program the mood in the beginning. Another positive side to your talent is the ability to have faith, faith in yourself and your future and perhaps, faith in those you love and touch with your deep caring.

Richard Rodgers (1902)

June 29

You are an organizer! There is a certain practicality to your nature but under that practical exterior lies a great mystical strength. You strive for both vocational success and financial success. Yours is not just vocational expertise but it has to have money with it. You are sharp, perceptive, and easily see through deceptive practices. This is why you are so good with people as a whole whether in business or personal. You know how to get value for money spent and seem to know instinctively a good thing when you see it. You are persistent with what you want, determined, and self confident most of the time, and as a result you do inspire others to grow and achieve with your excellent example.

Nelson Eddy (1901)

June 30

You have a lot of energy which you use not only in your own pursuits but in doing for others. Your effort with this should be achieving a balance between what you want and what you do for others. This influence makes you inclined to be somewhat of a humanitarian, and there is a lot of power that eventually can make you well known. Above all, you are a high minded person, interested in the pursuit of higher knowledge, music, and all the refined things of life. At some point in your life, foreign born people, or foreign affairs may become a great interest for you. Your foresight and objective impressions are quite a talent but be sure you do not force your impressions on others but just allow others to accept your impressions as is natural for them to do so, or not.

Lena Horne (1917)

The Day of Your Birth

July 1

There is a secretive part to your nature and because of this, few people really know you. You have quite a talent for business enterprise and can be a leader in that direction. You possess a great deal of self confidence and your apparent independence hides a very sensitive tolerant nature. With all your inner sensitivity you project a facade that shows the world you want your own way. Your drive for public success will stop at nothing to attain it. The important part of this is that your ideas always seem to be correct. You show your tolerant nature much more after you have found your secure and successful place in the world.

Leslie Caron (1931)

July 2

Your thinking and feeling world are much in balance in your life style. You are intellectual and use your reasoning power quite naturally but at the same time your feelings go out to others and their welfare. You have a good influence on others and seem to inspire others with your balanced outlook. There is a very energetic side to your nature with the ability to get things done. If you have a weakness it is your tendency to over-indulge in food, drink and sex. This is especially true if you are temporarily down emotionally or have been hurt. Use your fantastic insight for one of the creative arts, like music, poetry or dancing with which you can excel and also thereby control the emotional side to your nature.

Robert Sarnoff (broadcasting exec.) (1918)

July 3

You are a self starter. You may not always finish but you certainly are the pioneer in whatever you do. It all depends upon how much of yourself you actually put into what you are doing. This influence makes it easy for you to attract followers, those who so easily help you with your tasks whether vocational or personal. There is a certain charisma surrounding you that catches most everyone and everything in sight. There is much optimism in your nature that carries over to making a dull routine exciting. If something gets dull you find a new way of doing the same old job. You may, also, be the first one in your community or neighborhood who volunteers to tackle a project and at least get it rolling. You are no doubt the one in your family who says, "o.k. let's get at it." You are very intellectual and have an objective way of looking at things.

Pete Fountain (1930)

July 4

This position makes you very perceptive with an uncanny talent for tuning in on people and things around you. Idealism is your middle name. You possess vision, vision not only of the here and now world, but into the future. This results in your easy compassion with people and a tolerance for the mistakes not only with individual men and women but nations. A musical and poetic talent can show up if not early in your life it will be later in your life, but show up it will even if it is only a great appreciation of music, dancing, poetry, singing. You are poetic by nature, but this does not necessarily mean writing poetry but a strong appreciation of spiritual harmony for all people and a strong faith in the God Force. In other words being tuned in with the great super force that guides and protects us all.

Gina Lollobrigida (1928)

July 5

You have a very special talent at persuasion. It is very easy for you to influence others to your way of thinking. Most of the time your ideas are correct for you have foresight, being able to see the results of a given current action. This puts you in a success potential for writing, teaching, spiritual work and advancements for mankind. This is a talent you need to use well for the sake of humanity in general rather than just for some vain glory. The odds are that you will become involved in some type of higher mind study, whether scientific or spiritual which in your case is not separate. You have a mind that says we are all part of the whole, whereas we all have within us the instinct for the total truth where segregation does not exist.

P.T. Barnum (1810)

The Day of Your Birth

July 6

You are a hard worker, especially when you are really into something you care about. Your duties and responsibilities are important to you. You are a lover and are only a fighter when you are protecting loved ones against a danger of some kind. All artistic things delight you and you have a sense of all things cultural. Most of the time you are in the right place at the right time and this, quite naturally, results in success with whatever you are doing at the time. Whatever else you are you are dependable and can be depended upon in most every situation that confronts you. Abide by your own moral code and intellectual values and you cannot go wrong.

Merv Griffin (1925)

July 7

You are poetic, perceptive, possibly even musical and well able to express this talent in writing and/or entertainment fields. This position gives an easy instinct for tuning in on the intangible force all around us. You can express the inexpressible. By that 1 mean you can express those things others find hard to put into words. You also have a great talent for the spiritual world, whether in the ministry in religion or the spiritual world that refers to philosophy, astrology, psychic, or any other branch of the occult. You like to travel, see new and varied things and take an interest in everything around you. Being able to communicate in an ESP manner with animals and all other living things is another one of your potential talents.

Ringo Starr (1940)

July 8

You have a creative imagination either with writing or music. As a result it can bring actual cash profits for you. If you work on it you can achieve leadership in one of the artistic fields. Most of all you are a lover; not a fighter, except if someone hurts or touches something or someone you love in a negative way. You are in love with love itself. This is the reason you need use some of this excess for creative outlets for then you achieve balance with your affections and emotions. It is necessary for you to be surrounded by harmonious conditions. If too many conflicts occur in your everyday living, your health begins to suffer. Because you were born on this eight day, whatever talent you have can come to the successful attention of the public. When it comes to business opportunities it is well for you to follow your own hunches for your hunches can be very accurate and clear. When you are forced to follow someone else's hunches or ideas against your own, it doesn't seem to work out for you. You have a strong talent with money for there is a finely tuned instinct of what the public will accept and what will work. When it comes to those you are emotionally attached to, there is much responsibility you take in this direction so that you are not apt to shirk your duties toward your family or loved ones.

John D. Rockefeller (1839)

July 9

You have a talent for the psychic and the mystical. You are compassionate and have a remarkable ability for tuning in on human suffering and the heartache of others. You can be an idealist and a humanitarian with the potential to become well known if you work at it. You usually finish what you begin and have a very special universal and cosmic outlook on life. A great sense of freedom is a strong part of what you want for yourself and others. If there is anyone who is more thoroughly spiritually pure of heart it is you. Perhaps, your best expression would be the tremendous faith in the higher spiritual scheme of things. In other ways you can be somewhat secretive and a little mysterious to others. No matter what you say, there will be much you will not say. A need exists within you, to go off by yourself once in a while to recommunicate with the higher spiritual powers and seemingly get back on course with yourself. Your identification with others is so compassionate and tolerant that you may get pulled too closely to their suffering; hence the need to re-establish your own course of destiny. You never really lose your spiritual faith in life but there exists a need to refill your own cup at times. You are a complex person with a great desire for freedom but also with such compassion for all of the human race.

(1947)

The Day of Your Birth

July 10

This influence gives you a fine business talent. It also gives you a rather fearless quality in the pioneering sense. There is a natural tendency to feel some kind of cosmic destiny in relation to your experiences in life but also coupled with the ability to take courageous action to fulfill them. The discipline with self is very prominent with the result you can accomplish a great deal. You are responsible and serious with life and with whatever you do, personal or business. You do things others would not think of doing and as a result stand out in front of the pack. It is a very special combination of doing what you have to do, listening to your own directions and not listening to others telling you what to do if it doesn't sound right to you. In other words you do not copy them, they copy you. With this combination, GO FOR IT. The bottom line is public acceptance with whatever you do.

David Brinkley (news anchorman) (1920)

July 11

You are a person who may not be easy to understand for you seem to be operating on another wavelength than everyone else, or most everyone else. You have strong psychic power with the ability to zero in to all things of an intangible nature. Under a very disciplined surface is a person who is very sensitive and compassionate. You are also a person who can easily be hurt and this is the reason you do not always show how you feel and may hold back very strong feelings. You need harmonious conditions around you to be at your best. You cannot stand discord and if you get into a condition or situation in life where discord exists you should either resolve it into harmony or break away. On a positive level you can become a great humanitarian for you easily identify with the hurt others suffer. If you use your talent for some kind of artistic expression your strong sensitivity will not work so much on a negative level. You cannot understand why people have to hurt each other. When you are in a depressed or hurt phase you should exercise, take walks for exercise will reduce your depression like magic. This is true for all of us but especially people born on this day.

Yul Brynner (1920)

July 12

You are a person who seems more placid than you really are. In reality you are a very integrated person for you have just the right amount of aggressiveness to be able to handle life in all its facets. You are high-minded coupled with the ability to see reality. You do what must be done, work very hard when the need exists and take an adequate amount of leisure hours to dream or to play, but even play to you takes the form of some kind of productive hobby. You always have a dream, an ideal that inspires you in all phases of your life. You have a talent for leadership even if only among your friends and immediate associates. You always have an idea, are always willing to listen to others and share ideas, give and take. A home life is important to you, a place where you can be yourself in complete peace. It would be well for you to have an artistic hobby, such as writing, music, are poetry,crafts, etc.

Milton Berle (1908)

July 13

You have a quiet kind of spirituality, a spirituality that works in your everyday world not just on Sundays. You have insight and foresight that some would call psychic. It is a kind of practical foresight. Most of the time you are tolerant, compassionate but when pushed too far a burst of temper can show. You prefer the unruffled life where there is a more routine existence. You are very much in touch with the intangible forces of life. This is the reason you can lead a much quieter life than most people for you sense many things, many values beyond the material that others cannot tune in on. You can be in tune with nature and value life's silences as well as much activity and talk. There is a cosmic influence to this day and at times others around you will realize you may at times be marching to the beat of a different higher drummer.

Father Flanagan (clergyman) (1886)

July 14

Adventure and activity may be a big part of your life. You have a lively personality that magnetically draws others to you. You do not let any grass grow under your feet for you are usually always there when any first shot is fired. You are always in on the new things in vogue, whether a show, a person, a style, etc. Good judgment is part of your talent and also the ability to be objective about things is also uppermost. Love is important and you are always ready to gamble with love to the fullest. You have high values, and high ideals and are willing to give the ultimate expecting the ultimate in return. Because most people cannot measure up to these high standards, you are bound to have many hurts and disappointments before finding the right mate for you and also before you learn that you are only responsible for what you do under the sight of God and cannot be responsible for what you get back. Fear is not part of your vocabulary nor is it part of your life in any way. You are willing to gamble with the new, ready to gamble with the new phases of your life. Because of this you will grow a great deal in this lifetime, grow mentally and spiritually.

Gerald Ford (President) (1913)

July 15

Everything has to be solid for you. You are very creative and can possess many talents. Not only are you very talented, you have the ability to make constructive and productive use of any of your talents. You strive to achieve the highest for it is part of your nature to do the best that is within you. When you say something, you mean it. Others can depend upon you. Your word is as good as if it were already put into action. You are a master with all you do. Nothing is done half way. It is all or nothing. Life does not have any missing legs or missing links as far as you are concerned. You see to it that all things accomplished have good foundation to build upon and what you do or whatever personal relationship you get into is durable. What you need in return is a show of love and caring, and if you get that you are unbeatable. If you give love, quite naturally you expect love in return; love has to be mutual or you can have none of it. Yours is not sacrificial one sided love. Your key word is stability, and fifty-fifty.

Linda Ronstadt (1945)

July 16

Communication is your life blood. You move around a lot and because of your desire for change and excitement attract a lot of varied experiences in life. You like conversation, like to know what is going on in addition to learning about new things. This position gives you a positive approach to life, a positive approach that comes from a great inner faith. Because of your ability to communicate and your involvement in fun things, the the spiritual part of your nature may not be so obvious at first. As far as fun and games, sports, exercise, you may prefer to do these things with others rather than alone. You may also be artistic in some way and should also have a flair for the finer things of life. You are a social person with a great talent for being a good host or hostess. Get involved in some artistic expression like music, dancing, painting for in doing that you will have a beautiful outlet for your very creative soul.

Alexander the Great (356 B.C.)   Ginger Rogers (1911)

July 17

You possess a great sense of refinement. You can never do anything that would be in bad taste. You possess a great deal of generosity and consideration for others. Harmony has a lot to do with your philosophy of life. Most of the time you will always be kind and good natured. If you have a difficulty it is that you may not be discriminating enough with your choices. You take others at their word until proven otherwise. In one way this is a real asset but in another way you are naive and people soon learn they can take advantage of you. You have a strong business talent for you can create ideas that can work with the public.

James Cagney (1904)

July 18

The key influence for this day is your ability to make sacrifices. You have courage and the talent of seeing a vision of things to come on a social level. You have the uncanny way of seeing things casting their shadows on the horizon. This also represents courage of your convictions with the ability to take the lead to do something about your convictions and beliefs. You do what needs to be done at any given moment of time and will not be found doing something unnecessary or anything that wastes time. Visions mean something to you for it is as if you have a cosmic or divine connection.

Naturally you have a lot of faith and because you are willing to make sacrifices you get farther in the end than most others.

John Glenn 1921)

July 19

You have great business and executive talent. You have the potential to be a humanitarian yourself or you may become good friends with a person who is into social causes. You will attract many varied experiences in your lifetime resulting in the acquisition of a lot of knowledge and wisdom. This could give you leadership in some kind of spiritual work. One thing you have to watch is that you start things you may not finish. You will grow a great deal in this lifetime and can become a great tolerant, compassionate, understanding soul. You have the ability to discipline yourself when and if something is really important to you; otherwise if it is only a half interest you may drop it. Others will know when something is of great importance to you for you will stick to it.

George McGovern (1922)

July 20

You have a very fine nobility about you with a great deal of understanding of others. There is a certain unselfish quality about you. You have a generous spirit where nothing is too much trouble for you in relation to a person you care about. A very positive attitude with life invades your total being. You can be very active in any worthwhile cause and will cooperate with anyone for the betterment either of the community or just one single person. You have great insight with universal truth and can make a good teacher in this area. You work best when doing your creative talents with a mate. By that I mean any project is accomplished better when working as a team with a friend or a lover.

Natalie Wood (1938)

July 21

You possess a great imagination which can be served best in some artistic capacity. You also have a talent for leadership, saying your thing and attracting followers of one kind or another. You seem driven to express yourself, almost to a degree of being aggressive at times. Born on this day you are on the cusp of Leo, so will possess some of the Leo fire and charm of expression. You are also happy when entertaining others as a host or hostess. You will no doubt be surrounded by people most of the time. There is an element of good cheer to your nature that attracts others to you like flies to honey. One thing people can say about you is your ability to make yourself heard. You have an answer for most all things anyone wants to bring before you.

Ernest Hemingway (1899)

July 22

Your home life is very important to you and there is nothing you wouldn't sacrifice for it. You are solid and stable in relationship to your family and loved ones. There is also a cosmic and spiritual influence that surrounds you like a glow. Your twenty two number has cosmic connotations and can indicate a very highly connected universal soul. Your talents may range from poetry, music, psychic sensitivity, dancing because you are in touch with all the intangible forces all around you. Compassion and tolerance are a strong part of your character. Your birth date can bring you great acclaim because you have the ability to always be your own unique self. This day is also on the cusp of Leo and gives fire to your personality and makes you a more complex person than most. At some point in your life, you may have a great revelation and from that day forward dedicate your whole life to that cause. When that time comes you will know it without any doubt.

Karl Menninger (psychiatrist) (1893)

The Day of Your Birth

LEO
July 23 through August 23

The key words for Leo are I will. Leo is dramatic, generous, romantic and sometimes egotistical. They are good with entertaining, love fun and games and children. It is a positive, masculine, electric sign. Leo is fire and it is fixed. It is kingly, creative, flamboyant. Physical difficulties can be the heart and back. Leo people can be very ardent in nature but keep themselves under control. The zodiacal symbol is the lion. The ruler is the Sun.

The negative thing that Leo has to learn to conquer is false pride. Nothing is worse than when Leo expresses false vanity and seeks vain glory. At best they are loyal and radiant like the Sun.

The Leo jewel is the ruby. The flowers gladiolus and poppies. Their metal is gold. Leo rules glistening substances to which light seems synonymous.

Leo rules teaching, especially children.

July 23

You are very enthusiastic about life. Everything is done in a large way. Nothing is too much trouble for you. You have good judgment as to how things should be done. When you remember someone's birthday or anniversary the gift is usually first class. You are very expressive and have a host of friends. An instinct for the truth of things is very important to you and you will not likely sacrifice the truth by telling lies. Integrity and optimism are other characteristics that people see almost immediately. Behind your optimism and understanding is a true conquering lion. You also have a drive to learn and to understand higher spiritual and scientific values.

Max Heindel (1865)   Bert Convy (1935)

_____

_____

July 24

You enjoy your home and all the things you do in and around your home. The practical things in life are beautiful to you. Because you are cooperative, people in your neighborhood or relatives seek you out to help them do things, and you usually oblige. You always know how to improve situations and methods. Every once in a while a little jealousy pops up, but you soon learn to over-ride it by not acting upon your jealous emotion. You also can have some artistic talent. As with all July days whether Cancer or July Leo's there is a tendency toward being psychic with spiritual insight.

Alexandre Dumas (1802)

July 25

You are quick with your expressions and always have some clever little remark to make. To express yourself is as important as breathing. You can have some type of musical expression and may even be a good writer. Things have to move fast for you for you must be forever active. You need variety in your life for there has to be an element of excitement in your life or things get dull. Now they see you; now they don't is your motto. This influence attracts people to you for you are interesting and a bright, enthusiastic companion. You inspire others and at some time in your life may become involved in spiritual work or psychic experiences.

Frank Church (politician) (1924)

July 26

You have a potential talent for interior decorating and/or clothes designing. You may be the type of person who is interested in advancing your education with cultural study such as music, drama, literature and all things that give you a certain amount of class. If you love someone you can be very generous for there is no limit to how far you will go where a loved one is concerned. You may do a lot of entertaining in your home for you make an excellent host or hostess. There is a certain harmony about your nature in that you seem to create harmonious conditions out of discordant atmospheres.

George Bernard Shaw (1856)   Jason Robards, Jr. (1922)

The Day of Your Birth

July 27

You have exceptional tolerance which gives a calming influence upon those you meet. You have a strong intuitive talent and thus can become instantly in tune with any situation that comes up and because of this seem to be able to take appropriate action necessary. You should set aside a time each day for meditation and get in touch with the spirit so to speak. Most of the time you are at peace with yourself and your life, but once in a while you can get moody. When this happens do something different from what you may have been doing. Learn, also, to balance your life between the physical, mental and spiritual. You have fine mental and spiritual development but the problem, if any, is not taking action at times. Don't just think it or feel it, do something about it. Make the effort. You are a complex person in that there is a variance between what you do for others and what you do for yourself. The delay may happen when it comes to doing for yourself, making all kinds of sacrifices in situations with others, but not for yourself. Keep up with what is happening in your own world, also. You are a real paradox to say the least.

Keenan Wynn (1916)

July 28

You are a very active person and always seem to have something going. You like to move around and not get stuck in a strict routine. You want to be successful in public life but you do not want to be dictated to by society. This works best for you when you can take a leadership position in your community, doing your own thing, executing your own ideas and creating followers. You can easily take the good from the old ways and combine them successfully with the new, up to date methods. You are very innovative which if directed rightly could give a talent for financial expertise, resulting in success. You are adventurous but not so much that you lose track of the necessary concrete reality. When you believe in something, you usually always have the courage to go for it. Whatever it takes in the way of responsibility and discipline you can give it your all if you have decided it is important.

Rudy Vallee (1901) Sally Struthers (1948)

July 29

You can be described as having spiritual courage. You may even go so far as pioneering some new philosophy through writing, lecturing, teaching and preaching. Above all you are not a hypocrite. You have an interest in higher mind subjects including outer space research. In many ways you possess some of the humanitarian spirit. A true humanitarian is one who is able to be original and one who dares to express his or her own unique individuality. And because you are able to do that, you can become a leader attracting many followers. Your daring and magnetism results in many varied experiences in life. You are not afraid to live. If there is one word that describes you more than the others it is high-mindedness. You detest anything narrow-minded or petty and will put integrity to all things that cross your path in life.

Clara Bow (1905)

_____

_____

July 30

You are a leader. You show others the way with most situations in your life. It is rare if you ever take the back of a waiting line. You have an instinct for ideas that will work with the masses in general, whether these ideas are for making money or educational. No matter how small the idea you present to the world, it can forever have your name on it for the people who follow. This is a question of creative ideas put into concrete form so that others can enjoy the products of your mind. Sometimes this influence gives the ability to have inventive ideas that have practical workable results. You have the ability to gamble on something and because you see the thing at hand with such clear sight, it usually works out to not only your best interest but others.

Henry Ford (1863)

_____

_____

July 31

You have great cosmic insight. You have a feel for things in the intangible world that others cannot perceive. You are very idealistic and it is unlikely you have a selfish bone in your whole body. Do unto others is your motto and creed. In a simple word you are just a very nice person. When it comes to being tolerant and compassionate you are par number one. You see a child, a little puppy, loveable people, beautiful music and you are moved at times to tears. You are a sensitive which means you can be musical, poetic and psychic. When it comes to your taste in anything from people to material possessions it is top drawer. In many ways you see the best in others so that if you have to compromise, you accent the positive and ignore the negative; that is, if you have to do so. It is all or nothing most of the time, at least this is true if fate doesn't wield you something beyond your control. With you, it is quality rather than quantity. With all your compassion and tolerance do not under estimate the fact that you can be very stubborn when people least expect it.

S.S. Kresge (1867) Casey Stengel (1891)

August 1

At times you can show a great independent spirit which is best served in a leadership position in some way. You have a tendency to do things your own way. You can see behind what people say and do, and because of this you are way ahead of them. You have a quality of being able to look behind the facade. You have a talent for reading eyes, and it is no doubt the first thing you do when meeting someone or dealing with those you already know. You are individualistic and cannot be talked into anything but when you love someone, great sacrifices can and will be made but it may take love to do this. Use your great talent for leadership in the executive world of business to get the most positive benefits from your talents. If you are a man, perhaps the only person who can influence you is the woman you love, and then only up to a point. If you are a woman, the only person who can influence you is the man you love but he can influence you much more fully than the woman in a number one man's life. You can also act on impulse.

Herman Melville (1819)

August 2

You have a certain fiery spirit but a spirit combined with emotional consideration of others. Enthusiasm is your middle name and there is a lively quality to you that endears you to others. You do not let unhappiness take hold of you for very long for one of your greatest instincts is being productive. The wisdom you innately possess gives you the ability to see the right action to take. Action is your motto although you do not appear to others to be racing your motor. You have just the right amount of action and thought combined in such a way that will not let you get too far out of direction. You think things out, then take action and not the other way around. You are not likely to be the kind who takes action and then wonder why you did it. Each step you take is secure and firm. It is also not likely that you will go backward. You may tread water for a while but never backwards. As a result people around you know who to come to for a solution to their problems. You won't overdo in this direction because you are too much of a real humanitarian to allow yourself to become a crutch thus weakening them.

Peter O'Toole (1933)   Carroll O'Connor (1924)

August 3

You are the soul of honor and valor. This could give you, also, a talent for the diplomatic arts. One of your main philosophies of life is live and let life. You would fight for anyone's right to do what they have to do. Whichever direction your life takes, you have a certain faith in the ultimate good that happens, like blessings in disguise at times. You can be very sociable and may entertain in your home often. You are a strange combination of believing in the intangibles in life with the ability to be practical at the same time. In many ways this represents a talent for being productive and successful as a poet, musician, dancer, psychic. When it comes to situations that come up in your life you have the uncanny ability to see the beginning of a situation in addition to seeing the outcome; thereby being able to take the correct action.

Tony Bennett (1926)

August 4

You are optimistic, humorous and enjoyable to be with whether business associates or friends. You possess an understanding heart with the ability to understand others who come into your path of life. Because you can understand people and their ideas, this gives the capacity for bringing cooperation and understanding between people who may have been at

The Day of Your Birth

sword's points before. You have a love of higher education that makes you well learned but at the same time you also know how to have a good time. As a result you lead a well balanced life that is rarely negative, if at all. People all over the world are like one big family as far as you are concerned. To your line of thinking it is one earth, and we should all be one as part of the human family. There is a lot of integrity and honesty to your nature and others soon learn they can trust you.

Percy Bysshe Shelley (Poet) (1792)

August 5

You have great powers of communication and are interested in everything and everyone in your community. As you get older your world gets larger and larger because you take more and more interest in the people around you. You have a perfect talent for putting your subjective world in perfect balance with your objective world. In other words dealing with the here and now, but also having foresight into the future. Another part of this same talent is the ability to be objective about something you are very emotional or sensitive about. The understanding you possess is not just some inactive philosophy but you make it work in your everyday world. This is truly objective subjectivity. You could have a talent for writing or educational work. There is an idealism to your nature, an idealism that you make work, that you bring down to earth, so to speak, into a practical reality. You have the ability to inspire others and your greatest talent can be to teach and show others how they can make their dreams come true and how they can use their greatest potentials. Most people have dreams and reality separate. You do not and because of this you are likely at some time in your life destined to share this knowledge with others in a more professional capacity.

Neil Armstrong (1930)

August 6

More than anything else you are a person who likes variety in your life. If you have to stay too long in a fixed position (even though you are a Leo) or you have too much of the same thing day in and day out you get restless and extremely bored. You are a very active person and if someone wants something done, you are the one to do it. If there is a difficulty it may be that you do not stay with something long enough to get the best results from it. This can give you a combination of mind and matter in balance. If it comes to a conflict between your affections and practical logic your mind and logic will more than likely win. However, when you love a mate, and your family, logic may go to the wind and affection and love will be paramount. It is merely a question of the difference between those you deeply love, or those on the outside of your circle or those on the border line. Another consideration in point is how you feel at a certain point in time. You are not always that easy to figure out, and you are not exactly a humanitarian in the strict sense of the word. Just about the time others think they have it with you, they don't have it.

Lucille Ball (1911)

August 7

You are very perceptive concerning people. You have the ability to see through them so others cannot easily fool you. Even though you have the ability to do this, you are not an I-told-you-so kind of person. If you yourself make any mistakes you can admit it. You have an artistic talent that gives you the ability to make people happy; especially those you love dearly. By artistic talent I mean being able to produce the finer things of life. There is a harmonious aura to your nature which helps you make other people feel calm in your presence. You would make an excellent social therapist. People easily respond to you and they end up telling you all their problems. When you care for something or someone you possess the ability to make sacrifices for it or them.

Alan Leo (Astrologer) (1860)

August 8

You are a natural born executive with the wonderful talent for making and managing finances, not only yours but others in a professional manner. You take great pains to be responsible and attentive to your duties. Your ability to be compassionate and tolerant covers up your hard inner disciplined core but when people know you for a while both qualities become apparent to them. This not only gives great respect and pride in yourself, but it operates on the level where you can get very disturbed if someone you know is being cheated or abused in any way. So when it is all added up you are a practical idealist having the ability to make your dreams come true. Be sure that you balance your life between business success and taking time to smell the roses, or becoming involved in an artistic pursuit even if just for personal satisfaction or relaxation.

Esther Williams (1923) Mel Tillis (1932)

August 9

Born this day, you are shrewd and clever. Because in many ways you stand ahead of the crowd, if you work on it, you can become a great leader and humanitarian. Above all else you are an individualist. But even though you are a one of a kind type of individual, you do not force others into your way of thinking. Others will follow your lead naturally or you won't have any of it. There is another side to your nature which can get very serious or even depressive at times. However, in time you will learn to over-ride these moods and let the more positive philosophical part of your nature take over. One thing you must learn with this vibration is to try and overcome your pride and let others do things for you once in a while. You are loyal and faithful to those you love and when in love you will have the tendency to do something about it.

Robert Shaw (1927) David Steinberg (1942)

August 10

You are a very active person and know how to manage yourself and how to get the most out of your experiences in life. Above everything else you are optimistic. Nothing gets you down for long. You can be a leader and a pioneer in some cause. When you have a difficulty, a hurt, or a little unlucky incident, it only spurs you on to greater achievement and renewed vigor. One thing about you is your ability to start things, to be rather fearless in your efforts, but you also have the ability to follow through and see the results of your actions. Because you have good sense and excellent judgment your chances of fame and success are very real. As far as your vocation is concerned you have the variability to go into almost anything that takes your fancy. Your intellect is such that you can understand and accumulate all manner of knowledge and because you treat others fairly and squarely your accomplishments can be many and varied.

Herbert Hoover (president) (1874)

August 11

You possess a great deal of confidence in yourself and will usually initiate any action that has to be done. You are perceptive and have a more universal type of consciousness. Because you have confidence in yourself you would make a good leader in your community. One thing you must look out for is not to quit in midstream. You have a great deal of tolerance and compassion and because this is true you need to be aware who you allow into your life as friends or associates. Feeling sorry for someone is not an adequate reason for friendship. You must learn to attract those into your inner circle who are of the same caliber as yourself. You can have a high cosmic mission if you follow your own instincts and the instructions of your own higher creative self. When you follow and listen entirely to social standards you get off the track. This does not mean you should not be social, it simply means that you should learn to know the difference. However, in the end, the bottom line will be your tendency to lead. Your nature is more spiritual with strong feelings rather than strictly intellectual for it is much easier for you to follow your feelings than to analyze something intellectually or logically. Your ability to tune in on the intangibles in life is great; therefore, your spirituality can become of the highest degree.

Mike Douglas (TV personality) (1925)

August 12

Because you have a great way with phrases and words, people listen when you speak. You possess a high degree of objectivity which gives you the talent for arriving at the solution of any problem; therefore, you find yourself helping a lot of people who are less objective than you are. This influence gives you a good imagination but it also can make you psychic with great foresighted vision. All depends on how you develop this talent and use it. Your imaginative talent can take the form in music, poetry, dancing, dramatics, writing, painting, etc. If your talent for the arts is really developed, you can be very productive and do well financially with it. If you take your psychic and predictive talent into the spiritual realms you can become very well known in this area. You get along well with people because you are very tolerant and understanding and can put yourself in their shoes when need be.

Cecil B. DeMille (1881)

August 13

You have a very adventurous spirit with a passion for that which is not run of the mill. This influence gives you an optimistic, broad minded spirit. Nothing is too much trouble for you especially if that something is out of the ordinary and unique. You also want to stand out in a crowd in body, mind and spirit. In other words, you want to be known to others as good looking, strong mentally and spiritually in tune. Another thing this means is that your thinking is way ahead of others; your awareness of developing and reaching your full potential as a unique individual is very strong. You like things that are rare and of high quality. You cannot stand anything inferior (although you usually understand someone or something that is). You do not care what others prefer, but for you yourself, you like the best and that best is not only friends and associates but material things.

Annie Oakley (1860) Alfred Hitchcock (1899)

August 14

You have a combination of the practical approach to life along with idealism. If you have a quality above and beyond any others it is being fair with all people. Objectivity in any situation in life is your forte. You would be perfect in a vocation where you could be an arbitrator because not only do you have foresight and the ability to be objective, but you have the ability to keep all four corners covered. By this I mean you always have a strong base before you shoot for the stars. You can easily communicate# with others and they understand what you are saying and doing. You can offer a sympathetic and understanding heart at at the same time keep your feet on the ground in order to arrive at the best possible solution and resolution of either your problems or the problems of others.

David Crosby (rock musician) (1941)

August 15

You are very artistic and could do well in any of the expressive arts; such as acting, writing, lecturing. There is nothing you would not do to achieve harmony in the world around you; however, not to the point of denying yourself the fulfillment of your goals. You will go very far for others but will never bend where your own achievements are concerned. This position is like having an iron fist with a velvet glove. You know how to treat others with a certain diplomacy, but others have to know you for a while before they realize you have a certain stubborn determination behind your words and actions. This is the reason you can attain places of importance in the world of society. This is probably one of the best days to be born to give expression with one of the artistic forms.

Napoleon Bonapart (1769)   Sri Aurobindo (mystic) (1872)

August 16

You were born to be a lover for it is easy for you to bring harmony and caring to all you touch. You have a very special philosophy of life not to let anything defeat you. Music could be a strong talent either in the performance or the appreciation. Whatever it is you want to do in life, nothing is too much trouble or sacrifice for it. Your disposition is sunny most of the time and this is how you are to most people; however behind this sunny disposition is a temper at times. Your loving disposition is because you have supreme faith in a higher spiritual master, call it God, call it Jesus, call it what you will, but your faith in the positive force of the universe is above average. You have a great understanding which gives you the potential to be at one with most anyone you meet. A spirit of camaraderie is one of the greatest parts of your nature and you will not be limited in loving others.

Eydie Gorme (singer) (1932)

The Day of Your Birth

August 17

If you are anything, you are subtle. You make your point by being cooperative rather than aggressive. You possess a fine combination of psychic and the practical. You surprise less polite, less tactful people with how far you get with your cooperative methods. It isn't that you express yourself so fully, but it is doing and achieving results that count with you. Born on this day gives you insight and perception with the intangibles of life, the smell of roses, the starlit night sky, the smiles of a child. You don't miss a thing that could give joy. Finding a beautiful little wild flower in the woods can give you such pleasure. You do not have to go on a dangerous adventure to get excited. Life in all its little beautiful experiences gives you joy, a joy that is catching to the people around you. You are capable of a great deal of sacrifice for a loved one which seems to attract the same kind of love in return.

Mae West (1892)

_____

_____

August 18

You are a good organizer, with natural executive ability. There is a strong sense of pride in your nature that can get you in trouble once in a while especially when it is mixed with anger. Even though you have a disciplined nature, there is an element of adventure mixed in at times. If you can find the right mixture between discipline and adventure, you can be very successful. Good judgment is another attribute that you should develop to the fullest. While your judgment is good instinctively you should watch an attitude of "know it all" or not admitting a mistake. Do not let false pride take over for you will be cutting off your nose to spite your face. You can have the best of all worlds if you learn to balance the practical in your nature with your ability to be adventurous.

Meriwether Lewis (explorer) (1774)

_____

_____

August 19

You are a leader and "never a follower be". If anyone is to begin an action with a cause or a project, you are no doubt the one who will do so. As a leader you naturally possess qualities different from the average person, but even so you do not come off as pompous or egotistical. There is a double tendency with this influence in that early in your life because you feel you are a unit that can stand alone you may not let others assist you, but as you grow older you learn to be a real leader assisting and being assisted by others. When the chips are down, however, you can be a loner, love doing things on your own at times, like walking, reading, etc. You can get involved in spiritual work to the point of being a teacher of higher truth. In many ways you are a humanitarian, capable of teaching others to stand on their own and helping them to understand the way of all life. You can be a force in your life to be reckoned with.

Coco Chanel (fashion designer) (1883)

August 20

It is not easy for you to make commitments with others, If there is a negative influence to this day it is thinking your way is the only way. It is either all or nothing with you. Others are either for you or against you. You are never in between, that is the reason it is difficult for you to compromise in any situation. In a positive sense you will not let anyone influence you against what you think is best for yourself and your destiny. Because of this asset you can go far and especially can you have a good influence on people around you once they realize you will not go against your own self respect. Another part of this same influence gives you a talent for bringing out originality in others. If you have a disgust for anything it is seeing potential in others they will not work to fulfill and achieve. In the beginning you may not be popular with those close to you, but once they begin to see your unique ways of bringing out the best in them, they will sing your praises. Above all, you will not permit yourself to be a crutch for anyone, and you try to teach others they should not be a crutch either. This has nothing to do with compassion in the real sense, it has to do with individual strength.

Paul Tillich (theologian) (1886)

August 21

You were born on a day that has a high universal influence; therefore you have an instinct for knowing the truth of life. You can be perceptive, musical, poetic and possess a strong degree of tolerance for relatives,

The Day of Your Birth

neighbors and friends. You can get inspiration from the smallest incident in your day to day experiences, the smile of a child, the song of a bird, a beautiful sunset, etc. People take you into their confidences so that you end up knowing a lot of secrets about others which you do not disclose for you are good at keeping secrets. You can swing from being very extravagant to being very cautious with money. When you feel sorry for someone you may be very generous but then afterward you may think, "now I will have to economize to make up for it." At one point in your life you may take a strong interest in spiritual affairs. Depending upon the effort and the direction you go you could become a leader in spiritual groups and/or a good psychic.

Wilt Chamberlain (1936)

August 22

Optimism is one of your finer traits. This is a high quality day, a day that makes you who are born of this day very individualistic and independent. You call the shots like it really is, clear and to the point. If anyone knows their destiny, it is you. You go right to the point with no stopping in between. Because you also enjoy the lighter side of life, humor, good conversation, fun and games, you need to watch so that you do not take too much time for this to the exclusion of the universal leadership which you were born to accomplish. This is a high number day and gives you an instinct for things and situations as they should be. In other words, because you have been given more, more is expected of you by God, or The Force of us all. This doesn't mean you cannot have fun, what it does mean is the proper amount of time should be spent on achievement and positive results in your more universal destiny.

Claude Debussy (1862)

August 23

This is a day that is a cusp day which gives an influence of Leo and Virgo. This makes you a little more complex than a straight Leo or Virgo. One cannot call you a Leo or a Virgo (not really) for you have both characteristics. You possess the courage and drama of Leo, but also the caution and perfectionism of Virgo. You are not likely to jump into things as easily as a straight Leo for you will think things out first. You have a fine combination of strong feelings with excellent intellect. At one point you can be exceptionally generous with a loved one and at another time be critical and "penny tight". While you may be generous to those you love, you can at the same time take on the traits of Virgo and want perfection out of them, which can be a difficult tight rope for loved ones to walk. You are good at self expression and could either write, or be a teacher or lecturer. When it comes to material possessions you usually want quality rather than quantity. Even though at times one may not think you have your feet on the ground, you definitely have a firm foundation on which to operate through life.

Gene Kelly (1912)

VIRGO
(August 24 through September 22)

Virgo is an earth sign, mutable (flexible), feminine, negative (magnetic). Virgo is ruled by Mercury (for now) and its symbol is the Virgin gathering the harvest. Virgo is analytical, inclined to be of service, and at their best can become great technicians in some field. They can at other times be petty, discriminating and intolerant. They can work very hard, and are interested in health and diet. They have the tendency not to be able to see the forest for the trees, giving a narrowing influence. One of their main talents very definitely can be perfection, especially is they adhere to the higher positive side of Virgo. They should direct this talent into developing a craftsmanship. When they take a job, they do it well or not at all. A negative trait can be suspicion. They are computer-like in their approach to life.

The jewels for Virgo are amber and agate. The flower is the morning glory or the aster. The metal is aluminum and Virgo also rules the substance of glass.

The colors of Virgo are slate, soft browns, grays, mixtures of colors like plaid or tweeds, and some shades of violet.

Virgo rules veined substances or substances that when controlled can be very productive.

August 24

The art of communication is a strong feature of your personality. This day makes you a combination of Leo and Virgo being born on the cusp. Because of this you are a very complex person. You could be successful in drama, art expression, writing and because the Virgo part of your nature makes you critical and perfectionistic, you can produce flawless projects and go to the top of your profession. You can be discriminating, practical, but you can also be entertaining and fun loving. It is important for you to have a solid base to work from for you are not necessarily an adventurer in the strict sense of the word. You can be loving and kind, but sometimes when you love someone deeply you tend to criticize them. This is only because you want all that is best for them including their highest potentials. If loved ones know this about you, and understand the motives behind your criticism all will go along much more harmonious. You can easily find the mistakes in other people's art forms such as; writing, drama, music, whatever and for this reason you would make a good artistic critic. You would also be good at training performers, art students, etc. for you can help them perfect their craft.

Richard Cushing (clergyman) (1895)

August 25

You cannot stand inharmonious conditions around you. And if you have these inharmonious conditions around you for very long, it will affect your health. You have a talent for decorating and it is very likely that you will have a beautiful home, whether or not you get into professional decorating. It is very important that you indulge yourself to a cozy, well put together home. You seem to prefer doing things in your home, having all the conveniences necessary to enjoy your family and friends within your own atmosphere. You can be very perceptive at times to the extent that you know what people are going to say before they say it, especially in dealing with your loved ones. This influence also gives good communications with relatives, neighbors, and possible close ties with your mother. Of course, you can have a talent for business where you are providing some kind of decorating service, or a business or service where you are helping others make something or someone more beautiful.

Leonard Bernstein (1918)   **Sean Connery (1930)**

August 26

You have a very receptive nature for a Virgo. You have a sensitivity that is so highly developed that you respond to vibrations emanating from people and places that can make you very happy or very miserable, depending upon the situation at the time. There is a new word on the list of popular expressions these days and that word is allergic. It stands for hyper-sensitivity of some kind. It is important that you learn to throw off the negative vibrations before they affect your health. At times you are inclined to worry needlessly, but you seem unable to completely overcome this tendency. As far as your health is concerned, you should have a vigorous constitution but you must learn to throw off any vibration that negatively affects your health. When you are at ease or calm, you feel great, but when something upsets your peace of mind, you seethe internally thus making for a bad health climate. Use your great sensitivity for poetry, music or any of the other inspirational arts in order to more constructively use this part of your nature. If you work on it, you can have a very integrated personality, able to make your idealistic, dream nature work in the practical world of reality. If you do this, your sensitivity can work for you rather than against you. It all depends upon putting your sensitive nature to work.

Prince Albert (royal consort) (1819)

August 27

You are realistic and practical for the most part. You size things up immediately, seeing the real facts and doing something about it. As an executive you could be unbeatable. You are able to have a certain type of perception as to the outcome of a given new project or action, but you arrive at these deductions by the way of logic and method rather than in a psychic way. You mean what you say and are not apt to say something you haven't thought through first. You are not exactly imaginative in the strict sense of the word; therefore, you are not going to necessarily attract those who are. You should seek them out and listen a bit more to these perceptive, imaginative type people. They just may have an idea you can make work. Together you could be quite a team. However, the bottom line is all that interests you is what will work in the work-a-day world. If the rest of your astrology map shows you have some artistic ability of one kind or another, you can make it work in the buy and sell business world. If you do get into business, people can count on your honesty and integrity.

Samuel Goldwyn (film executive) (1882)

August 28

You are a natural born philosopher being able to measure the moods and actions of people, their plight and the truth about life itself. You learn through each experience you go through, seeing even the conflicts as part of the total picture of development. Because you are so gifted you need to share your basic and universal truths with others. You can be objective in your awareness of others and at the same time show sympathy when need be. This is a great quality to have and makes you capable of ultimate success in the area of counseling or any of the other human arts. If at times you are aware of a special destined role in life you are probably right. You can be a leader among men, for your integrity and practical approach to things cannot easily be equaled. All you need to do is develop all these potentials. You have a high opinion of yourself and will not go against your own code of ethics for anyone. This is the reason you can be trusted with any superior responsibility.

Johann Wolfgang von Goethe (1749) Charles Boyer (1899)

August 29

When it comes to taking action on something, you do not wait for anyone else to do it. As far as you are concerned that just wastes time. You do what you have to do always. You are the one in your group or neighborhood who may be the pace setter. Born this day can give success in a business of your own for you know how to make decisions without too much effort but are also willing to put action behind each decision. You have a certain amount of individuality to your nature making you stand out in a crowd, all other things in your astrology or numerological map being equal. You have a high degree of universal instinct. By that 1 mean you follow the beat of your own drum and seem to be listening to a higher spirit force of the cosmos. If you follow this higher voice, rather than others around you, you will stay on your destined path. You are an active person, always finding things to do. You give others freedom but you expect freedom yourself for you believe wholeheartedly in each person's right to be him or herself. You are not domineering with others and can be very congenial until they push you past your limit. Tolerance, compassion, and the poetry of life is also part of your nature but a poetry of life that is disciplined with an overall practical view. It is practical idealism.

Elliot Gould (actor) (1938)

August 30

You have all your bases covered. Body, mind, and spiritual awareness are in equal consideration. Enthusiasm is a paramount feature of your character but there may be a tendency at times for you to go to extremes. You can be a lively companion with a sense of humor and fun. If anyone plays a joke on you, or if life itself plays a joke, you can accept it and take it in your stride. You can be successful in dealing with community projects. You seem to have an extra fund of energy you can call upon when you have an extra big project to accomplish. With all of this you have a fondness for your home and a great attachment to your family even though your attachment is not strictly emotional but is beautifully balanced with your intellect and spirituality. If you try you could develop a talent for healing, intellectual leadership with teaching and spiritual group activities. You can be a natural in any one of these areas.

Jean Claude Killy (skier) (1943)

August 31

You certainly have power with words. When you talk, people sit up and listen. You have a certain charisma that attracts people to you; therefore, you should involve yourself in some kind of humanitarian work or the ministry. Integrity and self respect are among your main characteristics. Because you possess self respect you can easily respect others. If anyone has class you have, or at least it is a natural instinct for you. You have a kind of class that does not necessarily stand above the others in an egotistical way but one that shows the way to others. You could have a talent for acting, a type of acting that inspires others as well as entertaining. You can be very idealistic when it comes to human development,

The Day of Your Birth

whether your own or others. You may consider those you take into your confidence and affections as part of your family regardless of whether they are blood relatives or not. It matters not, for you see the world as one big family of humanity. It distresses you very much when you see potential in someone that is being wasted.

Arthur Godfrey (1903)   James Coburn (1928)

September 1

You are a very active person who knows how to get what you want from life. You possess the uncanny knack of foresight and seem to know how something is going to work out from the very beginning; therefore, this gives you the edge of knowing the right action to take at the onset. You are a leader, one who can initiate the action, but also a finisher. You are there in the beginning and the ending. If you start something you generally finish it. You are not afraid to pioneer into something new but since you are also a Virgo you have the fortitude, the courage, the dedication to work hard and the overall result means success. You have every step worked out well in advance. This doesn't mean that once in a while you can't throw the dice, so to speak, for you can gamble on things at certain times, but it is instinct with you as to what this may be. So there may be a question mark in other's minds as to whether you are really gambling even though it looks like you are. You are high minded and will not accept anything but the highest and the best, whether that best is material, physical or spiritual. This position can also give a talent as an executive in the business world. If there is anything you must watch it is "a holier than thou" attitude for despite all your nobility and integrity, which you always have, your high standards may cause you to look down on those of lesser quality. However, these same standards may cause you to get involved in helping others advance and improve. It is up to you which way this is going to work; it can work both ways. It may work one way earlier in your life and work the other way at another time.

Lily Tomlin (Comedienne) (1936)

September 2

You are a very tolerant person for a Virgo. You are a fine combination of a perfectionist and a collaborator and co-worker. You are adaptable, easily fitting into any situation. You combine intuition and intellect well. You have a strong interest in your home and family with the ability to work very hard for them but also to sacrifice if necessary. You have the ability to resolve any problem that comes your way. You may not have an innovative spirit but you are easily adjustable to other's ideas. Someone presents an idea, and you have a talent for knowing how to make the idea work. A difficulty with this combination is fluctuating between moodiness and positive intellectual activity. You have to work out a balance between the positive approach to life and the negative. Used at its best can give an instinct for business productivity. If you can use your intuition and sensitivity to produce success in the business world this can work greatly to your advantage. You can be very sensitive to the public and therefore capitalize by providing a public need.

Jimmy Connors (tennis player) (1938)

September 3

Most of the time you are positive and of a good disposition. In many ways you can be the life of the party because you not only provide humor but understanding. You possess one of the greatest virtues and that is the capacity to enjoy your own company as well as the company of others. You can be an adventurer or the person who enjoys doing things of a more simple nature like walking and reading. As a Virgo your spirit of adventure will be coupled with a productive motive. You may also be capable of being good at sports. Your understanding of the higher spiritual laws is an innate instinct, and because you are in touch with the truth could be a writer, a teacher or preacher. Another important facet of your nature is your ability to make the serious and important responsibilities fun. You are sincere and truthful and perhaps a little outspoken. You may be a Virgo but born on this day makes you more broad-minded than the average Virgo and not quite so critical and narrow minded. What an excellent balance this gives you. It gives you a talent for making an ideal practical and for bringing spiritual truths down to everyday integration.

Alan Ladd (actor) (1913)

The Day of Your Birth

September 4

You are a very serious person with a passion for perfection. You work very hard and accomplish much more than most others around you. However, you can be a little moralistic and at times suspicious. Above all you like a system and are not inclined to be impulsive but more inclined to think about each step taken beforehand. As far as time is concerned you are usually right on time, right on the dot, never early nor ever late. You do not act upon your emotions as a rule; therefore you do not have many obvious emotional outbursts. If something does influence you emotionally, you usually sleep on it in order to make a practical decision. You can be depended upon and are not inclined to shirk whatever duties you have to perform. Extravagance is not part of your scheme in life for you are a person who utilizes all things to the best advantage. If at times you spend more money than usual, it is no doubt for a worthy purpose or for a dearly beloved.

Henry Ford II (automobile executive) (1917)

September 5

You are the kind of person who likes to talk and have fun. If you use this ability to communicate in a professional way you could be successful as a performer, a teacher, lecturer, writer. You are interested in all manner of things within your community, which makes you a good neighbor knowing no stranger. Your Virgo Sun makes you serious and sincere even if on the surface you may not appear to be at times. Putting the qualities of your Sun sign and the day you were born together can make you fantastic. You are capable of discrimination and at the same time show consideration for others. You seem to know just what to do in dealing with others. Somehow, instinctively you have knowledge that guides you to the people you can get closer to and which ones you need to keep space around you. When you play, you play hard and when you work you work hard. Quite a combination and if you learn to balance these two seemingly diverse qualities of your nature into a workable unit, nothing can hold you back or keep you from ultimate success.

Raquel Welch (1940) Darryl F. Zanuck (film producer)

September 6

You are a lover above and beyond anything else. You appreciate beauty in all forms and perhaps have some artistic talent of your own. Giving parties, playing the host or hostess is your forte. Among other of your talents is diplomacy. A Virgo with diplomacy, that is what you are. You should work in clothing design, fashion, interior decorating or any of the other types of work where you are making someone or something more beautiful. You may not even have to do much studying you just have an instinct for it. If you take this influence to a higher octave, this talent can give you work in some cause for humanity in a very selfless service. It is your instinct to be of service to a loved one or valued cause. You cannot stand for unhappiness around you or any kind of discord. Your ability to cooperate with others is magnificent. Instead of being directly critical you are more inclined to offer suggestions which are stated in such a way, people seem to accept them. If you have a difficulty at times, it may be your inability to make up your mind due to your need to be perfect with what you do and at the same time desiring to cooperate. If you learn to work your Virgo Sun in combination with this beautiful six day, you can accomplish much in the area of service to loved ones or your fellowman in general.

Billy Rose (producer) (1899)

September 7

You are very intuitive with the ability to make sacrifices, if and when you have to do so, for the ultimate good of all including yourself. This represents a combination of the practical technician with sensitivity to the intangibles of life, like music, poetry, psychic, etc. You have strong faith and will not tolerate anyone trying to change your faith or water it down. You want top drawer with everything in your life and can wait patiently until the right thing shows up. You can be critical like all good Virgo people, but instead of being overly discriminating you have a knack for making the best of everything that comes your way. You instinctively know that things will change for the better if you just hold onto your dream long enough. The talent you have for original thinking makes you capable of following the beat of your own drum in life regardless of what others say or when others try to deter you with their sometimes erroneous ideas (at least ideas erroneous where your life is concerned). When problems come into your life you have the ability to solve them in very extra-ordinary ways. When it comes to material well being, you are balanced in that when funds are low, your faith in a new supply coming in always seems to work out to your financial favor. You also know how to economize when funds are low, but you will also spend when you have it.

Peter Lawford (actor) (1923) Grandma Moses (1860)

September 8

You have a talent for business and the executive world. Whether your talent is used in the business world or in your home you can be the one who organizes things and takes the lead. You get more out of a day than anyone else around you. A great sense of responsibility and duty are an integral part of your nature and anyone who shirks responsibility and duty can be offensive to you. Loyalty to the people you love is part of your high and noble spirit. You have a talent for financial planning and coupled with your business head can insure success with whatever you undertake. You know just what to do when it comes to important decisions in your life. In social situations you know how to be the good host/hostess without being gushy or overbearing. This day gives you a talent for handling other people's finances as well as your own, but you have to watch out so you are not too pushy with your advise. Wisdom you have but you have to wait for them to ask for it instead of pushing it on them. You see things so clearly it is difficult for you when you see others making mistakes.

Sid Caesar (1922) Peter Sellers (1925)

September 9

You are creative and full of adventure. With your talent for creative expression and your understanding of people, you can become a writer, a leader in some cause or religious group. You are a person who can ascertain the universal truth of our existence without formal study. It is instinct for you to understand the laws of life. You can have a talent for leadership within your community, whether with business or spiritual. Working unselfishly for others is the highest way you can use this talent. Everyone has a job to do in their lifetime that fits like the piece of a puzzle into the full scheme of things and it is up to each of us human beings in this mortal life to find out what that job is. With your high degree of understanding coupled with your ability to take action and work very hard, possibly even fame can result. You also have the ability to communicate with others and to express yourself in a very honest and straightforward manner. But even though you may be straightforward in your expressions with others, you never lose your sympathy for them. You have a great combination of being able to understand "where the other person is" along with putting objective truth to the situation at hand. No matter what you do in life you will stand out. You are inclined to be much more of a pioneer, an adventurer than the average Virgo.

Cardinal Richelieu (1585) Cliff Robertson (1925)

September 10

You are an original copy, making you one who is usually copied rather than you being the one who copies others. Among the qualities you have is the ability to get ideas and solutions to problems. However, in the long run this makes you an initiator of ideas which you do put into practice, but because you are so intensely interested in starting new projects you usually leave your projects to others. You could probably sell anything, but most of all you can sell yourself. Whatever ideas you get you also have the ability to see the way they can be executed at their best. Whatever dream you have you seem to have the know how to actualize it. If at times you appear to be selfish you are not; it is just that you may be preoccupied in some way and do not want to be disturbed or disrupted. When those you love understand this, they will never lose your support or loyalty but they must understand this. You will always be distinguished, standing way above the crowd.

Yma Sumac (singer) (1927)

September 11

You are a high universal spirit being highly selfless. Your compassion and tolerance is exceptional; however, others should not be deceived into thinking they can pull any kind of sob story on you, because you do know the point where compassion ends short of becoming a crutch. You have the ability to plan, organize and complete projects for the public. You have an instinct for what the public will accept and so can capitalize on this talent. You also have the talent for either working alone or working with others. Your flexibility in this regard is great. You are an easy judge of human nature, having the ability to understand where each person is at present but yet able to see the wider possibilities of their natures. You have a very well balanced nature making it possible for you to be aggressive when you have to be but also submissive when you have to be; therefore making you able to accumulate numerous varied experiences in your lifetime. Your mind is on higher things and even though others may not always know it, you do follow the beat of your own drums. Because you are so compassionate and able to help others on the spot; others at times get deluded into thinking you can be controlled; you cannot. Use some of your talent for the arts like music, dancing, poetry in a profitable manner.

D. H. Lawrence (writer) (1885)

September 12

You are fun to be with most of the time. You see the broad sense of things but can also get into the smallest detail of things, in other words you see the far and the wide in relationship to the most minute. You can criticize but get to the objective approach which is a very special talent. You have a very complex kind of talent for you can combine criticism with tolerance. In another way of explaining it is you can get by with saying things others would be crucified for saying. You understand things people tell you, or the things you study without being hit over the head. This influence also finds you exuberant, optimistic and at times a bit humorous. You can be a successful writer, publisher, minister or world traveler. You have the ability to bring out the best in others so for this reason you would make an excellent teacher. Whatever you do in life, organize and dedicate yourself in one direction and you can become a technician. You understand so many things that you may be tempted to put too many irons in the fire. When it comes to business and/or any other project that requires organization and team work, you are a natural for you seem to instinctively know what will work and what will not work. Because you do have a natural sense of humor or the ability to make light of a heavy situation at times, you can pull a difficult period through where others will fail.

Jesse Owens (runner) (1913)   Maurice Chevalier (1888)

September 13

You can be a fighter for you stand up for your rights. You stick in there for what you believe in and will not easily allow a temporary obstacle or set back stand in your way. If you are in a field of endeavor that is competitive, your determination and stick-to-it-tive-ness wins the battle in the final accounting. You are practical and have both feet on the ground. You have a well balanced attitude toward the physical, mental and spiritual responsibilities of life. You work hard, go through a lot, but somehow it is not as hard for you to do as it is for others. If you will but realize that you can be an inspiration to those around you, you can do more than just your own thing. Despite your seeming practical view of life, you do have quite a measure of idealism that keeps you going in hard times. You instinctively realize that the easiest and best way to grow mentally and spiritually is to put hard work behind and with your ambitions whatever they may be.

Mel Torme (1925)

September 14

You are a clever conversationalist. When you feel it; you express it. You have a special way of saying things enabling you to talk people into anything. You should use this very great talent with writing, lecturing or any vocation where you can use your ability to come across to others. It doesn't take you very long to decide upon something and it doesn't take very long for action to follow your thoughts. If you enter a condition that is boring that condition doesn't stay boring very long for activity and changes of activity are the spice of life for you. Because of your ability with conversation and entertaining others, you may appear to be more of a flirt than you really are; however, because you like variety and activity in your life you may not settle down in your 20's but wait until your 30's to do so. There is a hidden core of practicality to your nature where you do have both feet on the ground and when people know you a while they will discover this.

Hall Wallis (producer) (1899)

The Day of Your Birth

September 15

You cannot stand disharmony in your life and make an excellent companion for a mate or a friend. If you do not have harmony in your relationships you cannot get the most out of anything else you do. When others around you are upset, you try so hard to bring them into a happier state of mind. You also have a passion for making your home as beautiful as possible as well as keeping yourself attractive. Coupled with the Virgo Sun influence, love to you means on a conventional basis and also facing the responsibility it entails. Another outlet this day's influence can give you is talent in the fashion world or interior decorating. You also need a permanent home from which to operate in diference to an apartment. You are at your best when everything around you is peaceful and serene. If things are not peaceful and you cannot do anything about it, you may depart from the situation for your whole personality is inclined toward perfection and harmony. If a situation you get yourself into cannot be corrected, you usually leave it. As far as you are concerned you are wasting precious time that could go into some productive work.

King Richard the Lion-Hearted (1157)

September 16

You have a very integrated personality for you can be just as tolerant as you can be intolerant. One thing you need to watch is that you do not try to remake everyone around you into your own image. You use a great deal of force in trying to have your own way because absolutely no one can tell you that you are wrong. Sometimes, you are right when you criticize others and sometimes you are wrong, but right or wrong you stick to what you believe to the last outpost. You should get involved in some type of art expression or appreciation to balance and ease the pressure of your perfectionist drive. If you equally develop the psychic or intuitive side of your nature with the practical side you can become very wise and very accurate with your interpretation of things; however this may not be early in your life but later after you have matured and have had a few difficulties with people.

J. C. Penny (Merchant) (1875)

September 17

When it comes to business you have intuitive sense so that if you follow these intuitions you usually succeed against any pressure others may put on you. Any successful person has to have this perceptive sense of vision as to the outcome of a project. You have this talent to a very high percent. A lot of people have dreams; and a lot of people are practical but to have dreams and practicality work together is rare. You have this balance which makes you the practical idealist. You see a vision and you figure out exactly what it takes to make this vision a reality. You can be a little secretive about your personal affairs but this only makes you more interesting to others. Along with this business perception quite naturally comes the ability to do well financially. Business is not the only area of life you can do well for you can do well in the spiritual world, religion, or any other kind of inspirational work.

Hank Williams (1923)   Queen Elizabeth I of England (1533)

September 18

You are very high minded. It is a great passion within you to bring the universal concepts down to earth and get people to balance the mystical, universal concepts with their material lives. However, most people continue to value only the material much to your distress. When it comes to love you are direct and honest. You give a great deal of love but also want a great deal in return. Even though it is difficult for you to live in this material world full of competition you usually succeed in keeping your high ideals as well as being able to manage materially; but then you are a Virgo. You can be a fine example to all others around you of the integrated person. You can be a philosopher or some kind of counselor. When a problem comes into your life, you usually solve it immediately without hesitation or fear. Your Virgo computes, but faster than most other Virgos. If you take your life in the direction of some public works, you can become very well known in your community for your wisdom and the continuing development of your wisdom. You are conventional to a degree, the degree necessary without getting out of balance with your own individuality and universal concepts. When the chips are down your universal connection and concepts will win.

Greta Garbo (1905) Samuel Johnson (writer) (1709)

The Day of Your Birth

September 19

You are a leader who has more energy than ten people. You are willing and able to work hard for that which is either your duty or desire. You do not expect anything for nothing, but it does bother you when those around you do not extend the same effort as you do. Even though it is easy for you to do your own thing, and it bothers you if others do not pull their own weight, you do not offend people with your talents and drive. You have a certain unselfish nature and it also bothers you that others are not generous. There is a certain sense of equality about you; fifty for you and fifty for me. You can be generous and understanding over a longer period of time than anyone else but eventually if those you are generous with do not give back after several tries on your part, you begin to be intolerant and may even back away from the relationship. Behind all this is your ability to manage your affairs very well, home, business, money, love, enjoyments.

Emperor Augustus Caesar of Rome (63 B.C.)

September 20

Born on this day gives you a highly developed spiritual nature. Sometimes in order to arouse others to change and to action, you play the Devil's Advocate. You force people in this way, taking the opposite view, to own up to the desired action or theory you were trying to get in the first place. You are a master at doing this. When people expect you to do one thing, you do the unexpected. If there is anything you do not like it is for people to take you for granted. The minute they start doing this, you astonish them with something. This doesn't mean you do not have the ability to be loyal and responsible in a relationship but it does mean you expect to be an individual above all and you expect the other person to be so, too. You tend to be honest and frank and because you are honest and frank, things get straightened out in your life much faster than others who face their life's problems with lies, deceit or evasion.

Sophia Loren (1934)

September 21

You are a scholar because your mind is ever attuned to searching for more and greater knowledge regardless of whether that knowledge is science, philosophy, or religion. Above all, whatever happens in your life you remain optimistic and positive. Difficulties only make you grow and achieve all the more. You do not waste time and while you are dealing with current situations more fully than others, you have your sights on future developments and possibilities at the same time. You get the most out of every experience, every bit of knowledge and philosophy that crosses your path. You remain in wonderment with life. It is not important to you what works for others; what is important to you is what you believe and what your experiences have done for you. You do not retain anything in your life that is false. Discarding that which has no positive place in your life is easy for you. In many ways and with many things you can be skeptical until proven to you.

H. G. Wells (writer) (1866)

September 22

You are a high universal soul, capable of connecting with the higher cosmic force of life, if you but listen to the resounding voice of your own inner voice. The sun sign is changing on your day so you have a fine combination of Virgo and Libra giving you tolerance, diplomacy but also mastery of purpose and detail. Material things are important to you only in as much as they allow you to do those things that are part of what your mind and heart have to do. There is a certain magnetism about you that attracts others to you even though at times others you attract cannot put a finger on why they are attracted to you. Sometimes, people say you do not always seem like you are of this earth. At the same time you have a more universal vibration around you, you still have both feet on the ground which is quite a combination. This influence would also make you an excellent teacher of philosophy, religion, science and all those subjects that make people think of things beyond their own selfish interests. If anyone can do this, you can.

Ingemar Johansson (boxer) (1932)

The Day of Your Birth

LIBRA
September 23 through October 23

The ruling planet for Libra is Venus. It is an air sign, cardinal, active, positive, masculine. The zodiacal symbol is The Scales. Venus rules love, values, resources, counseling, diplomacy, jewelry, fashion, etc. It also rules partnerships, marriage and all other things artistic. The birthstones are the aquamarine, the jade and coral. The flowers are the cosmos, and the dahlia. The metal is brass. The colors are green and pastel shades. Libra rules substances that reflect (like mirrors) or that which takes high polish.

The ruling number is 6; therefore lucky days for Libra are 6,15, 24 of each month.

All Libra people are good at functioning as a host or hostess. They are congenial, and have the fantastic ability to put themselves in another's shoes, but always coupled with the ability to counsel when necessary in order to help the other person grow. They like harmony around them at all times including beautiful colors, gorgeous fabrics that show quality. They like clothes that are in good taste and are usually well dressed.

Above all else they believe in the philosophy of live and let live. They generally do not like anything that has to be hidden. They prefer all things out in the open.

September 23

You are the eternal student. You never stop studying or learning about life. You apply everything you read to your own real life dramas and have an analogy for everything. You could be a good writer for it is inherent in your nature to express what you have learned or to tell your slant of things. As well as you can express yourself in writing or communication work, you could also be excellent in the dramatic arts. You are very interested in your community and could become involved in many projects for the betterment of your community. You are a "neighbor" person, being very interested in the welfare of the people around you. You are also interested in the here and now, the today, but you seem to be able to balance this with the future, the abstract and the distant. This gives you a very integrated nature. You are close to your brothers and sisters and relatives but it is just as easy for you to consider your neighbor like a relative.

Mickey Rooney (actor) (1920)

September 24

You have artistic talent or at least you have a great appreciation of all things artistic. You can be very sociable and gracious. You dislike ranker and discord and try everything within your power to create amiable conditions around you. Gentleness is part of your nature with a deep sympathy and almost reverence for your loved ones. It is also easy for you to put your feelings into words. Even though you have deep sympathy and strong feelings you do go beyond the point sometimes of being able to manage them. You have a wonderful mixture of practicality and tolerance if you work on the integration of these two talents. You can make your loved ones very happy for you are a very special person to be around. At one time you can spoil the people you love, while at another time you can give them angry outbursts which surprises them at first but they soon get used to it. It is just your way of letting off steam and you do not mean for them to take it to heart. When you have an artistic outlet, you have a way of using this excess feeling toward a sense of beauty, creativity, and productivity; then it doesn't take a negative direction.

F. Scott Fitzgerald (novelist) (1896)

September 25

You have a strong psychic intuition and you also have a vivid imagination so you have to watch so you do not get these two distinct talents mixed up. You get hunches and the hunches that come in a quick flash are generally the true psychic impressions. Your imaginative ideas come more slowly and story-like. You are tolerant, compassionate and capable of sacrificing yourself either for a greater than life cause or someone you care about. You would do well in one of the healing professions or where you can show compassionate caring. Psychology would be good for you as well as some spiritual or religious work. You can be secretive and may not tell much about yourself. A lot of times you get caught in a dream world of your own and need to get pushed out of it once in a while. You may do very well working with and cooperating with a more high speed person for if you attract one like your rather low key personality, much of the time would be spent in fantasy adventures.

Glenn Gould (pianist) (1932)

September 26

You can be very organized, especially in the business field. One thing you must watch is the tendency to dominate those around you. You possess a great deal of self confidence and assurance; therefore you may tend to be a little intolerant of those who do not have your drive and discipline. You can make up your mind to what you want and stick to it until it is achieved. You like recognition for accomplishments; not so much for ego satisfaction but just because it is important for you to achieve. You think the world would be a better place to live if everyone had this drive for productivity. And in many ways, you are right. When you have this above average success you can be very generous; however, when you are still struggling for your place in the world you may not be so generous. When you can afford to be generous, materially and emotionally, you are, but but when you cannot afford it one way or another you are most disciplined in your outgo. The bottom line to your character is discipline and organization.

George Gershwin (composer) (1898)

September 27

You have a strong generous nature and above average taste. You are adventurous and enjoy making others happy. One of the greatest experiences you can have is to bring a shout of joy into the heart of another. Watch so you do not get too generous and lavish. If you had a billion dollars you would no doubt share half of it by doing special things for people. You fluctuate between being very active and ardent to being very placid and quiet. Your deepest and greatest dream may be the humanitarian par excellence. You cannot see why life is not meant to be lived in a happy joyous way. When people have fears and doubts you are bothered by this. You are bothered because deep within your own nature is something that fires you onward and upward beyond your own self interests, and you wish with all your heart that you could do something to make all of them feel better. Yours seems to be a mission in life and you feel this at times very strongly.

Jayne Meadows (actress) (1923)

September 28

You are a leader and a manager. You have ideas others haven't even dreamed of yet. If you do get into any kind of executive leadership you expect your orders to be followed to the letter. You yourself can carry out every order to the letter and your integrity with your vocation or your personal life is above reproach. Your word is a pledge that you will never break. You are best in a position in life where you are possibly using your brain instead of your physical exertion. This doesn't mean that you cannot function with sports, domestic chores or anything else physical, it simply means you prefer to do mental gymnastics with the competitive vocational world. You keep everything in its place, business to business and pleasures to pleasure. There is nothing you cannot organize with ease and perfection, whether it is a picnic, a cook-out, a committee for some cause, or whatever. You are the one in the crowd who is more than likely to start something. You usually take the initiative. It is also a possibility with your dedication that you can end up in life having a very prominent position because of your reputation for honesty and trust in what you do. Those above you in business will trust you and it isn't long before you have a high position in the executive world.

Ed Sullivan (TV Personality) (1902)

September 29

You have very universal ideas which makes you very intuitive where the real truth of a situation in concerned. You are expert at understanding others; therefore you have no problem following objective decisions and directions when necessary in your relationship to others. You easily identify with all artistic projects for you love concerts, paintings, dancing and any and all of the other art forms. You can be quite adept at anything historical or antique. This gives you the ability to do well in collecting and selling antiques because you can spot one a mile away. You seem to have been born with an instinct for just knowing what is valuable in this area and what is not. You can be an understanding and tolerant friend but only up to the point of being used to your disadvantage. This is not exactly cold calculation on your part for you sense that making yourself a crutch is not good for you or the other person in the long run. You have promise of great spiritual growth for there is a spiritual force that surrounds you like an aura.

Jerry Lee Lewis (singer) (1935)

September 30

Your integrity is of the highest degree and you will not compromise your ideals for anyone. You want the best things in life, not only materially but mentally and spiritually. You view your goal into the future and will make every effort in every way to achieve it. Nothing sidetracks you for long. With this talent is a fine sense of humor that endears others to you. When it comes to your associates, whether business or personal, the janitor can be as close to you as a president of some large corporation. What matters to you is the quality of the person and his or her honesty and high-mindedness. Status and social standing are not as important to you when you choose a friend. You would be excellent in any kind of teaching, legal field, spiritual work, or publishing. One of the best things you can be is a shining example to all those you touch. For your integrity, self respect and high ideals and your ability to work for those ideals finally influences others in a positive way.

Truman Capote (writer) (1924)

October 1

You are a very unique person, one of a kind. When the God Force made you he threw away the pattern for October 1 is very unique. You will work very hard, easily doing your own thing. You will never be afraid to take your own lead and travel your own road. Suddenly, when in your late 30's or early 40's the world may beat a path to your door as you can get some kind of recognition for your very special talents. You can be emotional, but that same emotional intensity can be taken a step higher enabling you to do something special for humanity. When you decide to do something or take a stand, you do not stand around for approval or ask questions, you just go ahead and do what you have to do. This is the reason that in the end you can become known as a leader. You are so busy most of the time doing your own creative thing in life, it is always a surprise to you to suddenly realize that you have a large following and are influencing others. Because of such self insight (unusual for a Libra) coupled with your Libra talent for relationships you can go far and become a very integrated personality.

George Peppard (actor) (1933)

October 2

You have a lot of integrity and are a very sterling character. You not only have a great deal of respect for yourself but for others as well, and because of this others are always glad to lend you a helping hand. No matter what you have to go through in life, good times, bad times, your own positive philosophical spirit maintains a balance because of your high degree of faith. This stems from a firm faith in yourself and your special spirituality. When the chips are down, when material resources are low, you never lose the highest of your values, belief in yourself and your God. When a difficulty happens to you, a loss or a sadness, it is only a pivoting point to a higher level, or a greater improvement in yourself. Defeat never stops you for it only signals a time for new growth. This is the motto you live by and will die by. In the end when your time comes to meet your maker, you will be ready, realizing the God of us all will have something better ready for you, that is how great is your faith.

Mohandas K. Gandhi (Hindu leader) (1869)

October 3

You are a very disciplined person, not easily showing any weakness. When it comes to any kind of personal affectionate or emotional expression whether toward a person, relationship to a project or even your work, you show how you feel by how much you accomplish or how much you serve. In other words you put your money where your actions are and not just your talk. Talk to you is cheap; work is not. You are able to give the very best that is in you where work is concerned. Above all else that you are, you build foundations, things that last, including relationships. You are solid and give others a feeling of security and well being. You may prefer to do things your own way and mostly by yourself (unusual for a Libra). You do not always have to be with someone to enjoy life for you like to study, do a little hiking and also a little meditating. Being a Libra you do relate easily to others, but being born on the third you do it your own way and as a result can be a very integrated person giving the same amount of attention to others as yourself. When you believe in something you do not argue about it, you do not make waves, but just go about quietly taking action. Your strength of character and courage is very nigh.

Thomas Wolfe (1900)

The Day of Your Birth

October 4

Above all else you like variety and as a result will attract a variety of friends for you relate to all people in all branches of life. Born on this day you are good at communication and conversation comes easily to you. You become so enthusiastic with your word pictures that you can easily lead others into anything you want. You are so curious about so many things that unless you have other more disciplining influences in your horoscope you may leave something before it is finished and on to something you think is more exciting. While on the surface of life you seek variety and do not always seem that disciplined, underneath you do realize that you need to have a more common sense approach. When life or curiosity get you too far out, there is something within you that brings you back to square one. If you get involved in some kind of professional work that has variety to it, you can use this curious nature of your to a more productive course; thereby making room for an outward display of discipline and responsibility. When that happens you will have arrived. In many ways there are two parts of you, one that is as enthusiastic as a child and the other part as disciplined and responsible as an adult.

Charlton Heston (actor) (1924)

October 5

This influence should give you a talent in one of the finer arts. You are fair, capable of accurate judgment and considered by others to be a well balanced person. It is true, for you do have a certain equilibrium with all you do. You get along very well in business and personal affairs for you can easily put yourself in the other person's shoes. People instinctively realize your innate ability to put things together so they usually step aside and give you the lead. You have a way of making people feel comfortable and so they cooperate before they realize it. The qualities you have in abundance that make for success with people is your ability to put management and innate understanding of others together in one package. Also, with your flair for the arts, you can be very successful in the expression of one of them to your financial profit. You may have a variety of relationships for you can relate to others on every level and are capable of immediately understanding what type of relationship each one is. You are rarely deceived about that.

Glynis Johns (actress) (1923)

October 6

You possess very spiritual qualities including the ability of prophecy. You are self confident but also tolerant and compassionate with others. It doesn't take you very long to make up your mind to something for you seem to have intuitive powers that give you the right answers on the spot. You are at your best with intuitive powers when difficult times are upon you. When things look darkest you always come up with the tiny spectrum of light that leads your way. You can be artistic either as a spectator or a participant. A large part of your nature is going to remain mysterious to others. While you are friendly and communicative, those you deal with always realize there will always be a large of you that will remain hidden. Only your dearly beloveds may know you to a fuller degree and what you are really all about. At some time in your life you have the ability to receive great recognition from the public for your trigger like mind, a mind that is very accurately intuitive not only for yourself but for others. This recognition will be to a greater or lesser degree depending upon your ability to project yourself, other aspects in your horoscope agreeing. But no matter what degree your recognition takes, your special talents soon begin to spread over your community like a light to a dark corner.

G. Westinghouse (inventor) (1846)

October 7

You are a person with great human understanding. You can easily relate to people in all walks of life and bring a peaceful condition to wherever you go. You seem to be able to touch the higher world of the spiritual for you easily feel and experience the subtle influences of the unseen world, but you do not let it go at that, you try to spread this spiritual understanding to others in the practical everyday, real world. As a result you could be a great humanitarian or dedicated spiritual teacher if not the whole world, your little world within your community. By spiritual I mean touching the great universal spirit where real truth exists. If it takes sacrifice to achieve peace and harmony, you can do this also and at the same time inspire others with your benevolent spirit. In other words you bring the spiritual down to practical reality.

James Whitcomb Riley (poet) (1849)

The Day of Your Birth

October 8

You get so involved with life in so many different ways that sooner or later there begins to be too many demands upon your time. Time in a day is never enough for you. You can see things clearly where a present action will lead to in the future. You have excellent judgment where things of the artistic world are concerned and would make an excellent critic. Your talents do not only extend to the artistic world but to the world of business. Because you instinctively know what appeal a book, a movie, an item of fashion, jewelry will make, your success is assured in any kind of promotions. You are organized with your work, but may find other people sometimes take up too much of your activity. Your best kind of work may be some kind of trouble shooter where you can easily find the errors in a situation or project. It is very satisfying to you to be able to straighten things out and make them work in high gear again.

Rona Barrett (columnist) (1936)

October 9

You are a leader with a strong mentality. It may not always be clear sailing with your leadership success for there are two parts of your nature that at times are at war with each other. You possess a very spiritual nature that has tolerance and compassion with a sense of true humility but there is another side of your nature that wants dominance over others. Until you have learned to balance these two parts of your nature you may just tread water until that time comes when you chart your course using both facets of your nature equally well. A very special marriage will settle you into very definite aims but until that time comes you may have many romantic attachments and much adventure. In many ways there is a fearless side to your nature willing to gamble with life and all life's by-products. Those who know you best will see the brilliance of the mystic side of your nature for you indeed seem to be attuned to the cosmic force. Your vitality is unlimited and perhaps one of your greatest talents is inspiring others with your vitality.

Camille Saint Saens (composer) (1835)

October 10

You have a good memory and a very great historic sense. You have the ability to inform others of past experiences in an entertaining but also an educational form. You make a good host or hostess and love to put on the feed for your social group. No matter what others may say, you seem to instinctively know what they are to the core regardless of what they may appear to be. Most of the time you are content, especially if you have a loving family around you. You are intuitive and psychic which generally makes you able to size up a situation rather quickly. You could do very well financially dealing with antiques. You may be the one in the family who retains all the history of the family, possibly many generations back. When it comes to someone who knows what to do and then take action you are the one who usually does. If there is any tendency you must watch it is not finishing what you start. You may leave it to others to finish, but as you see it someone has to take the initiative to begin and others should jump in and finish. There are the starters and the finishers and also the ones who follow through with what they begin. You represent those who dare to be the pioneer.

Adlai Stevenson III (politician) (1930)

October 11

You have a great deal of foresight thus giving you the instinct for taking the right approach with your first step. No matter what happens to you, you always have the ability to make a come-back and performing even better than before. Coupled with this ability not to be defeated is an inner optimism that what happens to you is part of a universal plan. Because you go through life with this rather fearless approach you attract a lot of experiences, good and bad. In other words you go where angels fear to tread at times. Nothing can squelch your ability to use your reasoning power, a reasoning power that is always on the level and always on target. One thing about you, you never lose your cool and if you do lose your temper on rare moments it never lasts very long.

King Richard III of England (1452)

The Day of Your Birth

October 12

You are solid and very dependable. You are the one who can make things work. Once you say you are going to do something, you can be counted on with your life, if necessary. You are loyal, responsible and are no doubt the most steadfast person in your family and community. Many times others give you their confidence and trust you with intimate things they tell you. You are a hard worker and put a lot of energy into what you do. Others don't know how you do it. You enjoy work and get full satisfaction with fulfilling and completing your work projects. When it comes to having a good time, you like the social life if and when it comes up, but most of all you enjoy what comes your way, whether work or play and take life as it comes. People you care about trust you and that is, perhaps, one of the most valuable possessions you can have.

Luciano Pavarotti (opera singer) (1935)

October 13

You are a talker and say things in a very glib manner that charms everyone with whom you come in contact. You make a good salesperson for you have the fantastic ability to keep the attention of whatever person or group you desire. You could sell sunshine to the Sun. This would also make you a good teacher for you have a clever way of holding the interest of your students as well. This does not mean you have to be a teacher in the strict sense of the word, but it does mean you teach others around you each and every day by your words, your deeds, your image, your inspirations. In addition to this talent you could do well in the writing field. Others like to be with you because you are mostly positive, seeing the brighter side of life rather than the negative or depressive. You have a good sense of humor, even laughing at yourself at times. Because you have this positive outlook on life and because you always see the better and positive way out of any situation or problem, you attract people of high station who are able to do special things for you and yours. You can have the world by the tail, so avail yourself of all these wonders life can give you.

Virgil (poet) (70 B.C.)

October 14

You are a lover of beauty and harmony. You possess the ability to make your home a thing of beauty and can decorate with a little touch here and a little touch there creating a lovely place that others would spend thousands of dollars on but not you, you can do it with very little money. You have a knack. The public knows you as the person who is very tactful and diplomatic. When it comes to your family and close friends you are the one who can see both sides and arrive at a favorable solution for all concerned, a natural born counselor. You have a flair for the artistic, crafts, music, fashion. Above all you have a soothing influence on the people around you. With you around things go smoothly; however, this does not mean you cannot take a stand with something you believe in for you can. When that moment arrives for standing up for something you believe, you can surprise others with the determination of your stand. Underneath your smile, the tactful words, is a determined heart and mind; especially when something is crude or vulgar that goes against everything you believe in.

Dwight David Eisenhower (president-general) (1890)

October 15

You can be interested in the mystical, the spiritual, the psychic and the occult. Your hunches and instincts about things are generally right on target. When it comes to your personal life, you may be a little secretive for you believe what and who you love should be more or less your own private business. You are disciplined with your feelings and emotions and are not inclined to go into an emotional merry-go-round. You are very loving and accept the sacrifices of love when and if necessary. One of the traits you can surely develop is spiritual love, loving another above and beyond the material and physical, loving another for his or her own sake and growth. Since you are capable of sacrificial love, and also capable of sensing how others feel without their saying it, you have to stop and think perhaps they can't come close to your talents in this regard. You may have to make an effort to express your own feelings to those close to you realizing some people need words, even though you may not. Use some of this inspirational talent to write poetry or get involved in dancing as a hobby.

Linda Lavin (actress) (1939)

The Day of Your Birth

October 16

You have a very serious nature and in the end you have the advantage over less serious people. Even though you accept responsibilities and duties easily, this does not mean you cannot have fun and pleasure, for you do when everything is ready for it. Perhaps fun is planned, or at least the time for it is planned. You do not generally act on impulse where fun and pleasure is concerned. It is not like you to run off to some pleasure pursuit at the drop of a hat, especially when you have work to finish first. You are the type of person who receives joy and satisfaction for a job well done. You are sincere and mean what you say and say what you mean. You dislike people who are dishonest and frivolous as life is serious to you. You seem to believe in a higher purpose with your destiny and you do what you have to do and do not really care what other people say or think. You have faith in yourself and the fateful direction life takes. You also believe firmly in divine justice and deep down you know that proper rewards will eventually be given out.

Noah Webster (1785)

October 17

You have a sense of adventure; however, it isn't always possible to satisfy this part of your nature so you substitute with artistic expression. You also substitute with movies, adventure or mystery books. With all your spirit of adventure you have a good business head and coupled with an imaginative instinct leads to success. You are spiritually oriented yet practical and realistic and it becomes a life long effort to combine these two qualities adding a flavoring of the adventurous making for a satisfying life. There is a secretive part to your nature that treasures all the fantasies of adventure and romance you cannot have in the real world. You should use this talent for writing your own adventure or mystery stories. You may be surprised at how successful you could become.

Evel Knievel (daredevil) (1938)

October 18

You always have to be active. It is difficult for you to relax at times. You have to learn to do some fun things at the end of a very hard work-a-day. You possess a goodly amount of patience and tenacity that pays off in business success. You need to be your own boss and be independent to do your own thing. In order to do this you need financial stability which you continually strive to get and maintain. You are a leader capable of initiating things others wouldn't dream of doing. After you put things into motion others seem to jump on your band wagon. You are an idea person and always have some idea worth considering. You do your own thinking and have a fearless quality to your nature. You have the ability to begin projects, to take the initiative but also to finish them and this is a rare combination. Original ideas, fearlessness, patience, tenacity are quite a good combination of attributes. You can't fail with these as part of your tools of life.

George C. Scott (actor) (1927)

October 19

You have an ardent and sensitive nature coupled with great strength of character. You do not waste time planning little things but plan big projects. Your vision is broad and long range. You have a strong interest in your home life as well as participation in community affairs. You are very loyal and faithful to a mate and if anything if offensive to you, it is disloyalty. You are efficient and productive in whatever you do. You have a fine combination of tolerance and psychic perception and the practical and workable so that as a result you can achieve some very unique things in your lifetime. Above all else, you have great business instincts for you seem to know what will work and make money; especially those new things on the horizon. You can introduce just the right product or service for you seem to know what the public will accept and what they will go for.

Jack Anderson (columnist) (1922)

October 20

You have a very domestic side to your nature, but another side likes adventure and travel. These two traits may not seem to go together but in

The Day of Your Birth

you they make for a very integrated person. You are true to those you love so you try to compromise your sense of adventure with your strong sense of duty to family. You can work hard but then when it is time to relax and play you can do that equally well. You cannot be accused of being all work and no play; nor can you be accused of all play and no work. With you there is a fine balance between these two parts of your life. You have a very understanding heart, and many come to you with their problems as you have the ability to sympathize with them emotionally while at the same time giving them objective advise.

Mickey Mantle (baseball player) (1931)

October 21

When you do something you do it right or not at all. You are practical and realistic. You enjoy entertaining in your home because you are fond of people and enjoy having them around. As a result you become quite popular because when it comes to socializing you do it up right. You are also a perfectionist when it comes to your work. When you work, it is not just for the money but you also do a good job for the pride of a job well done. You could do well at a job where accuracy is of utmost importance; perhaps in some scientific endeavor or computerization. In many ways, you can travel the road of the genius. Even though you are a perfectionist in what you do, you are more inclined to be more scientific than artistic.

Dizzy Gillespie (jazz musician) (1917)

October 22

You are a creative artist who has the ability to make your artistic creations profitable. Your gift of expression and way with words is very unique and could make you capable of being a writer. You seem to have the universal touch. Moving fast and always being in motion is an essential part of you. You are not that easy to understand for while you express yourself well and fluently, there seems to be part of your nature others sense but cannot exactly tune in on. You can become well known and attract fame and fortune if you concentrate on developing just one of your many talents. You have a built in method of self rejuvenation for when you feel sad or blue you get into motion, go somewhere, do something to change the mood. You speak up quickly, have a certain sparkling manner to your way with people.

Franz Liszt (composer) (1811)

October 23

You understand others and really care about helping them. You deeply love your family and loved ones and are extremely generous where they are concerned. You are talented in most all of the creative arts (or could be) and instantly recognize a genuine product from a second best; thereby giving you a talent for being a good critic of the arts, fashion, the entertainment world. Another pleasure filled hobby is music for as far as you are concerned music soothes most ills and can take you into whatever mood you desire depending upon what type of music you choose to become absorbed in. You can be very refined and attract to yourself all things cultural. You inspire others to grow by your caring. Others know you love them and as a result you can lead them to self improvement just by example and inspiration. You learn through your mistakes and experiences and are not apt to repeat mistakes. You are a lover; not a fighter. If you feel something you are most likely to express it. Because your day is the dividing line between Libra and Scorpio, you will possess some of the Scorpio intensity and strength of dedication.

Johnny Carson (TV star) (1925)

SCORPIO
October 24 to November 22nd

Scorpio has a strong, intense nature. They have great fortitude, are magnetic, heroic, and secretive. At times they can be jealous and vindictive. They have a talent for understanding the secrets of the universe. They make good detectives for they are interested in the secrets of others. In many ways they have a fatalistic attitude and can fight to the death for something they believe in rather than give up.

It is a negative-feminine sign, magnetic, and a water sign. Scorpio is interested in all things mysterious, like the occult, magic and the psychic. The ruling planet is Pluto. The symbol is the Scorpion and the Eagle. The higher attributes of Scorpio is ruled by the Phoenix which means they are capable of rises up out of the ashes.

Their birthstone is the topaz and the flower is the chrysanthemum. The metal is steel or iron and their lucky number is eight. Scorpio rules oils and all substances underground.

The colors for Scorpio are magenta, maroon, and deep reds.

October 24

You seem to be able to communicate on a plane others do not understand or perceive. There is a stubborn streak in your nature where your acceptance of the truth is concerned. You are blunt and say things like they are. Everything is the way you decide it to be and once you have accepted something or someone, it remains so. You are intellectually curious about many subjects and your ability to investigate not only book study but actual experiences with people and life is very thorough. You are somewhat of an unusual person with an air of mystery. Even though you are blunt with the truth and seem to be able to pick up easily on others, others may not get to know you that well at all. You can be gracious when you have to be, but not to the point where it infringes on the truth. You have some artistic talent; perhaps of the musical or poetic kind. You seem to be in touch with the intangibles of life, the occult, the unseen vibrations all around you.

Moss Hart (playwright) (1904)

October 25

You are intellectually curious and like things that others know little about or those things of study that tend to be oblique to others. You have a talent for doing your own thing in your own way. If what you do causes others to have an adverse opinion of it, or you, this doesn't bother you too much for you will do it anyway. However, if at first others do not easily see what you are doing or how you are thinking, your patient endurance wins them in the end. Above all other talents you may possess you are a good organizer with business and can be a good leader attending to your duties and responsibilities in an efficient manner. This is a good combination of being able to tune in on the intangibles of life in balance with the practical and organizing. It makes you able to sacrifice if necessary for either love or business; whichever is most important to you at the time. You can love someone in a very special way, sacrificing everything, even society's acceptance, if it comes to that. The same holds true of ambition with a vocation, being able to dedicate your 100% attention on it to the exclusion of everything else.

Johann Strauss, Jr. (composer) (1825)

October 26

You are more hard headed and not quite so tolerant. You are a person who is dedicated to truth, not some half-truth, or fable but truth, for in order to fully believe in something you have to be shown proof. In other words you are a skeptic, a skeptic who needs to see the total view, all the pieces of the puzzle put together in their proper place before you accept. This does not mean that you are without sympathy, but it is sympathy that will not allow yourself to become a crutch for anyone. Deep inside your nature you are aware that you weaken others when you make yourself a crutch. Before you accept anyone you have to be sure they are not false or deceptive. You have easy insight into the people around you. You will evolve and develop to the point that when you get into your latter years you can have very great wisdom. When anyone wants the truth about something, or someone, you usually have it for your drive to find the whole truth, the full picture gives you great insight, courage and others learn to respect you for this even though you can be hard-headed at times, hard-headed but never hard-hearted. There is a difference.

Jackie Coogan (actor) (1914)

October 27

You are a leader, always able to initiate an action for a project when others cannot. You possess a lot of courage and usually take the initiative in a given situation. You have an abundance of ideas, concepts and new ways of doing things. Along with these ideas, you have the organizing ability to put them into practice. You can be a trouble shooter, being able to get to what is wrong in a given situation. You will not take a back seat to anyone for on the whole you have a lot of confidence in yourself. Because of this people do move over for you and this makes you turn out very successful for you

The Day of Your Birth

get a lot of chances in life. You do express your opinions whether others like it or not so you may have to learn to do this with diplomacy and without anger. Learn to follow through and you have it made.

Isaac Singer (inventor) (1811)

October 28

If you were born on this day, you cooperate, and can be an ideal mate or partner. You are a person who follows through on things others start. However, even though you can carry out orders and other people's projects successfully, with a little help you can become a leader. You are excellent with your finances, knowing how to manage your income as well as attracting resources without difficulty. You usually know what you want out of life but go about getting it in a more diplomatic and tactful way rather than in a dominating, aggressive manner. There is an emotional side to your nature and it is important to you to have a mate beside you to make your life more meaningful. You are sensitive to conditions around you for you immediately sense the climate of people and react accordingly.

Jonas Salk (discoverer of Polio vaccine) (1914)

October 29

You are honest, open and above reproach and express your thoughts and opinions and stick to them regardless of any opposition. Your memory is excellent, so good in fact, once you see something or hear something you remember it instantly at recall. In fact the past holds more memory for you than current things. You seem to be able to sense the truth of things in a more universal fashion. You are sincere in most all you do. There is an idealistic influence to your nature coupled with integrity. An interest in all things philosophical and spiritual holds your attention always. You have a very special combination of independence and tolerance. You understand many things; therefore you would make a good writer, reporter, or any kind of adjuster of problems.

Fanny Brice (comedienne) (1891)   John Keats (poet) (1795)

October 30

You have a potential for writing ability and coupled with your acting talent can bring great success to one degree or another depending upon how much success you desire. It is all up to you. Your sense of leadership is excellent for you do not fear taking action and at the same time keeping both feet on the ground. You have a kind of creativity and leadership that has practical value. It is more than likely that in your world, however large you make it, you will have some type of prominence because something deep within you wants to achieve. You are ethical and never break your word once you have given it. You make plans but do not spring them until everything is ready to go into motion. Somehow you have the wisdom to realize you need to keep quiet about what you are going to do until the time is right. This gives you more strength and doesn't dilute your ideas with a lot of wasted talk.

Christopher Columbus (explorer) (1451)

October 31

You are a very curious soul ready to investigate anything new. Your life will include a large number of acquaintances. Your interests are so varied you either do not stay with any one thing for long since you do not seem to have enough time to devote to any one subject. It is fine for you to broaden your field of knowledge, but you should endeavor to specialize in one field. You like to move around a lot for travel appeals to you. Communication with others is a major part of your nature. You have to have activity in your life most of the time. It would not be well for you to settle down in life too young before you get the variety seeking and change out of your system. There is a strong duality in you which causes you to have two things going at the same time. You are very individualistic and strongly independent although you do not show your independent nature to others until they know you better. However, in the final accounting you will be able to take roots. It is just a question of sooner or later and with you it is no doubt later.

Alfred Nobel (philanthropist) (1833)

The Day of Your Birth

November 1

You possess a very optimistic disposition which causes you to be well liked by others. Born on this day you need a certain amount of freedom. There is also a certain amount of extravagance to your nature in one way or another; perhaps, not in all areas but you may have a certain item, or hobby where this extravagance shows up. One thing you need to watch is that you do not exaggerate things out of all proportion to what they really are. If you apply yourself you can become a great intellect, but also you can be very perceptive where the unseen forces are concerned. This is a combination of the scientific and the psychic which is quite a talent if you apply it in the right direction. With the proper amount of discipline you can become a specialist of some kind. As a result it can give you a very integrated personality. You possess great charm for your conduct has so many facets to it that others are generally amazed and even fascinated.

Gary Player (golfer) (1935)

_____

_____

November 2

You are a very hard worker with the ability to organize and see things through to the finish. You also have the ability to wait until the right opportunity comes to you even if it takes years. While you are waiting you continue to improve your craft through study and constructive experiences. Above all else you are dependable with a great sense of integrity. Your family means a great deal to you and there is nothing you wouldn't do to help them and protect them. Even though you are practical and responsible you do have a very creative quality and are definitely not a carbon copy of anyone else. You believe in the right of each individual to be themselves and even if they do not believe in what you believe, you fight for their right to do what they have to do, a very honorable and special quality that earns much respect from others.

Burt Lancaster (actor) (1913)

_____

_____

November 3

You are a person of expression personified; if you feel it you will more than likely express it but only to the point where the expression doesn't uncover your deepest longings and secrets. You are a very complex person in that you are communicative but secretive. You can say what you think to people but in a way that will not arouse any angry reactions. When you care for someone you will fight for them to the death if need be but also when you dislike someone you do not hesitate to show that also. Your words, your appearance, your timing is usually just right. You are good as a lecturer for you possess a high rate of magnetism when not only dealing with people individually but with large groups. You are interested in your community and do much to serve it. Your relatives mean much to you and you may be the one in the family with wit as well as wisdom. You are unique and can be objective as well as subjective.

Charles Bronson (actor) (1922)

November 4

You are an optimist and always full of hope not only for yourself but all who cross your path. You are artistic and well mannered. Your enthusiasm extends not only to your personal life but to whatever job you do with your career. You have a high sense of responsibility and duty to your loved ones and your employer. You are adaptable and always ready to accept any new circumstances into your life without getting upset. Your nature is such that you no doubt look younger than your years for it is in optimism we rejuvenate the body and stay younger and it is negativity whereby we deplete the body and age faster. You seem to know this instinctively. Even though you are flexible with life's changing conditions and like a variety of things happening you also have the capacity for concentration on a given thing at hand and following through. You are practical and artistic; logical and flexible; loving and courageous. This makes you quite a person who usually has a measure of success in all you do.

Will Rogers (humorist) (1879)   Art Carney (actor) (1918)

November 5

You are very idealistic and have a strong psychic talent. You sense a certain connection with the cosmic force and intuitively understand how we are all part of it. You firmly believe everyone should have or perfect a creative talent of some kind in order to regenerate our spirits from the daily mundane realities of each day. Your constant aim seems to be to make the

The Day of Your Birth

world a better place to live in and to instruct those you come in contact with how to keep in tune with their own higher force. You do this to one degree of success or another. Once you yourself find a philosophy that you think is the right one, you bend every effort sharing your ideas with others. Coupled with your ability to use words and express yourself, your ideas flow in unison one after another in perfect harmony making them very effective. You are sincere, well meaning, and very wholehearted; no half way measures for you. Every facet of life interests you from economics, sports, religion, art, music, poetry, dancing.

Art Garfunkel (singer) (1941)

November 6

Your ability to organize is very strong and you execute your duties efficiently and speedily. When you have a job to do, whether that job is your domestic affairs or your vocation you can be depended upon for you develop a reputation for being faithful and trustworthy. Therefore, you generally rise to a high position with your career. You are congenial to work with and generally do not make waves. The little details do not bother you for you understand them to be part of the larger project. You usually get involved in projects where church work or community affairs are concerned for with your organizational ability and dedication to hard work, others seek you out. Even though most of the time you do not make waves, when aroused you can be very domineering and aggressive and far from tactful. This is the other side of you. However, you will give things a fair enough chance until you take a more permanent stand. While you can overlook little petty disturbances that cross your path, if too many big disturbances come into your world, you can explode. Cultural, artistic, the finer things of life interest you for you have a sense of refinement and beauty to your character.

Sally Field (actress) (1946)

November 7

You are very selective in your choice of companions which results from your very idealistic attitude. You are interested in all the mystical aspects of life and fully realize there are many things going on behind the scenes in most people's lives. Because of this you make a good detective, a very perceptive psychologist or any other branch of research that takes keen awareness of the hidden motives of man. You instinctively understand the cosmic scheme of things and if effort is put into this direction you can become a great teacher, preacher, writer or leader in higher cosmic philosophy. There is a tendency for you to be secretive about your own personal affairs. You are compassionate and sensitive to others when you need to be, but when it comes to your own life you retain a selectivity with those you take close to you as friends and/or a marriage partner. When you do decide on a selective choice, you are prepared to make all manner of sacrifices for the relationship, whether personal or business.

Billy Graham (evangelist) (1918)

November 8

You are a leader, an organizer, and are happiest when you can initiate worthwhile and constructive projects. You do not stand still once you get an idea in your head for you will do something about it. With this talent is another talent for having instinct, a built in radar system that just knows what will work and what will not. People soon begin to realize this, and let you take charge. You need something going all of the time to retain your healthy attitude with life. If someone tells you to take it easy, you become restless and easily bored. To you being active and productive is the healthiest method and medicine you can take. It really matters to you that your community is functioning at its best and your greatest satisfaction and joy is to be part of it. The outer world of society and business is most important to you. You love your family but need to be an essential part of the whole community. You can take others rather casually except when you really want to make an impression that counts. You are better at initiating things than finishing them for it is easy for you to organize and instruct someone else to take over; thus giving you extra time to organize and initiate something else that needs to be done. A great function for you is to establish a system where a business or office work is concerned..like trouble shooter. You can organize, straighten out mismanagement then move on to another office, business, or corporation to conquer. It would be likened to being a doctor of business organization.

Katherine Hepburn (actress) (1909)

The Day of Your Birth

November 9

You have the innate ability to be very objective with your thinking. When it comes to a decision on something, you easily turn off the subjective role, move away from it, size the thing up objectively, get to the truth of the situation at hand. You possess a good sense of humor, but a sense of humor that is quick and subtle, calling on your higher mentality to see the humorous point, again taking yourself out of a subjective situation. Your humor and wit is never coarse or crude. You can be very optimistic by nature and always believe in the ultimate fulfillment of your most cherished dream. No one can ever take that away from you. You are very honest and truthful and cannot see why others can't see the value of being honest. As far as you are concerned you understand and believe in the good fortune that comes your way in facing life in this manner. Basically you have integrity, an integrity that does not lessen if someone does you wrong. In the end you succeed in turning most people around who cross your path with wrong values. Your belief, your optimism and honesty finally does the trick.

Florence Chadwick (Swimmer) (1918)

November 10

You have a great deal of talent in many directions and for a while earlier in your life tend to fritter away your time but once you decide upon a direction in life you become very serious about it, dedicating yourself and settling into the responsibility it takes. You have creative talents that could take the form of writing, or any other artistic expression. You may be successful in fulfilling more than one creative talent in your lifetime; thereby becoming well know for more than one achievement. You possess a great deal of talent for many things and may want to be adept in all of them, but you will at some point in your life take one talent at a time, bring it to a successful achievement and then go on to another creative development and so on, but never really completely losing touch with a formerly developed talent. While the greater part of your time and effort is concentrated on a current talent, you never completely take your fingers out of the previous pies. You are by nature gregarious and friendly and love to be around people. Early in your life this gregarious nature can conflict with the discipline and dedication to achievement but you soon mature and learn how to balance these two needs, integrating them to your best advantage.

Richard Burton (1925)

November 11

This is an unusual day and endows its bearers with great strength, intellectual, spiritual and emotional. Born on this day gives you a more cosmic connection and awareness. It gives great spirituality whereby you somehow sense the great importance of being in tune with the great God force. Along with this strong intellect and instinctive spirituality is staying power. Once you espouse an idea or a theory you have the fortitude to see the idea become productive. You have a combination of sensitivity and strength, an unbeatable team for success. You have just the right amount of instinct for knowing just how far you can push anyone or anything to the limit of its capacity. You have one of the highest numerical and astrological days of the whole year. Many great things can happen on this day in any given year and many great people are born on this day. You seem to have a drive to do the seemingly impossible for yours is a role of high leadership if you will but accept your cosmic destiny.

George Patton (army officer) (1885)

November 12

You like to be on the go most of the time. There is never a dull moment around you. You are a Scorpio, determined and forceful but along with this forceful nature is a curious flexibility not usually found in Scorpio. This naturally makes you very complex to most people. You are magnetic but at the same time electric, a kind of electromagnetism. You have a talent for words and expression, but can be sharp with your tongue. It is easy for you to get to the bottom of what people are really all about, seeing through sham almost immediately. Travel appeals to you because you get excited when the possibility of an adventure comes on your horizon. You could be an actor, an announcer, a lecturer, a writer, a teacher, or any vocation where you can electrify your audience. You may appear to be a flirt but this is only surface for underneath you are settled and loyal when you love.

The Day of Your Birth

Working with large groups in a leadership capacity helps work off some of your need for variety and exciting activity. Working with large groups can satisfy your need to spread the word, whatever your word or cause is.

Grace Kelly (actress) (1929)

November 13

You try very hard to have a congenial personality, You do not want to hurt anyone, but at the same time feel it necessary to follow your own conscience when push comes to shove. You are equally good in business and domestic affairs for you have a tendency to keep all phases in your life in balance. You are artistic, appreciate all the arts and have a drive for becoming a person of refinement and class. On one hand you may seem a little bit daring, but on the other hand you never lose your sense of responsibility and duty. Your charm is contagious and causes you to attract many into social circle, people from all walks of life for whether or not you have any form of discrimination in your soul, you do try to be fair to all types of people. If a negative or a prejudice of any kind shows up you immediately try to erase it by doing something positive about it. You are a Scorpio Sun sign but this position of your day makes you a much more benign and positive Scorpio, less inclined to be vindictive. You could become a great performer on the stage because your popular appeal with people is one of your greatest talents. You can also have an inclination for writing.

Robert Louis Stevenson (writer) (1850)

November 14

You have a talent for psychic consciousness, esp and any form of the mystical and seemingly intangible. To you, the intangible can seem very tangible. You could be very successful with these talents especially if you study and develop them. Any talent we possess should be cultivated and used in a given lifetime; otherwise we will have wasted the talent we were so generously given at birth. You could also be good at some form of musical expression or dancing. You have an uncanny talent for picking up on all the intangible vibrations around you. You also have an instinct for communicating with all types of animals. You seem to understand them and they understand you. There seems to be a silent kind of communication with them that is sparked. Not only is your talent in music paramount, but in composing your own original music you can become successful. You could establish an individualistic expression that could catch on easily. This can be true no matter how extensive your audience may be from only a few in your community to world wide. It is up to you. Much depends upon following your hunches and acting upon them instead of letting fear or others inhibit you.

Leopold Mozart (1719)   Prince Charles of England (1948)

November 15

You know how to manage money and to organize and manipulate a situation and persons in order to make opportunities for yourself (and sometimes others). You are clever in that you are aware of a money making opportunity others fail to see; therefore you usually end up being more successful with more money than the average person and with your Scorpio fortitude can knock down any barrier that stands in your way. Coupled with your ability to see opportunity, you do not deceive others for your ideals stand up under the pressure of success. You are willing to sacrifice a temporary discomfort, or a temporary lack of profit for a long range business or personal success. You have a shrewd sense where money is concerned and can do more with money than any other person you know. You are no doubt a letter writer, or a recorder of little experiences that seem important. You work hard when you work but you also play hard when you play for you thoroughly enjoy being with friends, parties, but you can just as easily get enjoyment and fun out of a given achievement in your work. You are not necessarily a work-a-holic but will not be under sold so to speak with the quality of your efforts nor will you waste time on the job. To you, wasting time is a grave sin of some kind.

Paul Simon (singer) (1942)

November 16

You possess a tolerant and sympathetic nature that draws people to you. Even though you are understanding of others and can give them a certain

The Day of Your Birth

amount of consolation, you do not do this to the point of becoming a crutch but in your own very unique way inspire them to develop a strength of their own, seemingly without their even realizing what is happening. Your instincts with people rarely fails you because you not only are able to put yourself in their shoes but never lose your own objective viewpoint. Along with this is a balanced nature enabling you to see the responsibilities of life but also the lighter side. Because of this you get a great deal of enjoyment out of life for you love what you do and do what you love. For the closest thing to your heart is being a well adjusted productive person. You have a talent for music participation and/or appreciation. You may also have a flair for dancing for somehow you can tune in on the finer nuances of life.

W.C. Handy (composer) (1873)

November 17

You have a tendency to be somewhat of an analyst, analyzing each event in your life and each person who crosses your path to one degree or another, in other words the whys and wherefores. You are very good at sizing up situations and people rather quickly and very accurately. What makes you so successful at this talent is that you have a good sense of humor along with it so that people take things from you they would not take from anyone else. You take what comes and let it go at that. You keep a healthy balance between the highs and lows of life, never letting anyone influence your peace of mind for very long, if at all. You have a lot of self initiative and are usually the one in your community who starts things and gets others enthused into joining you in these projects. You can be somewhat of a work-a-holic and need something going most of the time. You are good at business and could become a very high ranking executive if you put your mind to it. There is a fearlessness to your nature for once you make up your mind to something you will always be able to figure out a way to bring it about. You have a healthy respect for money and usually can manage your finances to your best advantage; therefore you always seem to have more money than you actually do simply because you know how to buy, how to save, etc.

Rock Hudson (actor) (1925)

November 18

You have a very high cosmic connection which makes you idealistic, poetic with a touch of tolerance and compassion. You like the outdoors, flowers, hikes, swimming and all those things that go on in the fresh outdoor air. You have a connection with nature in such a way that it almost seems like you are communicating with all things that grow. However, it is only that you experience the aura of the flowers, the trees, and the like and you seem to do something special for them. You have a rare talent in this regard. You should never go against your intuition for you seem to know when something is the right thing. You are psychic and mystical and may cater to these things like a duck takes to water. Because you are so much in touch with the universe itself, you enjoy things to the fullest thereby mostly remaining in a more calm state of existence. You can be somewhat of a humanitarian, caring deeply for the welfare of all men and women. In this way you are very unselfish, wanting all people to progress. This caring is not just for the human welfare, it is for all of life including nature and the balance needed in this regard.

Edmond Halley (astronomer) (1656)

November 19

You are enthusiastic and optimistic. When you feel something you are more likely to express it. You do not hide your light for at some point in your lifetime you may gain great public recognition. You have the ability to sway people to your way of thinking; therefore, you would make a good public speaker, television performer, theater, politics, whatever. You give off a certain strength and magnetism that catches on. Whatever the group you become involved in, family, business, or community work, it is easy for you to take the lead. Most of the time you are cheerful and companionable but once in a while you may want to get away off by yourself. No matter how long it takes to be successful and make your mark, you are willing to put effort into it whatever it takes, work or time. You are more of a flexible Scorpio than at first appears to be so; especially in relationship to others. When objectivity is needed in a given situation, you can step back from it and make an objective decision which results in you attracting people from all walks of life, people you help with their problems and decisions. In many ways you are the natural born psychologist.

Martin Luther (religious reformer) (1483)

The Day of Your Birth

November 20

You are sensitive and can be emotional at times. With your sensitivity is a companion trait of practicality. You have much creative talent that once you put this talent into productivity you can become very successful in a monetary way. You have a very special combination of determination, talent, sentiment with an instinct for taking action in applying them in the outer world of society. However, to help you bring out the best of your talents, you need a loving mate who satisfies your deep instinct for emotional security. Once you have this secure relationship with a mate, there is nothing you cannot accomplish. You need a mate to help you fight life's battles, not to fight your battles for you, but to work with you, side by side. If you do not have this special deep love relationship in a workable, everyday world, you may succumb to self pity to one degree or another. The destiny being born on this day seems to be working with a mate in a very creative productive way.

Dick Smothers (comedian) (1938)

November 21

You have a great deal of curiosity to your nature that leads you to investigate new fields of interest almost constantly. You are intellectual with the ability to express yourself very well even though you are somewhat of a secretive person. As a Scorpio you may keep many of the private things to yourself, but you do have the ability at expression in speech or writing. You are good with research; hence writing about what you research in science, art, history, community affairs will come naturally to you. A negative trait to your character lies in the fact that you like to express yourself and since you do not always like to say much about your own private life may find yourself engaged in gossip many times. You want to know about everything and everyone and in your growing up years especially you may have asked a lot of questions. You can be equally subjective and objective. This is a talent that can take you far because whenever a situation comes up where you must be subjective, you can do that and whenever a situation comes up where you need to take an objective stand you can do that also. You may have a talent for music and singing if you work on it. You have the ability and tendency to get involved in church work or community affairs.

Goldie Hawn (actress) (1945)

November 22

You are born on the cusp between Scorpio and Sagittarius so you may be either a Scorpio or a Sagittarius, depending upon the time of day you were born; therefore you may have the tendencies of both signs which makes you a more complex individual. You show the traits of stubborn determination of Scorpio but also the flexible, adaptable traits of Sagittarius. It depends upon the situation you are involved. You can have a talent for writing or participation in one of the arts. You have a particular genius for originality of expression. Many famous people are born on this day. It is a high number and gives a more universal or cosmic outlook. By this, I mean it is more likely you will follow your own instincts wherever and whenever possible listening to the higher directives of your higher cosmic self rather than those around you, thus making you the different one in your world. You may give the world a more adaptable and congenial self, but under that facade is a very sensitive, intense deep nature. You have a lot of strength and very high ideals.

George Eliot (writer) (1819)   David Grebner (author's son)

SAGITTARIUS
November 23 to December 22

You are optimistic and enthusiastic, very objective at times with a great deal of integrity. Above all, you do not like to be fenced in for you like your freedom. A philosophical trait is the greater part of your over-all spirit. You can be filled with the spirit of adventure and are usually willing to gamble on something, whether love, money, sports.

Other parts of your nature include unselfishness with the tendency to live life in a lavish manner. You are outspoken and truthful to a fault.

Your zodiacal symbol is the Archer. Your ruling planet is Jupiter. The nature of your sign is masculine, positive, electric, fiery, and mutable. Your ruling number is three.

The birthstone for Sagittarius is topaz or turquoise. The flower is the poinsettia, narcissus, or holly. The metal is tin. The colors are royal blue and deep purples. Sagittarius rules common and useful substances. Sagittarius rules the distant, and the objective or abstract.

The Day of Your Birth

November 23

You are very compassionate and have a high sense of duty to those close to you. When you believe in something or someone you have the ability for great sacrifice. You easily tune in on the suffering of those around you and do all you can to help with deeds of kindness and consideration. You would do well in the expression of poetry, music or any kind of psychic research. You seem to be in touch with the intangibles of life and sense a change in your environment immediately. You understand the needs of all people regardless of race, creed or color. You possess a certain generosity that almost depletes you of your own needs, but occasionally you are good to yourself and express a little extravagance. It would be well for you to study all things spiritual, find your place in the spiritual structure of man, and either write about it, teach it, by words and actions. With all your compassion, and expressions of sympathy and generosity there is much about yourself that is hidden for you can be very mysterious at times. You may even have a secret life no one knows about. Every once in a while you like to travel and perhaps even go off by yourself to rejuvenate and recommunicate with the higher spiritual force.

Boris Karloff (actor) (1887)

November 24

You are highly idealistic, but an idealism that is very workable with you. You don't just talk about it, you back it up with actions. You are a natural born executive and will take the lead in business deals and/or a humanitarian cause without any if's, and's or but's. However, with all this is also your other side that sees things so clearly that you may become too aggressive and not give others a chance to show some initiative. Generally you are usually right with how you have things figured, but others shouldn't get too dependent upon your expertise for it limits their own fulfillment and development. You also have some artistic talent if you desire to pursue its development. You believe wholeheartedly in the philosophy of human rights and generally become admired for the stand you take in this area. All this can lead to a high executive position or a very prominent position in your community affairs. You have everything going for you if you learn but one thing and that one thing is a little diplomacy.

William Buckley, Jr. (columnist) (1925)

November 25

You would be good in business, but the business world that deals with personal service, service that is on a one to one basis. You have a lot of intuition where people are concerned and this perception gives you an edge over others in that you know what they are all about; hence giving you the ability to take right action. Along with this are your instincts for becoming a true humanitarian. It isn't just compassion, it is seeing the potential in most people and becoming so moved by what they are or what they can be. If you truly believe you can help another person so improve his or her life and live up to his/her highest potential you would sacrifice much of your own time and money. However, you do not sacrifice so much that you yourself have to have help. You do what you can do but not to the point where you annihilate yourself and your own supply. Love on a personal basis is important to you but it has to be on the basis of allowing each other a certain amount of freedom to continue developing and pursuing personal achievements. Love for you has to have a measure of unselfishness to it. You cannot be dominated or possessed to the exclusion of what you yourself must be. Any relationship that tries to change you is wrong and doomed to failure.

Ricardo Montalban (actor) (1920)

November 26

You are a gambler with life, believing that life can and should be exciting. You are an inspiration to less adventurous souls. You easily start new projects for you are an idea person who puts action with each idea. You may not always finish these projects, but usually you turn over the reins to competent others. Your enthusiasm sometimes is catching but in the final accounting you will have been the one to dare to do and to be and to take chances. Even though you do gamble with life, there seems to be some spiritual protection over you that keeps you out of serious trouble, but on the intellectual plane you are clever and fast and can usually size up any trouble brewing before others are even dimly aware of it. If you want to achieve great things you must learn to devote some of the energy you use for daring to a specific purpose. This does not mean you have to control your adventurous spirit; it just means you should not allow it to take up all of your time, but only the smaller part of it. If you do this, you will be unbeatable on every level of your life. You are a way-shower and rarely, if ever, a follower be. You easily show others how to go about something in a way they never dreamed of doing.

Tina Turner (singer) (1939)

November 27

You possess a high degree of cosmic instinct. Whatever you do in life you are bound to be a success because you have a high degree of responsibility with whatever part of your life under consideration. You are successful in one sense because you are also flexible in that if one way doesn't work you adjust to the necessity to change the method but not the course. You have a great deal of nobility in your nature. You listen to other people, accept good ideas of others, and many times integrate them into your own endeavors. You are tolerant most of the time, understanding and are attuned to the higher forces of life here on earth. Forming successful relationships is another important facet to your character for you easily make adjustments when necessary to keep relationships in tact. To you it is just as important to have equity in relationships as well as in business and property. Your instincts with people are excellent and this instinct can be used in the counseling profession or just advising friends from time to time. Your responsibility and consideration for your family and home is very positive and inspiring.

Bruce Lee (actor) (1940)

November 28

You have a deep understanding of people and the situations they get involved in. You can make objective decisions easily and as a result many people come to you for solutions to their problems. You see through the facades people wear and as a result are not easily fooled. The truth is most important to you so that you can accept anything if you know the truth about it, but if someone does manage to fool you, you may not deal with that person again. You are constantly in search of knowledge which makes you the eternal student. You can be outspoken and rather impatient with those who do not listen. Your nature is for moving quickly, getting things done in the least amount of time. A drive deep within you needs an abundance of experiences in life. You have a tendency to cater to adventure and usually create excitement wherever you go in one way or another. You may not have studied a certain subject officially, but you possess an instinct for knowing something innately and can give an excellent critique whether in art, music, decorating, fashion, landscaping, whatever. A high degree of integrity and nobility pervades your spirit. You do not lie nor do you expect anyone else to lie to you. If they do, you are turned off immediately.

Randy Newman (singer) (1943)

November 29

This is a very special day to be born on for you have an instinct for universal destiny and duty. You are not one to waste your time for life to you is serious and you want to take advantage of all possible opportunities for growth and expansion, not only with your material world but the mental and spiritual. You are very perceptive and find life a little easier than most people find it. You usually know what you have to do and easily do it. All of nature appeals to you for you seem to be able to speak the language of nature. You are in touch with all of life and seem to have a calming influence on all things around you, whether animal, mineral, vegetation or human. The invisible subtle influences all around us seems to be very apparent to you and very real. You may be talented with music, dancing, poetry, psychic or if not a participant in these arts, there is great appreciation and understanding of them. The simple things of life appeal to you rather than the fast life. Your nature is serious and very constructive and when your job is finished on this earth plane, you will be found among those who have contributed a great deal, and even leave a great deal behind you from which others can profit.

Louisa May Alcott (novelist) (1832)

November 30

You are always on the go and create a lot of action wherever you go. You can see the humor in things and as a result people love having you around. You have a nigh degree of integrity not only with yourself but a respect and integrity extended to others. As a result you get a lot of satisfaction from life for you operate in a top-drawer-fashion with everything. You could be excellent in writing, or any kind of communication work. You are so good at talking that you can talk yourself or anyone else into anything. Your powers of observation are above average and your talent for expressing what you observe is exceptional. You possess an enthusiasm that doesn't know when to quit. Taken at its highest you have the ability to inspire all those around you so that if directed into the field of publishing inspirational, self improvement, and spiritual messages your works can extend far and wide. When you talk it is a mixture of humor and seriousness that is unbeatable.

Efram Zimbalist, Jr. (actor) (1923)

December 1

Born on this day makes you a much more methodical Sagittarian than you would otherwise be. You are practical and always seem to have a practical way of presenting either an idea or a philosophy. Yours is a mixture of enthusiasm and practicality. In many ways this is a very special combination for you can always see if a thing has the ability to be workable. You use care not only in your expressions with others but in your physical appearance. If you do say something seemingly outspoken as most Sagittarians are prone to do, you will have thought it out a little more than most other Sagittarians are capable of doing. In many ways you are a well balanced person. You can take the lead in any situation but if you do take the lead you are very sure you can command this leadership or you do not attempt it in the first place. When you express yourself in speaking and writing you can put words together in a most proficient manner. You are dependable and conscientious so that in business you can be counted on for what you say you will do for your word is your bond. All in all you are a pretty well integrated person and are definitely not inclined to be fly by night but will more than likely take roots a little more than most Sagittarians. You are fearless in your own way and cautious so that with these two qualities of your nature in such balance, success is assured in anything you do.

Lee Trevino (golfer) (1939)

December 2

When you work, you work hard; but when you play, you play hard. You do not waste time; you organize your work so that you utilize every moment, and as a result you have more time for relaxation and fun. To others who do not know you very well it appears that you are lax but this is really not true. When it comes to planning your day, you do your work first, start early, get fully into it for you really do not relax until your work is finished for the day. You do not like to mix the two and are not apt to be found mixing work and play. You have a natural flair for adventure and seem to need a very exciting adventure once in a while in order to give fuel to your proficiency with your work-a-day world. Without this indulgence into adventure occasionally you lose something with your work. You express yourself well and can be found doing your bit for the community in which you live. You love your family and easily tune in on a one-to-one relationship with a mate or a friend. No matter what experiences come to the fore within your twenty-four hour day, you are capable of handling them for you have a well rounded nature that never lets you down and a nature that can fit in anywhere, anytime with anything. You can either be the life of the party when that is in your focus or you can be the excelled worker with deep concentration. It seems you can turn this on at will.

Alexander Haig (government official) (1924)

December 3

You are an artist, whether this artistic talent is actual production of any art piece or great appreciation of it. Above all you have an optimistic attitude with life, can be humorous and objective. You have a calming influence on others in addition to giving them a great deal of understanding. Because you can give others this understanding, you expect them to understand you. If you do not get this understanding from them, a little flair of fire results (temper to you). You are able to go forward without looking back and dislike distractions or delays in your push forward. When you say something you mean it and most people realize this from the very beginning. Another side of you is the lover imbued with a great spirit of giving and sharing. Mostly you are a giver, whether it is love, works of art or putting yourself in service of something, a cause or a belief. You seem to be in touch with the optimistic spirit of the universe and when it comes to

The Day of Your Birth

philosophy and the spiritual you can be tuned in on the truth. Perhaps, your greatest role in life is to distribute this truth.

Andy Williams (singer) (1930)

December 4

You are very idealistic but an idealism that works in this very practical and skeptical world. Somehow, you are the type of person who can just make things work. When you have a dream you bend every effort to make that dream a living reality. God bless you for you are not only a dreamer but a doer, a rather rare breed. You work hard and the dreams reside in your heart and soul giving you inspiration and drive to work even harder instead of making you lazy. But your dreams, ambitions and goals are not just for yourself but for everyone who touches your heart in one way or another for you are very altruistic. You are one of those persons life calls kind and considerate. Your motto is truly DO UNTO OTHERS AS YOU WOULD HAVE OTHERS DO UNTO YOU. There would have to be very harsh aspects in your total astrology chart to dilute this influence of kindness and consideration. You will no doubt have an excellent marriage or any deep relationship because of your strong instinct to share. Because the spiritual is so much a part of your life, it is most likely that the GREAT SPIRIT will bring many pleasant experiences into your life, including out of the blue surprises. However, if you share and understand, you need a mate who is able to respond in like manner. If you do not have this kind of mate, it eventually pulls from your own spirit and can weaken you in body, mind and spirit.

Thomas Carlyle (Writer) (1795)

December 5

You are impatient and at the same time in other ways very patient. It all depends upon what you want and where you are standing at a given point in time. If you want something badly enough you can be as patient as Job, but if your interest isn't there or someone is standing in your way, you can be very impatient and even show a temper. You are excellent in the art of expression whether in writing or speaking and should be involved in a vocation where this talent can be used at its best and fullest. You can be very organized when you want to be and could be excellent in business as an executive for you like to give orders and people seem to take them from you. If you need to develop anything it is tact and patience You really do have an excellent mind and when you work at it you can be objective and subjective or whatever the situation demands of you. Working in and for your community is another direction for your talents. Above all, you are a strange combination of enthusiasm, communication, and responsibility. This sense of responsibility is in tact when you are not impatient. When impatience sets in, then anger, stop and count to ten or twenty and think, what other way can I handle this and you will find a better solution and accomplish more in every way.

Philip K. Wrigley (gum manufacturer) (1894)

December 6

You have a certain refinement to your nature; therefore you do not like to be around anything or anyone coarse or crude. You may have an instinct for the arts, whether in appreciation or creatively becoming involved. You need people around you most of the time but are rather choosey about who you want. There is a high-mindedness about you that requires nothing but the best with most things including intellectual self expression. You are a very active person, although at times it may be difficult for you to know exactly what you want out of life. From your early years on, your search for the best may limit you where a variety of growing up experiences is concerned; therefore while you are intellectual enough, you may not have developed enough understanding and common sense, an understanding and common sense that comes from living both the good and the bad experiences. Use your high degree of excellence in the pursuit of artistic achievement. This will satisfy your very refined nature so that other parts of your life can have more ambivalence but also more tolerance of an imperfect and inadequate world.

Joyce Kilmer (poet) (1886)

December 7

You have a very sensitive nature. You may even be an innovator in one of the arts, especially music. A talent for leadership has been bestowed upon you so that it is easy for you to take the lead with any action necessary. You may not always finish things, but you are sure to find someone to take over before you do drop something. It is your tendency to start things, get them going and then go on to something else. You are very sympathetic and compassionate most of the time. In many ways you can be easy going, but in other ways you can spin your wheels for want of action. If you put these two qualities together, you can not only be successful but well liked by most everyone. You have a cosmic connection and can be very psychic and perceptive. It is your nature to predict the future, whether on a small scale or a large scale. With all of this, you can be very secretive about your private life for there will always be much about you that is not known. You show only those things about yourself you want people to know. It is also your inclination to sacrifice for those things and for loved ones most important to you. You are very sensitive to the moods and conditions around you so that you are really not easily fooled. If you have a great talent it is being able to perceive conditions in their true light and not what people say they are. You can remove the facades most people wear.

Richard Warren Sears (merchant) (1863)

December 8

The influence of this day is very powerful. It would give you a great deal of idealism and instinctive knowledge of how humanity can be at its best. You would have power to be a leader for your ideas are way above and beyond average. You are a thinker and very philosophical. More than anything else you need to express your ideas and thoughts for it is your destiny to teach and perhaps even to preach. Courage is a part of your life style which in itself causes you to stand out among the crowd. Your intuition is excellent which can extend itself to money matters for you know how to manage money and how to make money. You are also capable of managing other people's money so you could find yourself associated with large groups, a large corporation or being a broker. You can put intuition and practicality together in equal amounts resulting in potential for success in whatever you undertake. With all this is an understanding nature that makes people come to you with all manner of problems which you are able to easily solve. This position also gives you cosmic and universal instincts, and a feeling of being connected to the larger scheme of things; therefore you never feel alone but part of the macrocosm.

Sammy Davis, Jr. (singer) (1925)

December 9

You are a true Sagittarian with a very positive Jupiter influence. It is the influence of this day to be philosophical and to want the best for all mankind. You do not think small, act small or live small. You are understanding, honest, with a great deal of integrity. While you have such a serious outlook on life you still have the ability to laugh, to enjoy your friends and are usually in a good mood. Nothing keeps you down for very long. You can be objective and abstract about anything that happens to not only you but those around you. In some way or another you are always working to promote or provide better conditions for humanity as a whole and are very much interested in the educational systems of man as a means to providing better conditions for us all. You cannot stand lies, or deceit of any kind and if anything turns you off it is someone lying to you. Most all of your life you will reach for greater knowledge thereby making you the eternal student.

Emmett Kelly (clown) (1898)   Beau Bridges (actor) (1941)

December 10

You are a practical Sagittarian. Whatever you believe in the area of everyday work, religion, or love it has to have a functional or useful purpose. No matter what is under consideration it has to work. However, as with all Sagittarians you do have a sense of humor which saves you from appearing to others as too cold or calculating. In one sense you may never admit you are wrong; however whether you admit it or not you do learn lessons from your mistakes. You are a more fixed Sagittarian and not quite as adaptable as other Sagittarians. You think for yourself. You may listen but in the end you will make up your own mind. Because you are so sure of yourself in many cases you may find yourself in a leadership position whether you want to be or not. There is a certain courage to your nature and in many ways you represent the pioneer, but a practical pioneer, establishing ideas that work.

Chet Huntley (newsman) (1911)

December 11

You have a knack for understanding the public and because of this understanding a great deal of fulfillment can be yours if you get involved in some public or community project or supply a public need of some kind. You communicate well with others as a whole and unlike most other Sagittarians can deal with the now and also the future and the distant. You also have a talent for being able to talk people into most anything. In addition to getting yourself in the midst of projects with and for the public, you like your home and your family for it is home and family that gives you the rejuvenation you need. In many ways you have an idealistic romantic nature but not so much so that you cannot see and adhere to practical considerations of said love affairs. One of your biggest and strongest ideals is the ideal of family life and how important it is to constructive personal growth. You may have a flair for writing or some other type of self expression. Being a Sagittarian you have a strong leaning toward the spiritual, the objective, the scientific, the abstract but born on this day gives the ability to express these things, teaching and writing.

Rita Moreno (actress) (1931)

December 12

You may have artistic talent of some kind. You understand all groups of people but also see the individuality of each person. You would make a good counselor helping people solve their problems. You are quite sociable and make an excellent host or hostess. You easily give affection and consideration to those close to you. Above all else you are, you are a lover and perhaps a very generous lover. Your kindness makes you charming and keeps you in some magic way looking much younger than your actual years or your personality gives the illusion of youth. It is your philosophy of life to inform others that attitude has a great bearing on health and looks. In other words you do not just get older, you get better. Yours is a great optimism with life with the ability to charm the very birds out of the trees if you so desire. You could also have writing talent, that if developed could bring profit financially.

Frank Sinatra (singer) (1917)

December 13

There is a mysterious side to your nature. People may think they know a lot about you, but there is much most people will never know. You have a talent for the psychic, being able to tune in on the intangibles all around us. Even though you are perceptive concerning the unseen, you have a practical side to your nature and are not apt to go off the deep end at any point in your life. When something is important to you there is no amount of sacrifice too much for you. You can overcome anything if it is a means to an end to something greater. You have a healing quality that others benefit from whether this healing is mental, spiritual or physical. You possess tolerance and compassion toward others which makes people comfortable around you. Poetry, music, dancing may give you a good kind of feeling and you seem to need one of these expressions in your life if not on a professional basis, as a hobby for relaxation. Above all you are fair with people for you give each person his/her due. At times you may be too idealistic which can cause you to be too trusting until you learn from your mistakes in this direction.

Emperor Nero of Rome A.D.37   Mary Todd Lincoln (1818)

December 14

You are a manager whether in business or on a personal basis. This would give you a potential for being an executive. Whatever idea you have you can put it into action in a very successful manner. You know how to make money and may also know how to manage it well most of the time. Being a Sagittarian you may get extravagant once in a while but not to the point of losing your common sense in the matter. You could be a director of communications in a large organization. Relatives look up to you for support and direction. Even though you are organized and face up to your duties and responsibilities there are times when you get restless and need to be on the move at a moment's notice. Adjust to these times, do not fight them. Be yourself as an organized person, but also take advantage of the part of your nature that needs variety and adventure. There is no doubt that you will always have security for you will see to it. You not only have the ability to handle your own resources but could get into handling other people's resources on a professional level. It is probably easier for you to give orders than receive them for it is natural for you to see the most efficient way to do things. Others do not always see this efficient way and it really bothers you when you can't activate your more productive system. Most of the time you are correct with your ideas.

Patty Duke (actress) (1946)   King George VI of England (1895)

The Day of Your Birth

December 15

You have artistic talent if you want to pursue it. It is very likely that you could excel in any one of the arts. If you do not express your artistic talent in a professional way you should at least express it as a hobby. Within your make-up is the innate power to become a great humanitarian. It is also your nature to try to make others happy even if it is just within your social group you become important. You possess a certain radiance that catches on to others around you. Having a good sense of humor helps. You also have a certain nobility of spirit that is its own reward. If there is any trait in your nature that stands out among the rest it is your ability to cooperate. Do unto others as you would have others do unto you is your creed.

J. Paul Getty (tycoon) (1892)

December 16

You are one of the more complex personalities not easily understood. In many ways you have x-ray vision in that you can easily see through people. However, this can bring misunderstandings because most people do not want to be seen through. This combination of easily seeing through others coupled with the Sagittarian way of being outspoken can be a blessing or a curse depending upon you yourself and how you control these two talents, positive or negative. If you use it creatively through writing or some other creative or inventive outlet it can have the result of becoming very lucrative rather than causing irritation for others. When it comes to the influence of this day it is up to you which way it goes and you alone. You are able to take the lead in things for you are definitely not a follower. You can be perceptive, intuitive with a high degree of creative intellect.

Ludwig van Beethoven (composer) (1770)

December 17

You have a special way of expressing yourself. Because you have a real affinity with nature and all the beauties therein, others are captivated by your descriptive word pictures of nature. You are a wonderful combination of duty, responsibility and tolerance. Cooperation is high on your list of attributes along with integrity. Yours is a fine team of instinct and good intention. This position could make you successful in one of the creative arts. You have a high sense of the cosmic for you seem to be in touch with the universal force. Spiritual work could become very important to you at some point in your life. You have a great deal of foresight into the affairs of man and because of this you could be a leader in humanitarian causes for the betterment of the human condition. If you have to you can sacrifice for any given purpose but can be humorous when it suits your purpose.

John Greenleaf Whittier (poet) (1807)

December 18

You have a very understanding nature. This day gives an influence of balance between the serious things of life like work and family responsibility and the ability to enjoy the lighter things of life. You are very spiritual in your own way but tolerant of others with a mixture of good judgment. You could be very excellent in an occupation that deals with counseling for you possess good judgment and others believe in you easily. You may one day have a serious one to one personal love, but that person must first understand your need to love all people in a detached way and not misunderstand the kind of love you give to people you help. You care deeply for the whole human race and are way above average in your agape love. Your ultimate mate cannot be a jealous person or it won't work in the long run. You are an active person and can accomplish more in a day than two or three people. Everything in your life has its place. By that I mean that when it is time for work, you work; when it is time for play, you play; and when it is time for compassion and spiritual understanding, you do just that. One thing is not apt to interfere with the other.

Edward Mac Dowell (composer) (1861)

December 19

This influence can allow you to lead a good life, understanding easily the difference between right and wrong. It also allows you to discipline yourself for constant improvement in every area of your life. However, you need to watch it so that you do not get self righteous or too critical of others. You can achieve great success in a given field of endeavor for you are capable of following the narrow path necessary. You can be conservative

The Day of Your Birth

and cautious where new innovative ways are concerned. You can be a leader, but a leader with tried and true way; not innovative unconventional ways. Common sense is one of your greatest attributes which gives a talent for being able to figure out the best ways of doing things. You may tackle a given project which you hadn't done before nor had any training, but common sense allows you to instinctively know how to achieve success.

David Susskind (producer) (1920)

December 20

You are flexible and adaptable to changes in your life, but you must watch it so you are not too flexible at the expense of establishing a firm base. It is easy for you to get bored and thus this can limit your potential for success, success you want so very much. Use your ability to plan ahead in a positive way instead of using your adventurous spirit too excessively. You have a talent for communicating easily with those around you which could lead to writing or some one of the other creative expressions. If you use your talent in this way it will divert the tendency for fickleness in your personal life, or keep you stable in your professional life. In this way you can get the acclaim and reward you seek. Community work is another way for you to get involved with your life and will give you the variety you need to feel whole and alive. You need a job where there is a variety and if you have this you will more than likely stay with the job.

John Milton (poet) (1608)

December 21

You are diplomatic, quite understanding and can always see the broad view of life. You would make an excellent teacher of abstract and higher mind subjects. One of your greatest characteristics is your ability to create harmony amidst arguments. You do not impose your will on others; therefore get more out of people in the long run than those who force their wills. Even though you are not aggressive, you know what you are doing every minute. You make a good impression on people but do not show your hand right away. You have a flair for the arts and could excel in one of them. As you go through life you are constantly improving yourself spiritually, mentally, and physically. You do not stand still materially either and in this way you are a great inspiration to others around you. Only by example do you influence others for the betterment, never by persuasion.

Jane Fonda (actress) (1937)   Chris Evert (tennis player) (1954)

December 22

This is a cusp day, so those of you who have it can be either Sagittarians or Capricorns depending upon the time of day you were born. Even so, you will have the qualities of both Sagittarius and Capricorn. You possess a great sensitivity that could give a talent for poetry, music, dancing, and psychic matters. You are in tune with the universe so may also possess an instinct for the way things should really be. There is a stubborn part to your nature that is not easily noticed by people when they first meet you. In using your spiritual talent you could become a great teacher in regard to living in harmony with the universe. You realize instinctively that man made laws are not always in accord to universal law. Others may think they know a lot about you, but chances are they do not for yours is a way of secrecy. You need affection but only that affection which is on a higher level and has an element of freedom to it.

Giacomo Puccini (composer) (1858)

CAPRICORN
December 23 through January 19

The zodiacal symbol for Capricorn is the goat. The ruling planet is Saturn. It is a feminine sign meaning it is magnetic. It is earth ruled and cardinal. The key words are I USE. Capricorns are ambitious, practical, and conventional adhering to society's standards. Other facets of their nature are seriousness, reserved social standing and status are of utmost importance. They are good at planning and organizing making good business people. The ruling parts of the body are knees, bones, teeth where the calcium intake can be affected. They are capable of hard work.

The birthstone is the agate, onyx, or garnet. The ruling number is eight. There may be a variance concerning the ruling number. Number eight rules business; thereby it is easily associated with Capricorn. The flowers

The Day of Your Birth

are the carnation, poinsettia, holly and snow drop. The colors are black, dark gray, sage green.

Capricorn rules dull or heavy substances. The trees are the pine tree, cypress, yew, and elm.

The metal is lead.

December 23

You are good at organizing things; therefore you would be excellent in the business world. You can make plans, get people together and get the job done. Coupled with the ambition of your Capricorn Sun sign and the foresight being on the Sagittarian cusp gives you should take you far on the road toward success. The results can be financial but the biggest satisfaction comes with a feeling of a job well done. You possess a certain wisdom that gets you through life's tough spots with the least amount of trouble. Your reputation is important to you so you are not apt to do anything that will smudge it in any way. You stick to tradition and the tried and true ways of doing things but this does not stop you from being inventive and introducing new ways and new ideas for you are somewhat of a pioneer. In the final analysis you understand what ideas will work and make profit and which ones will not work. You should always follow your own instincts on this.

Michel de Nostradamus (astrologer) (1503)

December 24

You have a very high minded spirit. You can be very disciplined but can combine discipline with tolerance, compassion and understanding. You are strict with yourself for you realize that the road to excellence lies in discipline and knowledge. You create harmony wherever you happen to be but it has to be a harmonious condition coupled with duty and responsibility to the tasks at hand. You finish what you start which eventually wins you attention and respect. Behind much of your actions and beliefs lies the humanitarian tendency. Friends and associates will be the kind that will bring mental stimulus into your life for you could not long associate with those who do not want to achieve all they can mentally and spiritually. Another asset to your nature may be excellence in the expression of one of the arts.

Howard Hughes (tycoon) (1905)

December 25

This is a special day on which to be born not only because it is the celebration of Christmas, but because it influences its bearers to be leaders giving great foresight, correct knowledge and organized method in starting projects. You are loyal and once your word is given you live up to your word. You are a person of high honor. Attracting followers is easy for you, so much so that you generally initiate action that others carry to completion. Influencing people to get into causes and crusades is your initial role in life it seems. You are psychic, sensitive and at times mysterious and not easy to know. In fact most people who are great leaders are not really that easy to get to know. Before you die you should have accomplished much for your community and in fact could even be honored in the archives of your community, being remembered long after your death.

Conrad Hilton (hotel executive) (1887)

December 26

Because you give a project or a person your undivided attention, you appear greater than you are. You are great, no doubt about that, but it is only that you have such discipline and concentration getting the very most out of a given interest that you come across as an expert. When your interest is aroused, your energy and endurance follows through all the phases necessary for completion of any project or interest. Absolutely nothing stands in your way for very long. You are intuitive and perceptive and when you follow your instincts you are usually right. You generally do follow your own mind, heart and spirit. You seem to be in touch with the higher cosmic force and usually know what to do and when. Having this kind of intuition about yourself and your directions and being able to combine this talent with your work force and dedication there is nothing you can't accomplish once you set your mind to it. For when your mind is on something heart and spirit are there also. You can be compassionate up to a point. It is easy for you to be perceptive about others also so you may find a path to your door from others who are seeking the right answers. There is the spirit of the poet in your nature and you may also seem to be in touch with the intangibles of life.

Steve Allen (TV personality) (1921)

December 27

You possess the ability to go far and wide. The small and narrow way is not for you. Most of your talent lies in the field of expression, whether that expression is drama, literature, music. Any form of communication will bring success. You name it, and it is yours. If there is a difficulty with this influence, it is your sticking to a given talent without getting bored. Because your talents are so many and varied this may happen, but if you program the disciplined side of your nature more, there will be no problems in this regard. Choose your greatest talent, the talent you feel the most comfortable with and the one that will bring you peace and happiness in the performance of it. You have a very complex nature in that you are sensitive, tolerant, but objective and detached. If you put your sensitivity and natural born intuition and hunches in a productive direction and use all your wit and optimism along with it, the world is your oyster.

Louis Pasteur (bacteriologist) (1822)

December 28

You are a practical idealist and believe in doing your part in the scheme of things and can't understand why others cannot do the same. Nothing daunts you with your image of the way things should be. Even if you have problems that would destroy others, you plug along with your vision, and try to make things with your work, your home, your family, your beloved mate as happy as possible. You are a hard worker and can achieve a great deal more than the average person. If you are in pain for some reason or another, you can stand more pain than anyone else. However, you should find time to do things with group activities, or some kind of community project for this will make your life more complete. At times you need to watch so you do not get into a set pattern to the exclusion of other parts of your life. Your will power is great and most of the time you have two feet on the ground. When something has been done, you usually initiate the action.

Woodrow Wilson (president) (1856)

December 29

You love good conversation, music, poetry, the theater, and all the things that represent a good time. You would be excellent as a speaker, or any kind of work that requires some type of expression. The ability to mix business and pleasure is an essential part of your nature. Another thing about you is that you do what you have to do, give what you feel like giving and expect no more, no less, in return for your honest efforts. Now this is true whether you get a return from others or it is just the satisfaction of doing a good job and being a responsible human being. You are intuitive, perceptive and seemingly in touch with the cosmic force. There is kindness and consideration to your nature. Involvement with neighbors, community, relatives is a major part of your life. You can work very hard for your community, your family, friends for you like to see things accomplished and like seeing people and things grow in a constructive, productive way and desire to be part of that productivity. You can take the quiet life at times and at other times you like the bustle and noise of activity.

Charles Goodyear (inventor) (1800)

December 30

You have a great eye for beauty and in the appreciation of all things beautiful which you remember to the last detail and then you describe this beauty to others. In this sense you can also write or it could take the direction of painting or drawing. Even though you see beauty to the smallest detail your specialty lies in the fact that you are able to view first and foremost the greatest and most important features of a thing of beauty. Just because you are able to see these small details does not mean you are critical for you are not. You believe in a harmonious well run community and will participate in whatever you have to do to help make your community a better place to live in comfort. You are polite and well-meaning most all of the time. One of your great talents lies in the fact that you can be objective and very understanding. In the final analysis you are a lover, not a fighter. Your sense of the cosmic is great and in your study of the higher philosophies your sense of duty is strong for sharing your discoveries with others.

Rudyard Kipling (writer) (1865)

December 31

You are somewhat of a mystery to most people. Much of what you are lies hidden to others. Many people will think they understand you but they will

The Day of Your Birth

not. If you have one or two friends in a lifetime who really understands you, you are lucky. You are sensitive, perceptive, and psychic. You possess the ability to sacrifice for anyone or anything you truly believe in and that sacrifice does not have a limit on it. If you do not want someone to understand your true nature and you feel they are beginning to zero in on you, you do everything within your power to confuse them. It takes many tests for you to accept a friend or a lover but once you do you are loyal and true to the end. You seem to have a connection with the intangible force of the universe; therefore your hunches are usually correct. Whether you use this talent for poetry, music, dancing for a vocational endeavor, it is still good for you to express yourself in a creative way as a release and a kind of rejuvenative force in your life even though just a hobby.

John Denver (singer) (1943)

January 1

You have a combination of practicality and enthusiasm. This is a rare team. Born on the first day of the year you do have the inclination to begin new things but you also have the tendency to do things your own way. Another team combination in your nature is courage and practicality. When it comes to starting new things you are sure to have a practical workable way of doing it. You may not always finish things but you certainly do like to set things up so others can take over. You may be a leader, but a good leader knows when to let others take over and you certainly do know how to do that. Leadership in religious or higher educational fields may be another part of your life that becomes important to you. You can be a leader in business for you not only know how to deal with the associates you work with but the public as well.

J. Edgar Hoover (FBI) (1895)

January 2

You have a talent for communicating with others in a way they immediately understand. Accented in your personality is a magnetism that is able to relate to all types of people. You are interested in just about everything and have a well rounded personality. At times, however, you may concentrate in going in too many directions at once; thereby not pushing a given talent to the ultimate of its development. You are here one minute and gone the next. Moving very fast for a Capricorn is part of your nature which makes you unpredictable for the most part. When it comes to being somewhere you are usually early. You are a ready mixture of charm, communication and reliability even though at times you may seem to scatter off here and there. When it comes down to the wire you usually always measure up. Writing could be one of your talents of which you can make practical use to the point of making money with it. You give generously of your time and talents; maybe not money but yourself.

Joseph Stalin (dictator) (1880)   St. Ignatius of Loyola (1492)

January 3

You seem to have an intellectual instinct for understanding and solving problems without having had to obtain any formal education with same. In many ways you have your feet on the solid ground and coupled with your talent for giving equal time to various parts of your life can make you a very well adjusted and integrated personality. Because this influence makes you capable of constructing things, you surround yourself with the equipment to do so. You believe in fairness and could become involved with the legal system for you can easily put all your efforts on the side of justice. One thing about you is that you have a mind that is not easily fooled as the minute someone asks you something, or appears on the scene you immediately get to the bottom of the situation without any if's, and's or but's. Even if you, yourself get into any difficulty or a temporary weak spot with your life, you can figure out the problem and correct it. You never stay in a weak spot for very long.

Stephen Stills (rock musician) (1945)

January 4

You are a Capricorn by birth sign, but born on this day makes you a Capricorn who is a little more speedy and flexible. Because you have a reputation for speed or fast decisions others try to give you scandal saying you are not accurate but this is not true. You are fast, practical and fulfill

The Day of Your Birth

your duties mostly without error. Others as a result of your very unusual talents may get jealous but this is of no concern to you. You do not waste anything and do not like others who do. Finding the simple, short, constructive, effective way of doing things is uppermost to you. You know how to communicate with others easily. In fact, you need to watch it so you do not always do the talking. Let others put in a word now and then. But because you have a sensible nature you know how far you can go "holding the floor" so to speak. Another one of your major attributes is your ability to mix business and pleasure. Use some of your communicative talent to write or teach. You may find you could be more successful with it than you realize.

Isaac Newton (physicist) (1643)   Jakob Grimm (folklorist) (1785)

January 5

In the top drawer of your talent is artistic creativity. You easily know the right colors to wear, to decorate your home with for there exists within your talents a natural inclination for color, design and beauty. You are easily in "love with love" and when you do love you are very loyal. Because you are so expressive, at first, others think you shallow but you are far from that. You like to make people happy for your nature is for the most part happy. Because of this you like to have parties and entertain. Part of you wants independence and the other part of you wants dependence on a loved one. As a result, you may get caught up with a mate holding too tightly to the deprivation of your freedom; however, you ever remain free mentally and spiritually no matter what others may do or try to do.

Konrad Adenauer (German politician) (1876)

January 6

You are very mystical in nature which results in strong perceptions and intuition about things. You usually know how something is going to turn out before it happens and in this sense you continue to represent a mystery to the people around you. It ends up by your becoming a kind of prophet in your area. By spiritual definition you are in touch with the universe in a way others cannot conceive. A proper name for your talent is seventh sight (psychic connection). All things ruled by this intangible connection are the things you become involved in doing; such as music, meditation, dancing, books, art appreciation. Because you are so sensitive you are aware of the troubles and worries of others, but also because you are, above all, a Capricorn, you will control this sensitivity. What you will do, is to do something to help others in a practical way, combining sensitivity for others with practical action. You are very idealistic but it is more like the practical idealist. You are generous up to a point, but perhaps, more generous with your time and your action rather than money.

Johann Kepler (astronomer) (1572)   Danny Thomas (1914)

January 7

You have the ability to be a fine executive because you have a talent for organizing and a seventh sight about money matters. It seems you can start something on a small scale and end up with it becoming bigger and better until you have big business with it. It is your nature to understand easily what will succeed and what will not succeed. Because it is so easy for you to figure out ways of accomplishing things, it is better if you do your own thing, or at least work at your own business. You also have a strong sensitivity, perhaps even psychic talent. You can be somewhat mysterious, not easily interpreted by others. As you get older, after a certain measure of success you may begin to be more philanthropic or become tremendously interested in educational pursuits whereby you train others. You have sensitivity but this sensitivity is coupled with great strength. If a given project or goal calls for sacrifice you can do it. If a given objective calls for discipline and a period of isolation from others, you can do this also.

St. Bernadette of Lourdes (1844)

January 8

You are a person who is realistic but also at the same time imaginative and fanciful. For this reason you could have a great career as a writer, an artist, an actor, musician. This position's influence makes of you a practical idealist, one who is capable of making his or her dreams a reality, but it also produces the ability to attract an abundance from his or her creative projects, abundance financially. You are a practical optimist if that is possible, or should we say an optimistic realist. Once you initiate a project, you usually carry it to completion. Yours is not for stopping in midstream. This is one of the most excellent influences for a creative executive. It gives the ability to make new and innovative ideas work and for that reason you could literally call the shots, opportunity-wise and money-wise.

Elvis Presley (singer) (1935)

January 9

You are independent and self reliant and do not like to take orders from anyone. You have the ability to lead and instinctively seem to know the right orders to give others. Attracting a multitude of varying experiences is also natural for you. You like to get things going, get others into action and then step aside in order to establish something else. You are optimistic generally speaking. Even though most of the time you will initiate a project and let others carry it through, at times there is a humanitarian goal that holds your interest to the very completion of it. You can be adventurous and in many ways are a gambler with life, especially when it comes to business projects. When you do gamble on something, you seem to somehow know it will work. Others may think you are gambling on the wind, but you yourself always have an ace up your sleeve they don't see or know about.

Richard M. Nixon (president) (1913)

January 10

You can work well with a boss over you if you have to do so, but you may prefer to follow your own ideas. You follow orders and do a good job while waiting for the opportunity to come to a position where you can give the orders. There is originality and cooperation both to your nature so that you are able to fit into whatever category you have to in order to better yourself. You equally relate well to others, but are also quite content to be by yourself at times. There is a rather fearless quality about you. You have courage and pioneering instincts meaning you are not afraid to start something new and unique and follow your own ideas. The beautiful part of this is that when you do introduce some original idea others are attracted to your ingenuity and may even copy you. This gets you promotions in the business world and attracts special relationships on the personal emotional level as well.

Charles Cornwallis (army officer) (1739)

January 11

This is a special day on which to be born for it gives the bearer great talent either in the arts or for that which is psychic and occult, or both. You have an instinct for things and can easily see into people. Your understanding of human nature is excellent and for this reason you get ahead in the world, whether in business, entertainment or psychology. No matter whether you direct your talent to entertainment, diplomacy or business, your genius and cosmic awareness will bring you rewards to the extent you act upon them. You know how to make people like you and therefore attract a large number of followers, acquaintances, friends and hangers-on. Knowledge of how to make things work to your advantage insures good luck surrounding you. You possess a certain amount of tolerance and compassion but not to the point you make yourself a crutch for others for your inclination is to help others use their potential and develop their own strength. Whatever you want to be, you can be, and this is the philosophy you try to impart to others.

William James (philosopher) (1842)

January 12

Your nature possesses a cross conflict between self imposed restriction and freedom. Don't blame others for this conflict, look to yourself for it is only you who can untangle these two opposing parts of your nature. When you use your talents, when you put your ideas into constructive concrete action, success will be yours. It is then that restriction turns into discipline and freedom turns into creativity. Do not just dream about ideas and don't let fear put chains around you, for it may be a question of fear or freedom. When you take fear and make it active responsibility to succeed and you take your need for freedom and change it into individualized concepts then at last you will have integrated your talents to the extent of being productive. Another way your talents can work is the positive trait you can have of common sense and wisdom coupled with objective understanding. In other words when you become more selfless and take the selfish isolation from around you and take the risk, finally, of considering others, you will have achieved the ultimate of what you can be.

Paul Revere (patriot) (1735)

January 13

Your nature can be one of extremes. It can bring self imposed obscurity or give you a certain amount of fame. It can bring financial security or financial insecurity. You have a great interest in your community affairs, love to participate in birthday and other celebrations for family and friends. When you learn to control your extreme ups and downs and stop secretly enjoying these emotional extremes, you can begin to give and receive the love you so intensely need in this lifetime. You have these extremes because everything stirs you so deeply. Learn to control your feelings more and to face each of life's experiences in a more mentally controlled fashion realizing that "this too shall pass away." Use some of your ability to easily sense the emotional climate of a situation for the theater as an actor, director, producer, writer. In this way you can more productively and positively use your ability at overplay. Get into some kind of artistic expression in order to balance your nature.

Horatio Alger (novelist) (1834)

January 14

Beauty is all important to you. You would create beautiful things wherever you go if you had your way and the time. In many ways you are in love with love and can be a great communicator of all things lovely. This expression could take the form of writing, poetry, music or whatever artistic creation becomes important to you. It could be directed to expression of love to a beloved mate. Being a Capricorn you may have great respect for conventions especially in the area of loyalty to family and duty, but not so that you lose your exceptional ability to perform your ideal of artistic participation which is an individualized need for you. Since this is a combination of functional artistic talent as well as its expression, you could become a great critic of the arts, realizing instantly what will appeal to the masses and what will not. You take great pride in your community and your environment and may find yourself beautifying the landscape if only your own flower garden, roses, flowers and shrubs of all kinds. In this sense you could become a great landscape architect.

Albert Schweitzer (humanitarian) (1875)

January 15

You have an instinct for tuning in on the intangibles of life and easily understand hidden facets of the personalities of others. A talent for predictions, and all things psychic is second nature to you. You like music, dancing, the theater and all things cultural. You may find yourself promoting the works of the finest composers, authors, and other creative minds and will bend every effort to do so even if it means sacrifice of some kind. There is a secretive part to your nature and very few know you for you only give bits and pieces to most people. In many ways you are like a puzzle that defies comprehension. You are excellent in helping your community grow in economic and social matters. When it comes to your relatives, brothers and sisters, you may be a soft touch. Money interests you only so far as giving improvement to your life style and not money for money's sake alone. But then the resources of your mind are just as valuable to you.

St. Joan of Arc (soldier-saint) (1412)

January 16

You are an excellent example of what your sign is all about, perhaps more than any other day with the exception of January 7. It is very likely that you will be the head of an organization or have your own business some day for your ability to organize people and projects is the top drawer of your talent. Your authoritative manner does much to instill confidence in the people around you. Another part of your talent is the artistic world and by artistic I mean either a participant in artistic expression or as a critic, collector or just plain enjoyment. In many ways you are very mysterious. Others may think they know a lot about you but chances are they do not

The Day of Your Birth

for much of your personal world you keep under wraps. You need harmony in your home life and will either have it or you will keep yourself so busy with your vocational world you will not be in your home much. You are loyal, devoted and a once given love will no doubt remain with you until death even though you don't talk about it.

Ethel Merman (singer) (1908)

January 17

You love to delve into the mysteries of the universe, the mysteries of life itself, religions and even occultism. You are inclined to be religious in the sense that you want to relate to all that is good and not evil. Your intellect is naturally knowledgeable by instinct for you seem to understand a subject even without ever having studied it formally. It just seems like you are connected to a higher source of knowledge. You are tolerant of those who cross your path of life and can develop into quite a humanitarian. There is no amount of sacrifice too great in your pursuance of God's world for the wonders of it ever seem to fascinate you. Born on this day gives more compassionate understanding to your Capricorn Sun sign.

Mohammed Ali (boxer) (1942)

January 18

You are a true leader with a fearlessness that takes you forward where others fear to tread. Among your various talents is the power of persuasion where you can talk yourself or others into anything. Any form of activity with the public or your vocational interests come above other things in your life. This does not mean that love, home life is not important, it is just that public success is very important to you and has to have a priority before you get too involved with personal relationships. Establishing new projects, new community programs is your forte; however once they are established you like to give over the power to others and move on to another world to conquer. You would make a good lecturer, writer, salesman, or wherever the powers of communication hold sway. Above all you are not a follower, but choose to be followed. If something has to be done, you are usually the first one to move forward to offer your services.

This does not mean that you blow your own horn, it just means you are not afraid to do that which hasn't been done before.

Danny Kaye (comedian) (1913)

January 19

You were born on the cusp between two signs so you take on the qualities of both so you will always be influenced by both Capricorn and Aquarius even though you are still a Capricorn. You are a lover and want love of the highest caliber. Your Capricorn influence makes you loyal, steadfast, but the Aquarius tendency takes love that is offered even though it may not be necessarily conventional; example, difference in age, background and maybe even race. You may outwardly conceal the deep need for true love and may appear very controlled but underneath is a great sensitivity. You never forget a hurt and may not forgive as easily as others. With all your cleverness and wit is a sparkling personality. You are nobody's fool and with it all end up with the prize at the top of the Christmas tree. At another point you can be selfish but at another time you can be selfless. Complexity may be your middle name, but magnetism is your first name.

Robert E. Lee (army officer) (1807)

AQUARIUS
January 20 through February 18

Aquarius people are inventive, independent, progressive, yet fixed, determined and somewhat unconventional. These people can always find original ways of doing something and do not expect them to do things like everyone else does. It is the sign of friendship, fellowship of man, and detachment. Aquarius is ruled by both Uranus and Saturn which means that in their fight for individuality and the unconventional they have an underlying influence of duty and responsibility to their individuality and inventiveness. Mostly they are honest and are angered when others try to cheat them. Once they set their minds to something, they are not easily changed at least not by coercion.

The Day of Your Birth

It is an air sign. It is fixed, masculine and positive. The ruling number is 22.

The jewel is the amethyst. The flowers are the violet and the primrose. The metal is Uranium or radium.

Aquarians are unpredictable and sporadic and it is not easy for them the adhere to a pattern.

The colors are silvery white or electric blue.

Aquarius rules all magnetic substances.

January 20

Your basic personality trait is optimism and because of this you are usually very popular. You were born with an instinct for being able to discern the truth in a given situation or philosophy. There is gravitation to all higher mind subjects. You have great sensitivity where family and home conditions are concerned. In your great desire to be objective, you may cater too much to others' ideas and make allowances for them instead of doing what you yourself DEEP DOWN know has to be done. When you work toward developing your higher knowledge of the world and its people you become successful and more self assertive. You can be adventurous with the spirit of gambling with life. In another sense you can be very much into sports and outdoor activity. Try to balance the objective with the subjective, keeping the concern you have for others in balance with your own drives and desires.

George Burns (comedian) (1896)

January 21

You possess tenacity coupled with intuition and courage. Working very hard for what you believe in, is as natural to you as it is to breath. You seem to work at your fullest one day at a time, doing what must be done, eliminating the obstacles as they come along. All this seems to surprise those around you for you can accomplish much more work, remove many more obstacles than the average person. This is an excellent combination for a realistic approach for making things work. It is creative ideas that are workable. The practical idealist at its best. This is an Aquarian you are, and that represents inventive ideas that have appeal for a wide mass of people.

You seem to know which ideas will take hold on a broader more productive basis. There is nothing small about you when you do something you do it not only with a passion but with a drive that puts all others around you to shame. With all your talent you can achieve great success for you have the drive, the ambition, the guts, the ideas that can make you far surpass most others.

Placido Domingo (opera singer) (1941)

January 22

You are the communicator, par excellence. Born on this day gives you the influence of cosmic awareness. Your world is not the ordinary or the mundane for you always seek to achieve more than average and that which is beyond comprehension of the ordinary person. In other words you are far ahead of the pack so to speak. You may find yourself at some point in your life doing a great deal for your community and may always have a cause you are wrapped up in. You are friendly, outgoing usually say what is on your mind in a congenial and diplomatic manner. But behind and beyond all your congenial and diplomatic manners is a person who is not that easy to interpret. You seem to be on the same wave length with everyone else around you, but everyone senses there is much more to you than at first meets the eye and ears. In many ways you are unconventional, individualistic, and independent especially when the chips are down.

Lord Byron (poet) (1775)

January 23

You are an artist either in participation or just appreciation of it. You express a kindly disposition to people and are well appreciated because of it. Your talents in this direction go another step for along with being kindly towards others, you are dependable. With all this is a way with others that could lead to success if you are involved in a vocational way with education or the healing arts. As you progress through life you can become more and more well known for your talent either in the artistic world or the sympathetic role as a healer. You will struggle along each day doing what has to be done with day after day, month after month, year after year until you suddenly look around and realize you are becoming very well known. One of the best things about you is that people are comfortable with you. Whatever position in life someone is in, they suddenly feel at one with you for you can understand and relate to all types of people.

John Hancock (patriot) (1737)

January 24

You are a very spiritual person with a great deal of faith. You can be very secretive when it is to your advantage to be so. Creativity combined with practicality can give great success in the business world. You easily adjust to any kind of circumstances in which you are involved. The gift of prophecy may also be yours and if used properly can give you exceptional foresight with your affairs. You can best use your talents in writing, television, the theater, or some form of creative self expression. Music is excellent therapy for you whether you perform it yourself or are just into the enjoyment of it. Life will bring you many experiences of various kinds for you are not afraid to live and sacrifice if necessary. You can deal with the hard world of reality and combine it with faith and compassion. Not many are able to do this but you are one of the fortunate ones. Success will be yours as far and as long as you want it, performing, achieving up until old age for you never want to give up.

Neil Diamond (singer) (1941)

January 25

You are an extrovert. Your interests and intellect is focused on the social and vocational world most of the time. The only time your judgment may be impaired is when you allow anger to get to you instead of using your fine intellect. You are ambitious and very definitely will make your mark in the world in some way. Executive powers are yours by natural right. You can be talkative and secretive at the same time. Perhaps, those things closest to your personal heart you will keep secret; perhaps, even from your beloved mate but those things dealing with ambition and outward success make you talkative and outgoing. Where your home life is concerned you are usually well organized and assume leadership. There is psychic and intuitive perception within your talent structure. All you need do is develop it. Even though success is assured in the business world, you possess the ability to sacrifice on the personal emotional level if you have to do so. Most people think they know you but most of them do not know the biggest part of your character which remains hidden except to a very, very few.

W. Somerset Maugham (novelist) (1874)   Jeffrey Wilken Shaw

January 26

You are a person who loves all of humanity. It is as if the whole world is one big family. The love you have to give is too big for just a select few. Deep within your nature is a drive to leave your mark in some social work, some civic endeavor, some cause. You can become a great religious leader or become very well known for your social service work whether just in your own community or the larger national scene, all depending upon your active efforts. You seem to instinctively know the weaknesses of people, but you also know where their strengths are. Your values are not necessarily monetary but living life in its fullest form according to your own development and desires. If your desires and intuition differ from conventional society you can set the pace for others to follow you. You are an innovator, always showing people another way. Funny part of it is, they listen to you.

Maria Trapp (folk singer) (1905)

January 27

When others are afraid to take the lead, you are not. The thing you have to watch is not quitting before enough is accomplished. You are very creative and have to do your own thing. Making decisions is easy for you and also giving orders is easy for you. You will be much more successful if you are more diplomatic and don't push your weight around. When you want to, you have a great understanding spirit but may also be very outspoken in your drive for truthfulness. You are a leader and coupled with your instinct for the right knowledge makes you unbeatable. You are sensitive to the intangibles around you including music, poetry, the emotions of others, and the spiritual values of life itself.

Wolfgang Amadeus Mozart (composer) (1756)

January 28

There is an emotional element to your nature and if you learn to control it you can avoid little panic situations when your affections are not returned to the same degree you give. You are generous and loving almost to the extreme and expect the same kind of devotion which is hard on loved ones. You can be jealous of those close to you, but in your impersonal, vocational life you have understanding without jealousy and excess passion. One of the most important things you must remember is to try not to be possessive of loved ones. Your home life is most important to you and you like a close knit family. Taking your talent into the world of the public or your professional life your instinct for knowing the public need and your know how in organizing can make you very successful. Pursuing a public life and family life in balance can make you a very integrated person. To make this all possible there is one thing more important than all the rest and that is you should resolve not to pressure loved ones.

Alan Alda (actor) (1936)   Arthur   Rubinstein (pianist) (1886)

January 29

You like a large group of people around you most of the time. You can never be limited to just a few people or with a life style that wouldn't have some excitement in it. You are happiest when you are the busiest and your greatest joy comes from the knowledge that you have accomplished something very durable for the greatest number of people. Great vision is yours as far as the total outlook for humanity in general. In many ways you are a philosopher which could have its outlet in writing, teaching, politics or social work. If one were to describe you in a couple words it would be a practical idealist. You have a sense of compassion, tolerance but also believe people should develop their own strengths and use difficulties as leverage. When it comes to your own growth, you can always move forward with few backward glances, if any. All of your lifetime you will be a student, always eager to learn about something new. You may also have an instinct for the spiritual truths of man; thus enabling you to be a teacher in the religious areas.

John D. Rockefeller, Jr. (tycoon) (1874)

January 30

You have a combination of being very mentally creative plus the ability to stablize and put ideas into action. Some would consider your talent imagination but it is more than just imagination which they soon find out. You possess two sides of the coin so to speak; however, be sure that when you put action and effort to a creative idea it is the idea you really want to pursue because many, many ideas will run through your head. Coupled with it you have foresight that if used rightly can give you the talent to obtain whatever goal you desire. Because you are a strong person, if something is important to you, you will let nothing stand in your way. Nothing will bind you if it in any way hinders you. You are able to accept the unconventional in love, but you are also able to be loyal to that love. It is a unique combination and one that can make you stand out from the rest. Use your talents well for if you have any negatives it is taking on too much, therefore diluting or limiting energy with the main goal of life. However, if this negative does exist in your nature it can correct itself by the time you are 30 to 35. You have another quality to your nature and that is getting the idea, accomplishing it; but then after the accomplishment a restlessness may set in, wanting to go on to other achievements. Be sure you review all the angles in a given situation before you do this. Use your foresight well.

James Watt (inventor) (1736)

January 31

You need to be in touch with people either as a speaker, a writer, entertainer, sales person or any occupation that deals with change and communication. You understand easily what people need and if you provide this you can achieve much success. As far as your affections are concerned you need communication to and from a loved one. You are honest and can build a wonderful image for yourself not only in the business world but in personal relationships. You possess a great sensitivity toward your family

The Day of Your Birth

and relatives but at the same time remain in free full control of your own individualism. You can be subjective in a rather objective kind of way if that makes sense. Perhaps, it is better to say you have an integrated personality that allows you to be subjective about your life, but your objectivity can step in when needed to keep you in balance. You can be tender and strong at one and the same time.

Anna Pavlova (ballet Dancer) (1882)   Norman Mailer (writer) (1923)

February 1

When a situation comes up for someone to step forward, you are usually the one who will do so. As a result you can become very popular with friends, community leaders and business associates. Somehow you easily know how to put your emotional needs in balance with your ego drives, and as a result you get along with both men and women equally well. You make an excellent host or hostess and as a result, you are invited out often yourself. You can be a natural leader and organizer for you have a very integrated personality. You like a lot of things going on, so you should have a job or situation in life that gives you freedom to have variety. This does not mean you cannot be true to a mate; it simply means you need a broad base in which to move and to grow. You can give extreme loyalty in love but also need someone who does not tie you to the post. You may run a business from your home, or at least this can be your potential. At least, you do your own thing in your own way. If you do not have a business in your home, your office or place of business may become like a second home to you.

Clark Gable (actor) (1901)

February 2

In many ways you seem like an open book, but when people stop to think about it, you really are not. For with all your openness and your talent with people you really are very secretive especially about those things that are very important to you. You are able to decide your steps on your own, believing each individual should keep his own counsel. You can work with others or work alone, whatever the situation calls for. However, those things you do in private, perhaps, are your greatest accomplishments because they are all yours. You love surprising people and doing those things people least expect. People take more from you than they would others because you have a charming way of presenting your eccentricities. You can be unconventional, creative, individualistic yet sensitive, at times emotional, intense feelings yet practical. You are a rather complex human being but very exciting to most people; that is, if you take advantage of all your attributes in a given lifetime.

Tommy Smothers (comedian) (1937)

February 3

You are somewhat of a fearless adventurer and ready to gamble with life any time, any place. Success is likely to come early because you are willing to take the risk, the action, the gamble. You are not afraid to experiment with an idea, a plan a system. One thing that will be very strong is that you will have a multitude of experiences in life for you will want to know first hand. As a result you will end up being a very wise mature person. You could find even greater success if you wrote about these experiences and who knows what success you could attain in your writings. You are interested in all manner of people so that you may go to countries, to sections of your city others wouldn't think of going. This will result in your attracting unusual friends. You have courage, a courage that doesn't stand still for if there is anything you do dislike it is boredom. Watch, however, so that you do not go to extremes with your desire for change, adventure, and expenditures of money. You have a right to be whatever way you want to be, but watch so you do not try to advise friends and associates against their own will. You are a strong individual and could over power many people if you so choose to go that way.

Norman Rockwell (illustrator) (1894)

February 4

You can be kind, considerate and charming. Because you can be so kind and considerate, you may be misunderstood by others as being shallow but this is not the case for your charm and caring is genuine. You understand people very well and can easily understand their motives and drives. However, when you offer to help people you do so in a way that is not

The Day of Your Birth

overbearing. There is another side to your nature that shows up when things may not be doing so well then you start trying to give other people advise against what they themselves really want to do. There are two sides to your nature and with effort the positive side of your personality can always be in the foreground. You are close to your family and a home base is very important to you. You care for others so much that sometimes you sacrifice what you want yourself. To say you are complex is an understatement. Don't allow yourself to become a crutch to others. Another influence this day gives you is the ability to be artistic and to make art projects pay off financially. You actually have both feet on the ground most of the time even though others may not think so.

Charles A. Lindbergh (aviator) (1902)

February 5

You have much hidden beneath the surface of your personality that does not show and it is this facet of your nature, the deep hidden side, that becomes rather mysterious but which also makes you very charming and magnetic to other people. Few get to the depth of you, but once someone does, you are loyal, sincere, and stable. Once you have established a relationship there is nothing you would not do for the person. This is true regardless of any faults that may show up in time. You may have a talent for psychic intuition. Your best expression of this intangible talent could be poetry, music, dancing, but not necessarily as a vocation but just as an outlet to your normally secretive nature – the therapy of expression. You can be talkative and communicative with most of the people you come in contact with but at the same time you remain very casual and abstract. You have a fine interest in your community and its well being and may find yourself at some point in your life attaining a leadership position. There is a strong compassion to your nature and tolerance with others.

Adlai Stevenson (politician) (1900)

February 6

You believe in following conventions even though you are an Aquarian who is supposed to be unconventional. There is a certain propriety to your nature. You usually follow the rules and if you do break them you have a very good reason. As a result you may be able to attain an executive position in some business or a leadership position on the political scene. When something goes haywire whether in your family, your business, your community, you can find the right answers and usually can come up with the formula to bring it back to success. You have a certain charm and refinement to your personality with the ability to deal with the social graces. You can also make money and handle it well. You usually can come up with a scheme, any time, any place where you can put something into profit financially. You can be stern, but kind; practical, but open-minded. This is quite a combination for one person to possess, but you have them all.

Babe Ruth (baseball player) (1895)

February 7

You have a deep compassion for others and in your own way can become a humanitarian. Your intuition and perception is good and if you follow it you can not only bring success to your own life but to many others as well. You would make an excellent psychologist. In many ways, however, you are secretive and private. You seem to know instinctively that in order to help others you listen to their problems rather than talking about your own. There is a sense of poetry to your nature; perhaps, not in the full sense of actually writing poetry but in the idealistic sense. Yet with all your idealism, you easily understand the weakness in the human spirit. You are active which means you act upon your ideals and aims and don't just sit back and dream about them. The combination of energy and action with your psychic sensitivity adds up to you being a person who is not afraid to pioneer some new cause for your community, no matter how small the cause or how large.

Charles Dickens (novelist) (1812)   Eubie Blake (songwriter) (1873)

February 8

You have ambition and the charm necessary to put your ideas across. In many ways you have strong hypnotic powers and can sway others to your way of thinking. Part of this power is dramatic, part of it is the way your words come across with such confidence. You can put imagination into practical form. By that I mean you have an imagination that floods your mind with ideas but also have the power to make these ideas work, not only for yourself but others. You possess great executive talent and can organize anything from a garden party to a sports event. People soon learn to trust your talent for taking responsibility and bringing about a successful accomplishment. You are a leader; not a follower. Nine times out of ten you show others the way for you are not afraid to initiate any new action that is necessary and as a result can develop quite a name for yourself in your part of the world. Your wisdom will grow as you get older and so will your ability to warm and inspire others like the rays of the sun itself.

Jack Lemmon (actor) (1925)   Evangeline Adams (astrologer) (1868)

February 9

Once you decide to do something, nothing can stop you. You do not know the meaning of the word impossible; that is if other influences of your star map do not dilute this tendency. This does not mean you push others around for you do not, unless they deliberately get in your way. For along with your motto of never letting anything deter you is LIVE AND LET LIVE. Once you decide on what you want from life, whether a career, being a parent, or whatever, you learn all about it giving it your fullest attention. You possess a healing talent, not only for yourself but others as well. This is true whether it is physical healing for yourself, mental stability, or spiritual growth. You never let a thorn in your side limit you; rather you will use any difficulty as a catapult. You seem to know instinctively that every so often you have to sweep unused or limiting things out of your path. In many ways you can be a work-a-holic for you are by no means lazy. You possess a great amount of talent with whatever you want to do so that you do not have to step on anyone else to get where you are going.

Ernest Tubb (country singer) (1914)

February 10

You have a delightful sense of humor that makes you popular with your set of associates. In many ways you retain a rather childlike glee in having fun. Now, I did not say childish, I said childlike for there is a vast difference. You have a good business head and are successful on a larger scale because you know how to mix the social with business contacts. Sometimes business contacts become social and social contacts lead to business opportunities and this works out very well for you where it may not work if others tried it. Watch so you do not promise too much that you either forget appointments or don't have time for them all. You may be a tinge extravagant with the tendency to exaggerate a little to make a point. But even your little foibles don't seem to bother others for they forgive you as your delightful personality makes up for any of your little foibles.

Mark Spitz (olympic swimmer) (1950)

February 11

You are inventive by nature and always know how to make something work out. If one way doesn't do it, another way can always be found. Not only do you find a way for something to work, it proves its worth in cash. This talent of yours finds its way this side of genius. This does not mean that the first time you try something it works; it means that you keep trying until you find the way. It is inventive talent coupled with determination. Above all you are not apt to be a carbon copy of anyone else for your innate nature stands true to itself. You can be stubborn and determined at the same time you are compassionate. However, your compassion does not go to the point you allow yourself to be a crutch. Your instincts are uncanny in so far as you know where compassion ends and being a crutch begins. You have much tenacity of spirit which gives great rewards in your life; however even though you stick to something longer than anyone else, whether in a relationship or a project, when you are finished with it, you are finished. Because of this rather complex nature of yours, you do surprise others most of the time. You are not easily deciphered.

Thomas Alva Edison (inventor) (1847)

February 12

You are democratic in the sense that you believe in the equality of each individual. In this regard you can be a true humanitarian. You do not discriminate between one individual and another. You may like one person over the other but you do not judge or criticize. You understand many things and not only have an instinct for the near at hand, the subjective, but can see long range visions in an abstract, objective manner. This can make you a leader among the people. However, the negative side of this is that you may risk or gamble big sums of money on an idea or an ideal and then lose it to those who have little scruples. You could be a writer, a speaker, a teacher who can come across in a very convincing manner. You get along well with people and especially with those of the opposite sex. There is a good balance between your ego (self confidence) and your emotional needs. Use this extra special talent of being able to deal with the here and now along with your foresight as a team and nothing can stop you from achieving your greatest desires.

Abraham Lincoln (president) (1809)

February 13

You like the finer things of life, like good music, art, books, fashion. You may be the one in your social set who sets the pace with fashion. You like romance and can be very romantic. Love means a lot to you and you may have many romances in your lifetime, but in the end you find that one that stands out from all the rest. When that happens it is a strong and lasting love. You do what you have to do in a quiet kind of way, moving forward without any dramatics so that in the end you surprise a lot of people with your complete success. The quotation BY THEIR HUMILITY SHALL YOU KNOW THEM stands well with you. You are not afraid to do things in a different way and it doesn't matter if people find out you have had a failure or two for you know that you will succeed in the end. You possess a practical kind of courage that endures throughout your lifetime. It is a courage that is steady and strong and not the kind of courage that is a flash in the pan.

George Segal (actor) (1934)

February 14

Regardless of being identified with St. Valentine's Day you do take love seriously with your whole nature being filled with thoughts of the ideal love, spiritual love. You are sensitive in the sense that you pick up the intangible influences around you for there is a psychic and maybe even poetic talent to your nature. Along with this psychic side are good judgment and very alert powers of observation. You are good with money and can easily manage any business or household. You are usually economical in handling your affairs but on occasion you may splurge. In every day life and/or with those in your immediate environment you are practical and realistic but this does not interfere or negate your great idealism with romance and love. Use some of your talent for observation and judgment in writing for if you do you could have great success in the easy way you can relate stories about your experiences with animals, babies, older people, lovers, etc.

Jack Benny (comedian) (1894)   Emma Duhs Prill (my mother)

February 15

You are a great advocator of progress in any form. You do not like anything to stand still and if it is within your power to move things along you do so. Business is your forte as well as instincts where financial matters are concerned. You are an original thinker, a crusader, and a courageous leader. If you direct your amazing talent of discipline, ambition, courage, and research you can leave the world a better place than when you came into it. You are an affectionate person and very loyal to those you love. If you have a great drive, it is the desire to give humanity something of value. You can communicate well with others and desire to share any knowledge you acquire with people. Your ability at communication makes you able to communicate your causes to others; thereby attracting followers.

John Barrymore (actor) (1882)

February 16

You are a very complex person. You exert a certain warm charm to others but with this charm is a certain mysticism that is very appealing. You can be secretive which only makes you more magnetic. All things mystical, philosophical and the occult would interest you and if you pursue it you could become very accomplished in this field. When it comes to love, you love deeply, not only physically but mentally and spiritually. As a result love to you is most satisfying because your tendency in this area is to give. Even to close friends and loved ones, however, you still keep a certain amount of yourself private. You are an active person, believing in getting things done. The older you get the more of a humanitarian you become for you readily respond to the sufferings of others. However, you not only respond to the suffering you do something to help alleviate it. You could be an excellent actor or actress if you choose to go in that direction. Your magnetism on stage or screen would easily come across to the audience, a kind of magic evasiveness that appeals.

Edgar Bergen (1903) Sonny Bono (1935)

February 17

You are a leader and your aim in life is to be the best you can be in every area of your life. You are capable of exerting every effort to achieve a full rich existence. But just because you want the best of everything for yourself, doesn't mean you are not generous and sharing for you can be. You should have some form of artistic expression such as; music, painting, writing so as to lend more balance to your nature. You could even profit financially by perfecting one of these talents. You possess sensitivity, compassion, but at the same time are disciplined and ambitious. Coupled with this is energy, action and leadership. This is a winning combination that can't fail you. You are no doubt generous with loved ones; perhaps, at times, you can be too generous. Overall, you have no blocks or barriers in your mind that limit your success. Rarely do you have doubts; rarely do you accept any impossibility.

Montgomery Ward (merchant) (1843)

February 18

You were born on the cusp and this means that you have characteristics of both Aquarius and Pisces. You have a powerful personality but also have to watch the tendency to overindulge in many ways. You will not easily be told what to do for if someone does try it you may end up doing something you may not have wanted to do in the first place; hence paying a big price for your stubborn nature. The positive side of this influence gives healing ability, physically, spiritually and mentally. You easily get to the bottom of things but others cannot keep a secret from you whether you want to know the secrets or not. Use your excessive talents for sports, science, research or some other difficult achievement that takes an over abundance of drive.

You have so much drive that if it isn't channeled it goes to extremes without purpose. Learn early in your life to channel your over enthusiastic and excessive nature to positive and constructive pursuits.

Jack Palance (actor) (1919)

PISCES
February 19 to March 20

Pisces is sympathetic, tolerant, compassionate and they seem to have a talent for telepathy. Their intuition is highly developed which some people call psychic. Pisces also appears at times to have some secret sorrow or secret. They are very idealistic which can cloud reality at times. They are capable of great sacrifice and martyrdom if they believe in someone or something. The negative side of this talent is that they can be subject to fraudulent experiences or people and Pisces people may depend too much on others. They are best when they are working behind the scene in hospitals, the film industry, or any other behind the scene activity. Music is another outlet for their very sensitive nature for music can give them a sense of release for their highly attuned nature.

Pisces is a water sign, mutable (flexible) and dual. Pisces is magnetic and sensitive. Pisces is ruled by two fish, tied by their tails each trying to go in a different direction.

The jewel is the opal and ivory.

The flowers are the crocus, and the jonquil.

The ruling number is seven.

The ruling planet is Neptune.

The metal is platinum.

Pisces people are impressionable and they have indelible memories.

Pisces rules all substances that defy analysis. The colors are lavender and white.

The Day of Your Birth

February 19

You were born on the cusp and this means that you possess characteristics combining Aquarius and Pisces. You have a very congenial manner so that you gather friends and associates likes bees to honey. You easily tell stories and make others feel very comfortable around you. You accept people into your orbit from all walks of life for you sense the equality of all men and women. You enjoy a variety of experiences that you share with others so easily. You could be very successful in a vocational kind of way if you write your stories and publish them. You are inclined to gamble with situations that come up in your life but things seem to work out for you because of your great faith and correct hunches. Something special guides you and perhaps it is your supreme connection somehow with the higher power. You usually listen to your own higher self rather than others around you. You are understanding of others' problems and compassionate and easily sought out for advice. You would make a good actress or actor for the stage which would be a good place to use your fantastic imagination, but you could just as easily be a minister.

Lee Marvin (actor) (1924)

February 20

You are independent and very individualistic. You have a strong sense of pride in yourself and what you accomplish in life. You are not likely to copy anyone else or to let anyone interfere with the things you know you have to do. However, don't let this go so far as to lack tolerance for others. Just because you are a Pisces doesn't mean you automatically have compassion and tolerance. You can be eccentric or constructively creative; either way you choose the pendulum to swing. You are capable of working very hard and putting your special creativity to work. You can also be brilliant in your strategy in getting things done and in your ability to direct people. So if you use your talent this way you will be productive and achieve much; however, if you use this same talent "turned around" it can be stubborn willfulness that can be destructive instead of constructive. You have a strong force that needs wisely directing like an engine in gear in an automobile. And don't forget what an important role it is to be the PERSON BEHIND THE PERSON. You don't have to be the top master to achieve for without the man behind the man, the master is lost. You are such a person.

Gloria Vanderbilt (artist and socialite) (1924)

February 21

You are a very active person who is always busy. You love to go places and see things. Life is always interesting for you because you generally find a way to bring activity into your life in some way or another. You have a very quick mind and can express yourself well. This expression of yours can take the form of just plain conversation, or writing. Whatever the subject you have the wit and common sense to converse about it. You are interested in your community and at some time in your life may play an important role in its affairs. Humor is also like second nature to you, but in an instant you can take on a serious tone. You get along well with others and can easily adjust if you have to do so. Home is important to you, but on occasion you like to travel and go to distant places. The final result of your personality means you are well adjusted and integrated.

Leo Delibes (Composer) (1836)

February 22

You can be a very diplomatic manager with a mixture of cleverness. You have leadership talent, a leadership talent that shows interest in the welfare of others rather than dictatorial leadership. You can be romantic and quite a lover when you want to be. This can give genius with writing talent if you make the attempt to perfect it. Even though all things romantic have appeal for you, your practical and realistic nature adheres to loyalty in love. You have an advantage over others for you are quite unique and individualistic, yet reliable and trustworthy. Others are drawn to you because of your very original and independent nature. However, even though you are independent you are understanding, lovable and considerate.

February 23

There is a sense of poetry to your nature which could lend itself also to music, dancing or any one of the other arts. Whether you participate in artistic expression yourself or just have a deep appreciation of it, it will always be a way of life that remains interesting for you. At an early age your parents may have noticed this sense of beauty you have. It may have taken

The Day of Your Birth

form by your interest in flowers, in the movement of birds, beautiful colors, etc. You have consideration of others that makes you easy to be around. If there is a weakness it is your tendency to be easily hurt. You can use your ability to perceive the intangibles of life in a productive way, or you can use your great sensitivity to being hurt and self pity. It is up to you. Regardless of how successful you may get in your life or your overall status, you will retain a certain humility of character.

George Frederick Handel (composer) (1685)

February 24

You have a practical and realistic side to your nature that makes it possible for you to be an executive and to be good in money management. However, there is another side of you that appreciates beauty, inspiration things, beautiful scenery which is the poetic side of you. Your inner nature enjoys these simple things of life, but your outer nature can handle the hustle and bustle of a busy, energetic business world. Because you easily understand the various facets of life, you handle your life beautifully and get the greatest benefit out of things as they are at the time. Because of all these qualities you possess you would make a good philosopher or psychologist. However, if you had to choose between the country scene and the simple life to the hustle and bustle of the larger city, you would no doubt feel the simple life has the most to offer in the long run.

Wihelm Grimm (folklorist) (1786)

February 25

You are impressionable and understand easily the motives behind people's actions. Because of this trait in your nature you could become a great professional psychologist. Along with this talent is sympathy. One thing you have to watch is that you do not become too sacrificial in your drive to help those who are suffering. If you keep this quality in control your ability to be a judge of people can be very successful. This sensitivity should be used in participation in one of the arts. As a result you will adjust and balance the tendency to be too self sacrificing. Television, or any of the other communicative vocations would be excellent work for you in vocational endeavors. You can easily express yourself, especially in regard to the intangibles around you that others only feel and cannot express. Make it a point to express the little subtle nuances and you could become great with this talent.

Bobby Riggs (tennis player) (1918)

February 26

At times you are a loner. Things have to be your way but by the same token you do not interfere with what others want to do. You do not force your way; others either take it or leave it. You are fussy who you choose for friends and associates with the tendency for quality rather than quantity. Even the material things you purchase have to be quality. You do not reveal your true self to just anyone for you have learned it is not wise to bare your soul promiscuously. This "real you" is reserved for those choice people dearest to your heart. You know when to speak and when not to speak which is a great asset to your successes. You also seem to know when to appear sensitive to a situation and when not to do so. You are by nature a leader; not a follower. Much of what you are, in a quiet way, is an innovator. The quality of doing things your own way, can be used for a higher purpose of helping others and showing them the way for a better life. Establish organizations, groups, clubs for the betterment of your community. You will probably hand over the authority to others after things are established but that is fine for you will just be free to move on to initiate other things.

Jackie Gleason (comedian) (1916)

February 27

You are very perceptive as you seem to be in tune with the higher universal and cosmic forces. As a result you may be an inspired artist who achieves much success not only monetarily but going to the top of your field. You can take a look at some raw material and immediately see what you can make of it into beauty. You will have a wide variety of experiences in life and will attain much wisdom and understanding that you will easily share with others. You may get into some teaching of higher mind subjects. One

The Day of Your Birth

thing that is important for you and that is when you have an experience of some kind, good or bad, you learn from it and are not apt to repeat a mistake. You are strong, powerful, mentally and spiritually, and could be in the healing profession, the psychological field or religion. Once you set your mind and heart on something absolutely nothing can interfere for you have the ability to look ahead so that you know what to do in the present.

Elizabeth Taylor (actress) (1932)

February 28

Your basic outlook on life is optimistic. Integrity is also on your list of attributes. You are socially acceptable because not only are you understanding but have a tendency to be humorous; therefore others enjoy being with you. You respect everyone's right to be individualistic and do not interfere or back people into any corners. You are generous and broad in your outlook so that this makes you well liked and you are even well liked by people who do not agree with you. You possess many talents. This will give you a variety of interests which means you may end your life having accomplished and perfected many things. If you have a difficulty it is getting bored because of your strong interest in so many things and because you do not like to be in a rut. You are interested in higher spiritual knowledge and scientific study and could make your mark in your world in either one of these fields. You have the capacity to understand things emotional but also have the capacity to discipline yourself with things vocational facing your duties and responsibilities with full force.

Mario Andretti (auto racer) (1940)

February 29

Born on a leap year day makes you a unique character from the very beginning. You are sensible and practical but at the same time very creative and individualistic. This results in your being a rather complex person. You are able to make any one of your creative ideas work and acceptable to the public. Others may take much more from you than they would from someone else because somehow they sense your strength. You like routine most of the time, but on occasion you do the unexpected and break the routine and do exactly what you like and not what is expected of you. This, perhaps, is your way of readjusting, of rejuvenation, of shifting gears. You have a great deal of will power with things you feel are important, a will power once set in motion others cannot break. When you have work to do you keep it up to date for you do not like delays or things carried over from the day before. Others may think you do not have an imagination and that you are too serious, but this is not the case for it all depends upon the situation at hand and the people in question. It also depends upon what purpose they are serving in your life at the time. There are those people in your environment who do see the imaginative side of your nature but that is because you "let them in."

Gioacchino Rossini (composer) (1792)

March 1

You respond to the rhythm of life easily as your senses are alive to all around you. Because of this you can make an excellent poet, musician, dancer, whatever. Not only do you respond to this rhythm but you can express what you feel in words and as a result know how to impress people, when, why, and how. Because your senses and awareness is so alive you really should find some artistic outlet even if only for your own enjoyment. You can take on a leadership role in spiritual work for you have the ability to tune in on the truth more easily than others. Most of the time you are optimistic so that others find it easy to be around you. With all this you can be practical and very realistic so that coupled with your talent for artistic expression it means you can bring all your little nuances of inspiration down to earth in a practical form for others to enjoy.

Nicolaus Copernicus (astronomer) (1473)

March 2

You can be emotional but do not always show it. You may show one side of your nature to the public and another side to those with whom you share domesticity. You can be romantic and may even over-dramatize a romantic interest. You should use this energy for the dramatics to write, or to get into the dramatic arts in a productive kind of way. This talent can go either

The Day of Your Birth

way, into self aggrandizement or toward success in expression such as; writing, acting, stage productions and even teaching. Use the control you have in hiding your negative emotions by disciplining yourself with some artistic expression and you may make it pay off in cold, hard cash. You can be close to your family and when you use your talent in having sympathy for others you can develop quite a compassionate, sensitive and tolerant nature and end up your life being considered quite a humanitarian.

Dr. Seuss (children's humorist) (1904)   Desi Arnaz (actor) (1917)

March 3

You can be very outspoken saying easily what pleases you and what does not. Your understanding of complex theories and ideas makes it easy for you to get into whatever line of work you wish. You can be mechanical and theoretical at one and the same time which results in your being an inventor. This means you usually are able to make your theories and ideas work. When you want to you can be very sociable and usually take the initiative at these times. When it comes to running an office, your home, or your work place wherever that is, you can usually find a unique way of organizing and executing your routine or your way of accomplishing things. You can be lovable and caring overall but most of the time you have to do things in a big way, your way. Yours is not the small, narrow approach.

Alexander Graham Bell (inventor) (1847)

March 4

You have a combination that is unbeatable. You are practical, realistic yet possess an abundance of faith, compassion and tolerance. You believe in the intangibles as well as the tangibles of life and know how to put the two together making you the practical idealist. You inspire others because you do not give up, retaining your faith even in your darkest hours. You can always find the practical rational way out of a difficult situation. You can be wise beyond your years when you are young and wise beyond the average person as you mature in life. Your common sense and unmatchable faith makes you sought after by friends, associates, and strangers who have heard about you. When a situation comes up in your life that gives you problems or aches and pains, you find a way out of it for it is not your nature to put up with a bad situation. As an advisor to others on a professional basis could bring you great success.

Knute Rockne (football coach) (1888)

March 5

You have executive talent and would be successful with your own business or in a high position in a company other than your own. You desire to earn money, to live more than comfortably and to obtain a high station in life. You can work hard, discipline yourself for whatever it is you want to attain. You plan your life for you do not want to live in a haphazard manner. You accomplish much more in a given day's time than most people and so you deserve every success you get. You know how to handle your income and so obtain much of the good material things in life. However, you do enjoy taking short little trips for pleasure, talking to friends, neighbors, visiting relatives and generally taking time out for fun for it is your motto that all work and no play can make you a dull person. You communicate well with people, and others are able to understand you; therefore you do well giving orders since coming from you orders sound logical and workable. Even though you can give orders you do not sound nor act like a "know it all," nor are you demanding in your attitude. The bottom line is you know HOW, WHY and WHEN.

Heitor Villa-Lobos (composer) (1881)

March 6

You are full of energy, wit, and charm. In many ways you are an example for most people. You understand the human condition and do all you can to help others become as much as they can be. You are an active person who gets things done. You have foresight and because of this you can take action in a present situation that either leads to greater success or prevents difficulties. You can be artistic, refined, and loving. Sometimes your feelings and sympathies are so strong you go too far, but in the end your sympathies help make people better for it. If there is any complete person in your circle of friends, associates and intimates you are it. There are many sides to your nature, artistic, business, psychological awareness, psychic talent. As a result, you can fit in anywhere, anytime.

Ed McMahon (TV personality) (1923)

March 7

Above all else you can be a leader in your world. You are perceptive, psychic, but in the sense that you see things for what they really are and not illusion. You are capable of great spiritual love and possess a great sensitivity to all of nature and her creatures. You can be scientific; yet spiritual. This is quite a combination which makes you a very unique person on top of your world. Your observations are quite good, for you miss nothing. Because of this talent you can end up becoming very wise and quite a philosopher. Your talent for being able to perceive the intangibles around you is very acute. To you, all things large and small, animal or mineral, have life and in your own way you revere it all. One thing you may have to realize is that others are not as perceptive as you are and you may have to exercise your tolerance a little more. You can be scientific but also spiritual. You use the scientific approach to life in that you like trying to find ways things can work. You get poetic and musical inspirations which you manifest into the real world. This is what you are all about, making the intangibles tangible. If you use this to your advantage you can go far toward success.

Maurice Ravel (composer) (1875)   Luther Burbank (1849)

March 8

You have a clever way of handling people and as a result will either be good in business or politics. Everything you do has a purpose and every purpose has a friend or an associate behind it or with it. In other words relationships you form have to have significance for a given purpose or you are not interested. You can transform anything you come in contact with to your purpose at the moment. You are a master of conserving things for a greater productive purpose. You also have a kind of heroic strength. Nothing deters you if you are truly interested. You have the ability to attract others into your orbit of living who are strong and who seem to either inspire you even more to your purpose or they stand beside you and help you directly. A cosmic and universal awareness is yours which seems to give you a magnetism that draws others to you even if they are not fully aware of why they are drawn to you. Underneath all this is a sensitivity and emotionalism that doesn't always show. It only shows itself at those quiet times with the people you love the most. You are good with business and seem to have a flair for it. The public image you have may be decidedly different than your private personal image. It is almost as if you were two different people.

Lynn Redgrave (actress) (1943)   John Elmer Prill (my father)

March 9

You are dramatic and if you use this talent for the professional stage you can become very popular. You understand others very well and instantly know the nature of their personalities and what will work best with them. This does not mean you sacrifice your own desires and your own nature, it simply means you know how to get the most out of others and perhaps, put them at their ease. While you are helping others be themselves, you are completely aware of your own purpose at all times. In other words you are never so compassionate you lose yourself. As a result you end up having a multitude of friends and associates that at times you have to weed out. Because your magnetism is so great, others are drawn to you, and it causes times when it may keep you from your main activities. When that time comes that is when the fur flies. You are optimistic, humorous, and have great integrity. The thing you have to concentrate on doing is to try to find your hierarchy of values and direct all your energy into a more singular pursuit; hence creating success and productivity. You tend at times to scatter your energies and talents which is understandable since you have so many talents.

Bobby Fischer (chess player) (1943)

March 10

You have your two feet planted in the ground at all times because you are realistic and practical. However because part of your nature is sympathetic and compassionate, you remain in constant respect for other people's feelings. This is true except if it infringes upon your own values and feelings. You can be a very well balanced person, balancing the realistic with the idealistic; the practical with compassionate tolerance. Others know that you will give it to them straight and that they can count on you for a certain accuracy of decision. When it comes to friendships, romance, marriage you are loyal and are not likely to be promiscuous. When it comes to opposite sex relationships you are sensitive, yet practical; realistic, loyal, yet romantic; intelligent, yet imaginative. Others know from the beginning that you are sincere. You do not necessarily go for the glamour in a person but see inside to the center of their soul for you seem to know instinctively which relationships will last and which ones will not. As a result you are ahead of the game every time. Once you do give yourself to a relationship and you believe in it, you can make any kind of sacrifice necessary to maintain it.

Pamela Mason (actress) (1918)

March 11

You have the ability to express yourself very well and because you have the talent for putting your inspirational or imaginative thoughts into understandable language it could profit you by being a writer. This could take the form as an entertainer also. You enjoy going places and doing things and no doubt have something going most of the time. No matter where you are or where you go, you are capable of making your point or attracting attention. You do surprise people, however, for you make changes rather quickly and suddenly which may or may not always be to your advantage. Use some of your magical and expressive energy to do something for your community. This could take the form of informing the public of important things to be done, pulling people together for greater strength in a given project. You can do this by the magic of your words, and the magic of your ability at communication. Another thing you can do is to get involved in any one of the communicative fields. You can be perceptive, psychic, poetic and when you meditate in your quiet times you can discover you have cosmic connections that can lead to cosmic consciousness. The older you get the more involved you may become in universal truths and concepts. Having faith is also another one of your more positive attributes. If you have someone around you who needs someone to believe in them, you seem to give them this faith resulting in little miracles not only for them but for you. You possess something special in your firm and beautiful belief which you wear for everyone to see like a shining armor.

Lawrence Welk (bandleader) (1903)

March 12

You are artistic and should have some form of artistic expression even if it is only for your own entertainment and emotional release. However, if you concentrate and perfect this artistic talent it could profit you financially as well. Some form of artistic release is an innate yearning of your very soul. All that is beautiful and harmonious attracts you like bees to honey. You are affectionate with the people you choose as friends or lovers and are loyal to them once the relationships have been established. All you seem to desire in life is to be of service to a loved one and to have a loved one help you with a given project. Yours is not the working alone scene but yours is to cooperate with others, to understand, to blend. You have a great deal of higher mind understanding as it is associated with science, religion, philosophy. You also seem to have a fine balance between being subjective and being abstract and objective.

Liza Minnelli (singer) (1946)   Walter Schirra (astronaut) (1923)

March 13

You are a very sensitive person, sensitive not only to people but to the atmosphere around you, whether that atmosphere is a rainy day, a sunny day or disturbed or happy people. Try not to become too hurt by anger or any other excess emotion you hear in another's voice. You can work hard and you get things done that have to be done. You can be practical but also idealistic. You are practical when it comes to doing your job, but idealistic when it comes to relationships. You have a high idealism on how people should behave and present themselves. The capacity to give a lot of love is also one of your attributes but you also need a lot of love back in return. When you have this special love in your life, you are happy, fulfilled and productive. However, if the chips are down and you have to make a decision of what is the most important thing you desire in your life, it would be love; not money. Anyone who has great sensitivity needs a creative outlet to be at his or her best. Find yourself a creative outlet such as: dancing, playing a musical instrument, writing poetry, acting. When you find this outlet you will be healthier and more extroverted with all the other parts of your life. Somehow the creativity will give you more confidence and more emotional support. It will teach you to take the more positive approach to relationships and life in general rather than becoming depressed at the drop of a hat.

Percival Lowell (astronomer) (1855)

March 14

You are business minded for you seem to know what will sell and what will not sell. Your timing is absolutely correct when it comes to buying, selling, or trading whether this buying and selling is a product or a service. You can be good at organizational work for you are efficient and clever. There is also the ability for hard work in your nature, but you also have the capacity to sacrifice if necessary to achieve results. Yours is a combination of instinct and hard work. This is quite an unbeatable combination and produces a genius where results are concerned. But, along with with these two talents to be at your absolute best you need romance in your life, a love you can count on from hour to hour, from day to day, from year to year. You are loyal to your chosen mate, but if you do stray it may only be mental straying like regular stimulating conversations with one of the opposite sex. You may be extremely loyal to your original mate but others may misinterpret. You are excellent in organizing community affair projects and getting results. When it comes to shopping, you can spot a bargain a mile away. Loyalty to your brothers and sisters is another one of your special traits.

Albert Einstein (physicist) (1879)

March 15

You always know what is going on around you and are very perceptive where other people are concerned. You seem to know instinctively how people will behave and react. This may find you giving advice to others and people will soon learn to seek you out. This talent will give you a certain kind of power over others all your life so you need watch how you use it. You are energetic and active which results in strong sexual powers. You can be rather demanding of a mate which means you may want all of his/

her time. You may share everything you have but your mate. You really should develop a hobby and other interests, things you do with friends other than your mate in order to put more balance into your life and also give your mate a certain sense of freedom and breathing space. When you hold on too tightly to a loved one, you smother and can lose him/her. In another sense you are very accurate with the advice you give others and you grow even wiser the older you get. You are expressive, and could become very successful if you write or teach your innate understanding of human nature to others.

Andrew Jackson (politician) (1767)

March 16

You may appear to be more detached from others than you really are. You are a leader, do your own thing, but when it comes down to the wire, and a friend needs help you will give it and be very tolerant and compassionate. You are more capable of deep emotions than you show and although you appear calm and collected most of the time, this may not always be what you really feel. Perhaps, it is the best way for you to be because as you put it, it is a waste of time trying to acquire sympathy from others for they are too caught up in their own problems anyway. When your deep feelings and your ability to discipline these feelings is sublimated into some creative work, your chances for improving conditions in your life is unbeatable. While you may appear to be selfish and self concerned, you are really just the opposite for your inability to show your feelings is only a cover up of a very sensitive, caring person. Used in the right way, the sum total of your talents can bring you into a very satisfying productive life.

Jerry Lewis (comedian) (1926)

March 17

You have great strength with most every situation that comes up in your life. Once you set your mind to something, you do not get off the path. You have healing power not only with yourself but give it to others. Others feel strengthened after they have been around you. When it comes to your friends and your close opposite sex relationships you are rather selective but once you choose someone you stick like glue. You are loyal not only to

The Day of Your Birth

your friends but your ideals. You can put up with a negative trait of a loved one above and beyond average. You can be stubborn and determined but in a positive way this same stubborn and determined nature of yours can be heroic when conditions warrant it. If you have a cause you can devote unlimited energy and devotion to it, above and beyond any bounds or barriers that may come up. Early in life your strength, determination should be directed. When directed you are limitless, unbeatable. This great strength and power needs directing at a very early age. You have an instinct for what is right and what is wrong so should be in a position of authority where you can use this talent to the best advantage.

Rudolf Nureyev (ballet dancer) (1938)

March 18

You are foresighted, objective and abstract with your visions. When you have an idea, you can determine just the right action to take to get the envisioned results. You are humorous and pleasant when dealing with those around you. However, there is a certain need for freedom. When others try to hold you too tightly you may rebel and pull away. You are adventurous and like travel, meeting new people, new experiences. No one should ever try to hold you so tightly you are limited from doing whatever you have to do. If someone should try to put you in a cage, you would be a most unhappy person. Never allow any emotional attachment to keep you from fulfilling the highest image you have of yourself. If you are given this freedom from a mate, your integrity, your loyalty and devotion knows no bounds. You are intelligent, an original thinker, an educator of abstract truths, even if only in your immediate circle of friends and family. All of your life you will be interested in spiritual truths, and all that makes us humans tick. There may be a talent for the executive branch of business or politics.

Edgar Cayce (psychic) (1877)   Ovid (poet) 43 B.C.

March 19

You will have a balance with your experiences in life; love, business, happiness, loneliness, family, friends, the arts. It is your nature to want a balanced life in order to put all the four corners of your life into an organized reality. As a result of all your multitude of experiences you have throughout your lifetime you will become very understanding in the process. You are basically practical but you always have an open mind, always open to new experiences, new discoveries. You may end up becoming a great philosopher, even if only in your little world. Many people will ask for your advice and you may give it profusely. You have a lot of energy and vitality which you use well. One thing you will no doubt have is happiness because you will go after it. You do your own thing, follow your own dictates, look around and lo and behold others are either imitating you or following you.

Richard Burton (explorer) (1821)

March 20

This is a day on the cusp between Pisces and Aries and will take on attributes of both signs. You communicate easily with the people around you and possess a kind of social charm. Others like you around because of your wit and your ability to converse easily with all sorts of people. You make most people feel at ease. If you see something wrong in your family, your community, you quietly without fanfare help to correct it. You have a way of getting people to agree with you, whether you are correcting a community flaw or on some pleasurable excursion. If you have a talent that supersedes all the others, it is your ability to get around people, making them think it was their idea in the first place. You could be an excellent politician or in any profession that has to influence people such as advertising. Because you were born on the cusp between two signs you will possess qualities of leadership, pioneering instincts, fearlessness, ideas that are in abundance. In other words you have the beginning (leadership) and the end (tolerance, compassion, and humility). What a good combination for success. For more information on cusp signs, see my book EVERYTHING HAS A PHASE.

Sepharial (astrologer) (1864)   Carl Reiner (comedian) (1922)

//
Year of Your Birth

People born in a given year have a group destiny in common, whether that destiny is conscious or unconscious.

1900-2000

1900 is a number ten and is ruled by the Sun. It is cosmic and introduces a new era for mankind. It not only introduces a new decade but a new hundred year period. A ten year will always introduce a new ten year period and end a previous one. It is the sign of the times for the next ten years. Since this is Sun ruled those born in this year either have a problem with ego or they can be very good at initiating new things, but they are more likely to listen to their own higher instincts rather than others around them.

1901 is an eleven and is ruled by Pluto. It is more universal in its value. These people are intense and deeply interested in all things mysterious and occult. This is the year of people who are difficult to understand for they seem to be tuned in on a different wave length. The year gives these people an interest in healing and many of them could introduce newer methods of healing to one degree or another or many of them will be interested in newer methods of healing. They feel nothing is impossible. At times they seem to belong to another world.

1902 is a three and is ruled by Jupiter. It is a combination of one and two with an underlying influence of the Moon (emotions, feelings, sensitivity) and the Sun (ego, confidence, positiveness). Those born in this year may have a new kind of spiritual belief. They are optimistic with the ability for integrity but there are those among them who are extravagant, stretching the truth, unduly adventurous. The positive side of these people and this year is their capability of teaching and disseminating higher truths and scientific things. The world expands its knowledge and scientific values under this 1902 influence. Those born in this year have a natural talent for balancing their relationships to the best advantage of all concerned.

1903 is a number four and is ruled by Earth. This is a combination of one and three. There is an underlying influence of the Sun and Jupiter which means that on the surface they may be practical and realistic and seem to have both feet on the ground, but behind this is the expansiveness of Jupiter and the ego confidence of the Sun. Whatever the people born in this year do, they do in a big way and get concrete results. Since Jupiter has some influence with the scientific world, scientific projects were introduced during this year that proved to be of great significance for practical use on earth. Number four people and number four years can make ideas for the greatest practical use. Coupled with the Jupiter influence any idea started in this year can give far and wide expansion. During this year a broadening of foreign affairs and the beginning of ego troubles among countries and leaders would manifest but would manifest in a strong way in 1912.

1904 is a number five and is ruled by Mercury. This is a five that combines a one and four. So we are talking about a Mercury that has a mixture of Uranus (creativity, originality with a touch of practicality). These are the people who always find a workable solution to a problem. They are talkative, neighborly and can be involved in community betterment projects. This is a time. when cities began to grow all over the country from small town status to larger cities. This year also introduced vibrations where new methods of communication came into being. It was a restless year with a lot of short little comings and goings. People born in this year had a different way of communicating with others and would also have a very curious nature, interesting in many things.

1905 is a number six and is ruled by Venus. This is a combination of a one and a five. It represents an underlying influence of communicational talent and also a talent for the arts. It is a year of people who are interested in fashion and art. This was a year where there was a new introduction in fashion, music, art. The people born during this year are loving, needing and spreading harmony through their world, whatever the size of their world. They are lovers. This is a year when much would have been written on love, much to-do concerning romance, music, and all things inspirational.

1906 is a seven and is ruled by Neptune. This gives an underlying influence with things artistic. People born in this year can be mystical, poetic and interested in dancing. They seem to flow easily with the rhythm of life. This period during 1906 may have introduced new dance steps and great interest in the film industry. These natives can be interested in psychic matters and things occult. They are capable of making great sacrifices for those they love or that which they believe. Mystery and new psychic discoveries or values could be important during this year. They are either very spiritual and are capable of tuning in on the intangible ray of the universe. However, the negative side of this same influence can make others among them deceptive and given to "con artist" schemes, all depends upon the evolvement of their total astrology chart and given aspects therein.

1907 is a number eight and is ruled by Saturn. These natives are business people given to discipline towards career. They are interested in industry, commerce and all outer world accomplishments. Many new types of businesses may have been established during this year and/or the people born in this year can be very disciplined, serious and conventional; however, they do have inner faith, compassion with a tendency to follow some inner hunch where vocational or business affairs are concerned as well as

The Day of Your Birth

with their personal lives. It may seem like they are serious and tough, but under that exterior is great sensitivity.

1908 is a number nine and is ruled by Mars. Those born in this year are active, having energy that is well disciplined because a secondary influence is Saturn. At times these people can be very assertive and aggressive. They are very daring and may be interested in sports or things like horse racing, cars. Some strong ones among them have pioneered in the car industry or did much to spur things on in that direction. The negative side of this year would give some who can be argumentative. However, at times, a negative influence shows up making them feel depressed or fearful instead of their normal discipline and organization of their actions and energy.

1909 is a ten and is ruled by the Sun. This is a cosmic number so this begins a new cosmic or universal decade. When a number ends in zero the influence is representative of people being interested in outer space or all things that have to do with the astro-world. The people born in this year stand before the crowd in leadership, no matter how large or small the crowd may be. These people can have a talent for the entertainment world, are fun loving, good at teaching others. Whatever they do, they are good at self expression.

1910 is an eleven and is ruled by Pluto. This is a cosmic year and gives strong universal influences to its people. New potentials in healing and health would have been introduced in this year and the people born in this year may be very interested in health efforts and healing. They make good detectives if they put their minds to it, and are capable of doing the impossible; at least what others think is impossible. This year of 1910 represented a new period in the financial world. Any given year's influences affect the people born in that year because they are a sign of their times and they carry this influence throughout their lives to one degree or another. They are either conscious of the drive towards what the year represents or they have an unconscious drive. The negative side of this Pluto year could be people who are dominating and with a very small portion having the POTENTIAL at being mobsters, killers; however there will be those among them who would become heros, healers, and psychologists. It would have been a new ten year period when great psychological advancements would be made. We will have another Pluto year in the year 2009. Many advancements will have taken place in this 99 year period for physical and mental health. All these things take place whether all the people are aware of the influences or not. Only the very enlightened are more aware. Another influence in a given Pluto year would be sexual interests or enlightenment.

1911 is a number three and is ruled by Jupiter. This is a one and a two and represents an underlying influence of the Sun and the Moon; male, female; negative, positive; electric, magnetic. All these seemingly opposing influences are in balance in this year. The people born in this year can achieve harmony in their lifetime and in their world. They are optimistic, objective. It is a great year for expansion, society getting out of a rut, introducing new worlds to conquer. It is a year where there is an interest in a broader view of life. A new philosophy may be introduced in the area of religion or spiritual matters, or a new religious cult may make its entrance upon the scene. The people born in this year do not like confinement and they also like a lot of space and freedom. They may be interested in foreign affairs and travel. Some may have destiny with science; others with religion and still others with publishing or teaching and writing of higher mind philosophical subjects. New methods of travel were introduced for the decade. Some among them may have been (in mind only) are first space cadets.

1912 is a number four and is ruled by Earth. This is an underlying influence of the Sun and Jupiter. These people are going to be very solid about what they believe. Whenever you have a four constructed from a one (Sun) and a three (Jupiter) you have solid expansion, solid concrete beliefs. This was the beginning of world wide expansion, getting out of the rut of isolated countries. A past lifestyle would begin to drop away and the beginning of a more world wide pattern of communication,ideas, foreign trade would take place. From 1905 to 1912 Neptune was opposing Uranus. This started the first wave of opposition, errors in standards and values which started confusion among the people. Error was introduced through these years, errors against real cosmic spiritual values. This was a conflict between materialism, spirituality and cosmic enlightenment. The cosmic creative ideas were sent forth but many did not receive these ideas accurately; thereby erroneous beliefs were taught and people began to live by them. In other words materialism began to be in vogue gradually losing the balance with true spirituality.

1913 is a number five and is ruled by Mercury. These are people interested in community affairs and much was done to develop small communities and the advancement of educational systems. Some people during this year were destined to be writers, leaders in community affairs or newspaper and telegraphic work. These 1913 people may be a restless lot, anxious for things to happen. It was the year when things concerning communication started to advance. We are like the time we were born from macrocosm to microcosm. The macrocosm being the influence of the outer planetary combination. Example: those born with Neptune, Uranus opposition or Jupiter, Uranus conjunction are related to each other as a group influenced by the same cosmic planetary influence. First comes the influence of the year, then the sign, the day and lastly the hour. The macrocosm represents the influence of the planets; the microcosm represents the influence of the hour of birth (the ascendant) and the Moon.

The Day of Your Birth

1914 is a number six and is ruled by Venus. This is a one (Sun) and a five (Mercury). These people influence fashion and some among them may have introduced new fashion in their lives, new values. They are the lovers of the decade. In the year 1914, fashion, money, artistic objects were the influences presented for the decade. The underlying influence of the Sun and Mercury gives the power of expression for writing or simply expressing love. If you were born in 1914 you are a lover, not a fighter unless you have some pretty harsh influences in your chart to offset this. Music or some kind of artistic expression is also important to these people. With love, they are fulfilled for loving is as important to them as breathing. Relatives and community affairs will play a big part in their lives.

1915 is a number seven and is ruled by Neptune. This is a one (Sun) and a six (Venus). These are the people who are interested in dancing, music, psychic study and the poetic view of life. They can be somewhat mysterious and not easily understood. This is also true of those born on a seven day (25th), (16th) and (7th). During this year a new dimension in psychic understanding would have come about. Neptune represents the intangibles of the universe so this may have been the year many unusual things happened. Since the underlying influence of this year has an influence of Venus these people may have a measure of artistic talent and be capable of spiritual love or sacrificial love.

1916 is a number eight and is ruled by Saturn. This is a one (Sun) and a seven (Neptune). This is a business year, discipline, organization. These people are very ambitious, disciplined and in many ways austere. They are good at making the intangibles concrete like painting, music, poetry, dancing. They have intuition, an intuition which they can make work for them. This represents a combination of the guarantee, the concrete, but coupled with the ability to believe in a hunch, an idea, a person, just somehow knowing. This results in their being the practical idealists. It is a year for the vision, a vision which becomes reality, or the illusion corrected. You could call these people the trouble shooters.

1917 is a number nine and is ruled by Mars. This is a combination of one (Sun) and an eight (Saturn) as an underlying influence. These people are energetic and active. During a Mars year it is either very actively productive or argumentative and war-like. It may make the people born in this year have an interest in sports and/or heavy sexual experiences. Either way these people have a lot of energy to use one way or another. The Sun and Saturn rulership gives a lot of discipline with action; perhaps it gives the ability to follow through and not just be a flash in the pan. These people, then, can accomplish much in sports or any other area that requires discipline in action. You can be sure they will always achieve results with whatever they do.

1918 is a number one and is ruled by the Sun. This is a combination of a one (Sun) and a nine (Mars) which gives it an underlying influence of Mars (action). These people are leaders, pioneers in one field or another. They are the people who can put the best of both decades together, the previous decade and the new one, blending the old with the new, new ideas, new fashions, new entertainment tendencies but not completely throwing out the old ideas. Sometimes, people born in a one year have a tendency to be showmen no matter what they do for a living. They can be egotistical. Action is their greatest characteristic for you will never find them with their hands in their pockets.

1919 is a number two and is ruled by the Moon. It is a zero and a two. Everytime you have a zero come up with the years it represents some kind of cosmic influence. The people born in this year are ones who seem to be listening to the beat of a different drummer. This represented a period where a new type of family life was introduced via the cosmic influence. The people born in this year seem to have insight where emotional or family matters are concerned. They have a feel for the public need and can profit from this knowledge financially. They may even be a bit psychic.

1920 is a number three and is ruled by Jupiter. This is a one (Sun) and a two (Moon). This represents a new wave for higher education, religion, publishing, and foreign affairs. These people are optimistic, enthusiastic and well able to be objective in their affairs. They see life in a more holistic fashion even though the word holistic would not be used until some fifty years hence. It may be that many born in this year planted the seeds for the holistic movement which would bear fruit much later in time. They are honest people, at times outspoken. They are interested in philosophy of all sorts and have vision, a kind of abstract foresight. This foresight gives them the ability to know how an idea, an action, will turn out in the future.

1921 is a number four and is ruled by the Earth. This is a one (sun) and a three (Jupiter). You can observe these people being generous and somewhat adventurous at times. Being ruled by the Earth, they would take life very seriously but coupled with a strange and unique combination of optimism and practicality can get them very far in life. These people get things done and no doubt do things in a big way. It is a good year for business success if they choose to go in that direction. They have spiritual and religious insight and would make wonderful teachers in this area. A total broad view of life and truth brought down to earth is their greatest talent and potential.

1922 is a number five and is ruled by Mercury. This is a one (Sun) and a four (Earth). Those born during this year have an instinct for communication in all forms. During 1922 a new facet of not only communication but interpersonal relationships began. It was a year when more and faster travel would begin to take place. The people during this point in time

The Day of Your Birth

began to get around much more. It was a restless year as the people born in 1922 verify by their restless personalities. Good writers or speakers can come from this year's crop. The people born in this year also have a passion for talking and dashing here and there. It also is representative of the great subjective awareness of these birthday persons. They are truly the NOW people, people who live in the present, taking life at its fullest NOW.

1923 is a number six and is ruled by Venus. This is a one (Sun) and a five (Mercury). This is a year dedicated to fashion, love and lovers, and creators of artifacts of all kinds. The people born during this year would take their love of fashion and music through their lives. Many of them may be trend setters with fashion and decorating. They can be diplomatic and will make attempts to create harmony at home and in their social world. They have strong loyalty to relatives and their home community. Those born in this year will no doubt remain forever young in their attitudes with life. They will certainly always be lovers in the real sense of the word.

1924 is a number seven and is ruled by Neptune. This is a one (Sun) and a six (Venus). When we is dealing with Neptune there will be influences of self pity, alcohol, and the extremes of sacrifice among its natives. The positive side of this 1924 influence ruled by Neptune is high spirituality, poetic talent, and a spiritual kind of exalted love which may be also defined as unconditional love. Born into this year are dancers, psychics, musicians and spiritual healers with great compassion and tolerance. There is also an underlying influence of harmony and an artistic sense of beauty. People born into this year need a secret place where they can regain their strength through solitude and meditation.

1925 is a number eight and is ruled by Saturn. This is a one and a seven and has an underlying influence of the Sun and Neptune. These people are doers, the achievers, the responsible people of the decade. However there may be more of an idealistic part to their nature than is at first perceived. At its best there can be those who are the practical idealists, able to make dreams come true not only for themselves but others. There may be the negative people among them who are depressed a lot. The year itself will have been a business year, but the hidden influence may be things were not what they seemed and this is true of the people born in this year; perhaps, much more sensitive than others think they are.

1926 is a number nine and is ruled by Mars. This is a one and an eight and has an underlying influence from the Sun and Saturn. This represents action and aggression but action coupled with the ability to discipline and achieve. There are those among them who are very combative and those who are very constructive with their actions. These are the people who are into challenges and the pioneering of new things. This year of 1926 would have been a very active year for everyone. It was a year of much physical activity, sports, exercise, body building, accomplishments, ambitions, and work-a-holics. From the years 1920 through 1929, Neptune was inconjunct Uranus. This was spirituality, inventions, science and the beginning of a lack of balance between the spiritual and the material. Inventions and science started to take prominence over the spiritual as well as slowly but surely these paths seemed to be going in a different direction.

1927 is a number ten and is ruled by the Sun. This is a one (Sun) and a nine (Mars). Wherever you have Mars somewhere in the line up you have action. However, the ten makes this a cosmic influence. These people are very energetic and begin a lot of new ideas and achievements. This was a sports year that brought forth sports people and a lot of new leaders were born. As with all ten years, it is the old mixed with the new. Those born in this year have a great deal of creative talent whether in writing, entertainment, teaching. They look ahead and do not look backwards. They may even be hard to keep track of and others are certainly not going to easily keep up with them.

1928 is a number 20 (2) and is ruled by the Moon. This is a two and a zero so again we have cosmic influence where the people seem to be on a different wave length. They are domestically oriented and it would introduce into the year a new family influence and considerations. The year itself would have had something to do with new home styles, architecture, feelings, with great sensitivity to surroundings, environmental conditions. The people of this year would make good home decorators, nutritionists, restaurateurs. They can be emotional but not necessarily emotional in the weak sense of the word. Weak and emotional are two different words and two different moods and are not synonymous with each other. It is that these people are sensitive to their surroundings and any nuance of change. They are good parents, but may be even considered cosmic parents. This means they can feel protective over all children not just their own.

1929 is a number three and is ruled by Jupiter. This is a number one (Sun) and a two (Moon). This is the year of the great financial "bang" and wouldn't you know it would be a Jupiter year when the bubble burst. The people born in 1929 may be a little extravagant in some way, but not necessarily with money. They may also feel the grass is greener on the other side of the road so to speak. Sometimes in a Jupiter year things go too far past the middle (beyond balance) which results in walls being broken down or things getting out of control in some way. This is especially true where people's lives are concerned. In a positive respect this can represent the co-existence of the positive and negative, male and female, ego thrust and passive emotions. The year may start out being competitive between these opposites but cooperation and balance come by the end of the year. It represents a year when the natives born to it have a great need for peaceful balance not only with a mate but with the other parts of their lives. They spend a lifetime trying for that balance. Balance is

The Day of Your Birth

the underlying influence with these people, an influence that doesn't easily show for they have a facade of opulence. Where these people are concerned, don't make a judgment until you know them better or "have walked in their moccasins."

1930 is a number four and is ruled by Earth. This is a one (Sun) and a number three (Jupiter). It was in this year an effort was made toward practical realization of what happened the year before and to get back to the basics. Jupiter in the sense of this year's influence would represent understanding, truth, objectivity. It was an entirely different Jupiter than 1929 Jupiter. The people born in this year are friendly but detached. They are people who cannot easily be bound for they need freedom to do their own thing whatever that may turn out to be. They can be practical, realistic in their outward facade but spiritual, understanding and optimistic on the inside. They are understanding as long as you do not infringe upon their rights. If you give them this right they can be very generous.

1931 is a number five and is ruled by Mercury. This gives an underlying influence of four (earth) and one (Sun). Communication with them is an art as well as a necessity. They may get involved in community endeavors or neighborhood situations. People born in this year are talkative, but even though talkative are practical and realistic with all they set out to accomplish. They do a lot of traveling in and about their immediate community and may be somewhat restless for new things. It is in this year that major teaching establishments were formed; and the people in this year would teach in these special learning centers; or become involved in the continual growth of such establishments. This influence of teaching holds true even if they are only involved in activity with relatives or neighborhood children.

1932 is a number six and is ruled by Venus. This is a number one (Sun) and a number five (Mercury). These people are good with fashions and art. This talent is coupled with the ability to express themselves easily in any phase of the artistic world they choose. People born in this year are the lovers and can be found most of the time trying to keep the peace. If they are not directly involved in the art world they have great appreciation and make excellent critics. Financial interests are also part of this year's influence, whether for the people in general or those born in this year who may be actively involved in the financial world. Direct involvement in their community affairs is also part of these individual's lives. It gives a special love for brothers and sisters to these birthday people.

1933 is a number seven and is ruled by Neptune. It is a number six (Venus) and a one (Sun). The Neptune years represent the spiritual, psychic, music, poetry, dancing and all the other intangibles of life. This year or the people born into it can introduce new methods in any of these things. They can become leaders in these areas. One of the influences can be spiritual love with the ability to sacrifice for loved ones. But on the other side it may represent confusion and a certain negativity. There is positive as well as negative moods among these birth people and as a result they will either approach their destiny productively or destructively. These people need a creative outlet in order to direct some of their excessive creative energy.

1934 is a number eight and is ruled by Saturn. It is a number seven (Neptune) and a one (Sun). This particular Saturn year has a complex interpretation. It is dedication to some achievement in regard to the public or a career. It presents discipline that is directed toward betterment. In many ways it is discipline plus sacrifice if necessary. It is taking responsibility and facing a duty with faith and belief in that which must be done. It represents a year of business efforts and those born in this year would have a tendency to be leaders in whatever business they choose. However, there may be an element of trusting a hunch at some point in their lives that will be a major turning point for them. The success they strive for is not just money but the personal satisfaction of a job well done.

1935 is a number nine and is ruled by Mars. It is a number eight (Saturn) and a one (Sun). These people can be very active in sports, and may achieve prominence either in sports or some other area because of their innate ability for discipline. They may have strong sexual passions but passions that are backed up with responsibility and duty. They are aggressive, and capable of selfless activity for others, at least the high minded people born in this year. Those responding to the negative influence of this year are going to be more argumentative and stubbornly aggressive.

1936 is a number ten and is ruled by the Sun. This is a nine (Mars) and a one (Sun) and has an underlying influence of action. This is the ending of a decade and the beginning of a new one. It introduces a new group of leaders into the world. It may also introduce new forms of entertainment, and produce a new popular entertainer, who comes into his popularity during this year and/or one born in this year who will obtain his prominence later. Some people born in this year are egotistical and others make good teachers, entertainers and lovers. Both types born in this year are confident and fun loving. They are charming and self confident most of the time.

1937 is a number twenty and is ruled by the Moon. These people are more emotionally disciplined than they at first appear to be. They are very sensitive to the needs of others. This is a domestic year and creates a new type of architecture for homes and business offices. The people born in this year are geared to more every day matters, enjoying their homes very much. This is the year of the woman and a year that had a tendency to be in line with more feminine fashions and instincts. The people born in this year make good parents for they know how to love and nurture all living things.

The Day of Your Birth

1938 is a number three and is ruled by Jupiter. This is a number one (Sun) and a two (Moon). These people are optimists. They are ever ready to gamble with life and usually end up having many adventures during their lifetime. This is a year geared to religion and higher education, science, all new ideas and techniques in every field. Those born in this year may be educators and those who do things in a big way. They are humorous and have very objective approaches to life. Not only did the year produce good men and women relationships throughout the year, but the people born in this year would have a tendency to be open and aboveboard with relationships; hence, lucky.

1939 is a number four and is ruled by the Earth. This is also a number twenty two and is co-ruled by Uranus. Twenty two years are always cosmic and produce people not easily understood. Having a cosmic approach to their lives they follow the beat of a different drummer. They sense instinctively that they have a cosmic purpose to their lives. It is not always easy for them to relate to others on a mundane level. This year of 1939 is important in breaking a mold, breaking a pattern for society which would represent a dawning of a new way of life for humanity in the years to come. This is the year of the humanitarian. It represented the exposure and discovery of highly creative knowledge, scientific technology, computerization and a new purpose for man. A twenty two year is always a year that is very much a break through. From the years 1939 to 1945 we had Uranus trine Neptune. This would have introduced a new wave of the esoteric, art, music, new visions in philosophy, new ideals, new spiritual insights. Things started to turn a little, getting back into a balance between the material and the spiritual. This doesn't mean that everyone was aware of this happening but it meant that souls were born who would have great insight into cosmic vision. New vision was given to a very few during these years even though as the public observed we were at a height of the golden material age. After 1945, the seed that was planted would grow bringing about a balance between the spiritual, mental and physical. However, this seedling would not bear fruit until many decades later.

1940 is a number five and is ruled by Mercury. It is a one (Sun) and a four (Earth) and has an underlying influence of a practical Mercury. These people born in this year would be able to easily communicate and deal easily with relatives and community affairs. It was a year where subjective values would reign. These individuals are the NOW people, people who deal with immediate now situations, having all things at hand in focus. It would introduce a new ten year period in communication, papers, radio, television. People born in this year would be practical and can make a success with whatever they do.

1941 is a number six and is ruled by Venus. It is a one (Sun) and a five (Mercury). These people like clothes, jewelry, and all things artistic. They are harmonious, peaceful, diplomatic human beings. They strive for affection and love. During the year itself love stories would abound and music would be softer, more gentle, and the people born in this year would lean this way, also. This represents a combination of artistic talent with the ability to express said talent with confidence and ease. Their over-all destiny is the expression of love in all its phases, whether that love is toward a human being or an expression of art.

1942 is a number seven and is ruled by Neptune. This is a one (Sun) and a six (Venus). These are the people who are talented with music, poetry, dancing, psychic instincts. They may also be very compassionate. It is a year when the unusual may have happened for people in general. The people born in 1942 can be rather mysterious. They are spiritual and idealistic but some would respond to the negative influence and be subject to illusion and deception. The higher part of their ability is being able to give and attract spiritual love. The negative part of this influence is being deceived and disillusioned by love. It is up to the person him or herself to grow in awareness. World War Two beings.

1943 is a number eight and is ruled by Saturn. It is a seven (Neptune) and a one (Sun). This is a business year and is also one of the war years. It represents people born to it who are disciplined and attentive to duty but also who can and do undergo great sacrificial periods in their lives. These people are dedicated to producing something of value, something practical and stable, but with the Neptune influence always hovering in the background this could be trial and error. The year itself represents faith and duty in its highest sense. In its more negative sense it would bring sacrificial responsibilities. This year is symbolic of authority figures, the great father. This is the authority figure who is sincere, self sacrificing for an ideal or an authority figure who is cunningly deceptive. It was a year with war where discipline and sacrifice was called upon for all the people.

1944 is a number nine and is ruled by Mars. This is a one (Sun) and an eight (Saturn). People born in this year are active, aggressive at times, and somewhat of a pioneer. They have a fearless attitude about life, or at least that is the way it appears. However, behind this aggressive spirit is temperance and discipline that doesn't show to most people. They know what they are doing at all times even if you don't think so. In one sense they can be classed as humanitarians and in another sense they may be sports minded and given to the discipline needed for great feats in sports.

1945 is a number ten and is ruled by the Sun. This is a nine (Mars) and a one (Sun). These people are leaders and again this is a year that ends and begins a new esoteric decade. Those people born in a ten year are the ones who are influenced by two decades in their values. They are the people who establish new things and have the ego and the energy to do so. However, they may establish new groups, new causes for others to take over leaving

The Day of Your Birth

them free to move on and clear other paths. As a whole they are self confident, sports minded, sexually in high gear, or vibrant for a better word, with an aura of energy that attracts people of all ages and all calibers to themselves.

1946 is a number twenty and is ruled by the Moon. This is another cosmically influenced year. The people born in this year are domestic. They love good food, family life and would make good counselors of family problems. They have high emotional ideals and values. This year rules women, and may introduce a new decade where feminine values become slightly different. A year that is a two or a twenty is always good for relationships on a more equal basis so these people are excellent with others; however it can go the other way in a negative fashion. If it goes negative then they will expect the mate to do all the adjusting. Either way, this moon year can go negative or positive. Much depends upon efforts by the person or conditions at the nurturing stage of his/her life as a child, the how and why of their childhood.

1947 is a number three and is ruled by Jupiter. This is a number two (Moon) and a one (Sun). These are the people who may be very interested in education, higher mind subjects, foreign affairs, and religion. They can be very objective and can always make an objective decision when need be. It is a year for publications, books, magazine interests. The people born in this year may get into these things as they mature either as a vocation or an avocation. Foreign affairs or foreigners would have become prominent during this 1947 year and foreign affairs would be important to the people born in this year. Above all, the people born in this year are optimistic, have high integrity and open-mindedness. However, they can deal in exaggerations, extremes of one kind or another, and gambling either with money, love or life itself. There is an underlying influence of the Sun and Moon making these people good at relationships. They have a stroke of luck in man and woman type of relationships.

1948 is a number 22 and is ruled by Uranus. There may be an underlying influence of four (Earth). This is a highly universal number making the people born in this year difficult to understand. It is a cosmic year generally speaking which means at this time there was a great division in man's purpose on earth. It represented a division in time and man's values. The people born in this year are different as all 22 year people are for they march to the beat of a different drummer. They seem to have a different method of communication. They seem to possess the gift of mental thought transference and early in their lives cannot easily understand why others do not have the same talent. I keep lovingly saying these people are from a different planet in earlier lives of their souls. When 1984 came these people found an important turning point in their destinies even if only a full mental awareness of what they have to do. A high order of things would begin in the year 1948 when as a people we began to go across a bridge to a slightly different purpose for man or the beginning of the need to awaken to higher values. The people born in 1948 seem to be out of the ordinary in some way. If you know one you will understand this. They have different attitudes with life and are very self willed. In this year of 1948 the beginning of the individualistic movement began. These people have a practical business head and can get very far with this talent if they so choose.

1949 is a number five and is ruled by Mercury. It is a two and a three and is co-ruled by the Moon and Jupiter. These people may be very good at communication of one sort or another, talking with neighbors, brothers, sisters, writing or even public speaking. Their destiny could have something to do with their immediate communities. They can be in the communication field professionally or on the lower scale, gossips. All of this year's people are NOW people. They deal with the day at hand, mostly forgetting yesterday and believing tomorrow is not yet in focus. They have a tendency to be somewhat nervous at times for they have a lot of nervous energy that has to be used. They move around a lot, always on the go either in travel or talking. Taken at its highest influence they can become great leaders of truth, religion, science, publishing. These are the people who have a very integrated personality, living today but with an understanding of the direction they must go in the future. They see the pattern of their future but do not dwell on it for fear they will lose the immediate, the now. They get more out of a single day than most others around them.

1950 is a number six and is ruled by Venus. This is a number one (Sun) and a five (Mercury). This influence stands for clothes, jewelry, music, and all things artistic. They are loving, gentle people who need harmony in their lives and need to have relationships where communication is uppermost. They are lovers; not fighters. Interior decorating, fashion designing, dealers in artifacts, counseling are only a few of the things in which they can excel. This is a year of love and romance. The people born in this year seem to be in complete touch with their environments and at one with all living things. They vibrate in unison with nature rather than cutting themselves off from nature as most of us do. Just because they are gentle does not mean they are not strong for they have a gentle strength.

1951 is a number seven and is ruled by Neptune. This is a number one(Sun) and a number six (Venus) and is co-ruled by this ego influence and the love influence. This is the year of the psychics. These people are perceptive and idealistic. It is the cosmic year where growth comes about spiritually for man and where the great need is faith. Music is a part of this Neptune influence as is the talent for dancing. The people born in this year are either good with music or dancing. They either appreciate these things very much as part of their inspiration in life or are good as performers. They are mysterious, and many times hard to figure out. Compassion is

The Day of Your Birth

their middle name and they seem to have a natural talent for healing. Another attribute is their ability to give and attract a spiritual love. If there is a negative influence with this year it is loving someone and assuming that person is like they idealize them to be; whereby they are hurt later because the veil of illusion falls away.

1952 is a number eight and is ruled by Saturn. This is a number seven (Neptune) and a number one (Sun). There is a combination of the realistic and the idealistic with this influence. They can be very much given to ambition and vocational success; however, the underlying influence of idealism can make them the practical idealist. While this is a business year, meaning these people need to find their place in the outer world of business and commerce. Even so it may not be easy for these people to do that. It seems the test lies in faith given to an ambition before any guarantees or success comes into their lives. Faith always comes before the guarantee in anything. If anyone thinks they will give the discipline, duty and loyalty to a person or a thing after they GET a guarantee, they are wrong because BLIND FAITH COMES FIRST. The underlying influence of Neptune keeps wiping them out until they learn to recognize both influences of faith and discipline and give each their due. The people born in this year can do this by dedicating themselves to an ideal or by coming to a place where they have great confidence and stamina in achieving a goal.

1953 is a number nine and is ruled by Mars. This is a number eight (Saturn) and a one (Sun). These people are much more disciplined with their actions than they seem to be at first. They are the work-a-holics. They can be quite humanitarian minded in their outlook on life. They are energetic and very active with something going on all of the time. During this year of 1953 humanitarian efforts were prominent among certain people. It introduced new sports stars, either in that year or ones born in that year who would gain prominence at a more mature age. Whether the people born in 1953 are active in sports themselves they are interested as spectators. Many of these people are successful in business because they have the energy and the discipline necessary. Those who have gone before them with similar traits are 1899, 1908, 1917, 1926, 1935, 1944, Those who will come after them will be 1962, 1971, 1980, 1989, 1998.

1954 is a number one and is ruled by the Sun. This is a number one (Sun) and a nine (Mars). This begins a new decade and finishes a previous one. The people born in this year are born leaders and generally speaking they lead and others follow. They definitely do not follow. In many ways, it is difficult for them to put themselves in other people's shoes. They have a kind of fearless quality (like Aries) and are not easily defeated. Children, entertainment and all other types of fun and games are associated with this year and these people. The positive side of this influence is leadership and inspiring others to grow and to achieve by their example or the negative side of selfishness in gaining their own purpose.

From 1950 through 1959 Uranus squares Neptune and these people born in this period mean well but they are very self-willed, and sometimes they go to extremes with drugs, sex, food, or the opposite extreme of self denial. During this period was introduced a problem where spiritual values began to change, where extremes to one end of the spectrum to the other was common. Those who were not involved in the drug and sex scene during this period and who were on the higher positive side were individualistic with unusual beliefs, not likely to follow those born before them. Their beliefs may not show through their behavior necessarily but when the chips are down they expose a high cosmic connection. This period either produced those who may experience some delusions regarding the father or authority figures or they go to the extreme opposite and idealize their father. Used in the positive constructive sense these people can be very creative in writing, music, art, poetry possessing the talent to introduce new forms of art expression. The opposite end of this spectrum are those who go to extremes with some form of fanaticism. The things of the spirit were at cross purposes with creative thinking. This was preparation for the decade of the sixties where Uranus became dominate and Neptune (music, drugs, excessive idealism, fantasy) was harnessed by Uranus, the influence of individualism and willfulness, and also the other way around, the idealism of the brotherhood of man.

1955 is a twenty and is ruled by the Moon. This is a cosmic number with an interest in more universal values. These people are interested in the home and children and possess great domestic tendencies. They can be emotional at times, but they seem to have enough cosmic strength to rise above, adjust and make difficulties work for them. Some born in this year are dedicated in a positive way to raising a family, home decorating, or any kind of vocation dealing with the home and home supplies. This year is mother ruled and the year is feminine, magnetic and has a lot to do with concentration in nurturing all of nature including plant life, gardens, etc. They have a strong tendency to produce things, gardens, children, artifacts, construction of clothing, etc. They can be good with relationships when they set their heart and mind to it.

1956 is a three and is ruled by Jupiter. This is a two and a one and is co-ruled by the Moon and the Sun. The people born in this year are geared toward higher education, religion, science, the abstract. In their over-all interpretation of life they are objective, foresighted and able to see the broad view of life. They can be interested in foreign countries or become involved with foreign born people. The year itself introduced new interest in higher education. When we have a Jupiter year professional people take the foreground and scientific leaders come to prominence out of this year's crop. Jupiter represents getting out of a rut, so a major experience in 1956 could have world wide importance at a later time even though the people were not aware of the importance of this experience at the time. People

The Day of Your Birth

born in this year are good with relationships especially dealing in man and woman situations. They are able to successful combine ego needs with emotional needs.

1957 is a twenty two (4) and is ruled by Uranus. These people understand 1948 people very well. The people born in this year can be very unique and inventive. Very definitely they are not carbon copies of anyone else anywhere unless it is their 1948 front runners. The 1966 people who come after them will also be similar. The people born in this year have more cosmic values. They will bring about great changes at some time in their lives. During this year great changes may have started to take place even if at the time they were only slightly felt. The 1948 changes will be much more apparent in 1957 and the 1957 changes will be much more obvious in 1966. The people born in this 1957 year are not ordinary, nor do they want to be considered average. They are psychic, sensitive, musical, and possess the ability to express themselves in music, poetry, dancing, psychic expressions that can make some of them become great.

1958 is a number five and is ruled by Mercury. This is a two (Moon) and a three (Jupiter). These people are natural born communicators. They can be humorous, optimistic and very enjoyable company. They are open to everyone for no one is a stranger to these very expressively vital people. Many of them will do a great deal for their community in which they live. They are so open that at first they may be very naive so that they have to learn not everyone is as trustworthy and honest as they are. I compare them to little puppy dogs for they are so cute you want to cuddle them no matter how young they are or how old they get. They may deal with transportation, traveling, or anything that deals with traveling in a secondary way. If there is a negative it is the tendency for some to be extravagant, or to exaggerate. Some of them will travel to foreign countries in their life times which will have a profound effect upon their lives after that.

1959 is a number six and is ruled by Venus. This consists of a two (Moon) and a four (Earth). Love, beauty, art, and the magic of all that inspires in love, or the arts is the core of these birthday year people. These people can be talented with music, dramatics and even counseling others for they are kind, considerate and understanding. With all this is a practical side to their natures that makes any kind of artistic attempt pay off in cold, hard cash. They have a flair for fashion and love is as important to them as breathing. New fashions may be introduced by them for they have a way of leading others in this direction; thereby making money if they get into business. They have a great deal of charm and are very economical. The year itself generally speaking will have some economical bearing on later years. There is an economical thread that ties 1959, 1968, 1977, and 1986 together. Our national economy takes a different turn in 1986.

1960 is a number seven and is ruled by Neptune. This is a number 6 (Venus) and a one (Sun). This is a spiritual year. The people born in this year have a more universal connection with new higher influences for spiritual growth. Not only does this influence have a great bearing on the natures of those born in this year, but the whole of 1960 had a spiritual influence upon all the people. This is the year when the psychic force may have been stronger for those capable of picking it up. Those born in this year can be psychic, musical, poetic, idealistic but there may be those among them who are given to self pity, drugs and alcohol. It all depends upon other configurations in their astrological chart or their childhood background. Dance is important to these people and many of them excel in this art. These birthday people have loving personalities and are quite capable of loving someone spiritually and sacrificially. There will be those among them capable of making money with psychic research or fantastic musical achievements and fame.

1961 is a number eight and is ruled by Saturn. This is a number seven (Neptune) and a one (Sun). This year is father ruled, authority, social standards, and vocational considerations. Each number in each decade that is similar has LIKE values but the difference lies in the fact that man is progressing or changing. As this number eight in the sixties is going to have different social standards and a different influence on authority figures, different from the fifties. This is also true of vocational considerations from the fifties to the sixties. Business outlooks were good for this year and the people born in this year will have a definite flair for business and public success. They are capable of sacrificing if they have to in order to make the business, the vocation a success. There is either strong idealism for the father, or strong differences of belief. An eight of one decade understands an eight of another decade to one degree or another, as does sevens, sixes, fives, etc.

1962 is a number nine and is ruled by Mars. This is a number eight (Saturn) and a one (Sun). The difference lies in a further delineation of the year itself. The year 1953 is also an nine but the root numbers are a five and a three. The root numbers for 1962 are a six and a two. The 5 (Mercury) and the three (Jupiter) gives a mental influence. The six (Venus) and the two (Moon) gives a more emotional root influence. The 1953 people are capable of thinking and doing things in a big way leading to great expansion. The 1962 people are further defined by an influence of love and money with their vocation so that their approach to the public, business involves a sixth sense about what the public wants and needs and catering to this need can make them do well financially. Over-all 1962 is a Mars year which means action, sports, with a certain fearless quality. They are people born to be leaders who will not take a back seat to anyone. Dealing with 1962 as an eight we discover 1926 is an eight. The difference in interpretation lies in the generational differences. In 1962 Venus (love,

The Day of Your Birth

money comes first; in the 1926 year, the Moon (family and emotional considerations come first. It is a question of sequence of events in proportion to their importance. Take for example: 1911, 1922, 1933, 1944, 1955, 1966, 1977, 1988, 1999. These people may identify with other years that have the same final digit but they are more unique and much more individualistic. Their destinies seem to be very strong ones and are not easily pulled from the path of destiny. They have a more singularity of purpose where the inner drive matches the outer action fully. The interpretations I am giving for the years are general ones for the particular year. One can always delve into the year and get a finer more in depth interpretation. There are steps, layers, like outer influences and more inner hidden motives. As the total and final digit of the year is the outer influence, the underlying numbers making up this digit is the inner nature not always apparent.

1963 is a ten and is ruled by the Sun. This consists of a one and a zero. These people would introduce a new ten year period. They are very self sufficient or it would appear so. They have a great deal of magnetism just like the Sun that warms you on sunny days; however, sit in the glow of the Sun too long and it burns you. This means that Sun people have a tendency to take over. When they are in a leadership position in life and their ego world is functioning in a positive manner, they can have a very inspiring influence on others; however, if they are not satisfied with their lot, they can become over bearing. As far as the year 1963 goes, it begins to unravel a new destiny for man as a whole.

1964 is a twenty and is ruled by the Moon. These people are domestic and are mother influenced, generally speaking, but there are always exceptions to every rule. They are more given to emotional outbursts, catering to their feelings. It is a year that deals with home situations and family problems. It represents a group of people born in this year who are geared toward partnerships, togetherness. These people seem to have more feelings, emotions and just plain psychic instincts than most. Home means much to them and when they finally settle down they can be very satisfied just staying home at night. The best of them make good parents for they are excellent in caring for others.

1965 is a number three and is ruled by Jupiter. This is a two (Moon) and a one (Sun). This represents concentration on higher education, foreign affairs, optimism, sometimes extravagance, adventure, gambling. Both 1965 and 1956 are number three years, with underlying influences of the Sun and Moon. The difference lies in looking a little deeper at which influence takes priority, Mercury or Venus. In 1956, Mercury came first with communication, environmental conditions, community affairs, relatives. In 1965 Venus came first with love, art, money. Both these years represented years where new innovative methods came about for communication, foreign affairs, and higher education. A Jupiter year always gives understanding to his people and also gives the ability to be objective when experiences warrant it. These people do things in a big way. They are never held down by a narrow limited view of life.

1966 is a twenty two and is ruled by Uranus. This is a cosmic year and therefore attracts a more universal outlook. This is a new cosmic influence where love and finances are concerned. These people were born to adapt to a higher cosmic force in order to adjust and change current conditions around them. The influence would be more inclined to deal with love, material values, and. artistic endeavors. These people may get involved with progressive movements that would initiate the Aquarian Age. They instinctively understand the Aquarian way where human values are concerned. How much they get involved would depend upon other configurations in their astrological map at birth.

1967 is a number five and is ruled by Mercury. This is a two (Moon) and a three (Jupiter). Quite naturally this five represents "expressive" caring with the ability to understand emotional situations not only in their own lives but others around them. Sometimes, these people can overdo or be extravagant. They are subjective and at other times when you least expect it can be objective which results in quite a mixture of moods. The objectivity surprises people because they come on at first in an emotional and subjective manner. They are able to communicate well and know no strangers. This year introduces new mind improvement influences and newer advancements with computers (Virgo and Jupiter combined influence), integrating great detailed information into the system. These people born in this year may have a lot to do with the much newer computer age.

1968 is a number six and is ruled by Venus. This is a two (Moon) and a four (Earth). These people have a different concept of art, music and love than the six people born nine years earlier. The people born in this year are artistic and need harmony around them in order to function at their best. They can do well with some art form that can not only give public success but financial benefits; however, whether or not they choose an art expression for their life's work they should have it in their lives as a hobby and a relaxation. On the whole they are lovers, not fighters and make good partners for they are very loyal. They can also be in touch with the financial world and seem to know instinctively what to do, where to go, when and how much in order to make money. From the years 1963 to 1970 Uranus sextiles Neptune, introducing more of the metaphysical advances. This period marks a joining of the spiritual and the physical influence, bringing back together the influence of a belief in a balanced harmony between the two. This also represents creative mind with the psychic and intangible Neptune. It is enlightenment and new awareness of the spiritual truths.

The Day of Your Birth

1969 is a number seven and is ruled by Neptune. This is a two (Moon) and a five (Mercury). This year deals with spiritual values. The people born in this year can be mystical, tolerant, musical, poetic, and given to the dance. They are compassionate and may either express the seemingly inexpressible or lack the ability to express themselves. They are never in the middle; it is to one extreme or another. They are not easily understood. On one hand they are able to express their feelings, emotions and sensitivities of the psychic or unseen world or suffer silently. Both these qualities will show up at various times in their lives. They may find at some time in their lives they end up teaching all those who will listen concerning things in the realm of the spiritual. This represents an influence of being in touch with all of nature. It is as if these people can communicate with plant life, animals, and may even be able to hear the actual music of the spheres. They are capable of making great sacrifices for relatives and any other situation in their communities that touches their sensitive, caring hearts.

1970 is a number eight and is ruled by Saturn. This is a one (Sun) and a seven (Neptune). This year is father or authority influenced. It deals with the public good. The people who own this year can easily be leaders in their worlds and well be able to make sacrifices for whatever their causes. This does not mean these people are not interested in domestic life, it simply means they are more interested in vocational and public areas of life. They are the practical idealists, capable of making dreams come true; also capable of seeing a vision and actualizing it. The drive of ego status may be important to some but to others born in this year it means just being the very best they can become in this lifetime.

1971 is a number nine and is ruled by Mars. This is a one (Sun) and an eight (Saturn). These people are active, aggressive, ambitious, with a lot of energy. They can fight at the drop of a hat if their rights are invaded or threatened. They love sports and possess the discipline necessary to excel in some type of sports or competitive activity. They are fearless at the same time, cautious. It is quite a combination which if channeled and used rightly. can give them a great deal of fame, semi-fame or notice in their world. The year is masculine in its outward influence, but there is a softness to these people that doesn't, at first, show. They may not be quite as fearless as they appear to be. The influence with this year gives the struggle to go forward into achievement. This is over-all very positive when this energy is used for productivity. The negative influence which may show up with some people born in this year would be fighting, and arguments.

1972 is a number ten and is ruled by the Sun. This year is geared to a new ten year destiny span. These people can be leaders for they have a fearless quality when it comes to doing their own thing. They make good leaders because they are not afraid to introduce new things. They are the in-between people capable of understanding all other generations easily. They represent the ability of closing one door and opening another, putting the best of both worlds together. Most of the people born in this year have a good self confident ego but there may be some among them who are egotistical. They will either warm you or burn you.

1973 is a number twenty and is ruled by the Moon. This year is domestic and mother influenced. It is emotions, feelings, sensitivity to others. There may be accent on foods, eating, restaurants. New conditions with housing may have been initiated this year. The people born in this year are good with relationships and have the ability to understand other people. Two year people do not like to stand alone for they are at their best when doing something with a partner whether business, pleasure, or love. One thing about them is they understand the public and if they use this instinctive knowledge for business they can do well financially.

1974 is a number three and is ruled by Jupiter. This is a two (Moon) and a one (Sun). This represents higher education, philosophy, religion and foreign affairs. The people born in this year cater to all things abstract all their lives or at various times in their lives. They are usually very optimistic, objective, and at times humorous. Extravagance and over indulgence plays a part in their lives, either a prominent part or a minor part. This year adventure holds sway. Much depends upon other considerations how much adventure. These people can be honest in the extreme but also exaggerative and untruthful. It will be either one way or another. It will depend upon the situations into which they are caught. People born in this year are capable of relating to a mate with exhuberance of their own kind of integrity. This year's influence represents a balance between self confidence and strong feelings making them well integrated personalities most of the time.

1975 is a twenty two and is ruled by Uranus. This is a cosmic year making the people born into this year much more universal in their outlook on life. They can be inventive because they are awakened to higher creative knowledge. Because they are also in a strange complex kind of way, practical they are capable of putting their inventive ideas into practice. They are extremely individualistic in their thinking. It was in 1975 that began a new era where a faint dawning of the approaching Uranian (Aquarian) age was casting its shadow. It would be in 1998-2000 when Uranus would take over the rule of the sign of the times, a rulership Neptune has had for 2000 years. The Aquarian age will be when man will realize we are all one earth and not a collection of isolated countries upon this earth. The year 1984 was the next step to awareness, and then 1995 is the final step before the door is closed and a new one opened. The people born in this year, or any 22 year, seem to have a subtle understanding of all this. They can be psychic, musical, perceptive, mystical with the ability to express all the intangibles in one way or another. They are different and stand out among the crowd in their own way. They have a spirituality that is more cosmic and universal rather than social or temporal.

1976 is a number five and is ruled by Mercury. It is a two (Moon) and a three (Jupiter). This is different from 1967 because the underlying influence is Venus (6) and Neptune (7) finds the year 1976 having Neptune's influence first in importance to Venus. They will easily tune into the intangibles of life around them including music. Whereas the people born in 1967 will have Venus (love, money) first; then Neptune. Above all these people in both years will be capable of spiritual love or if they take the negative road deceptions with love and values. In the end, however, they will understand and reach the higher level of truth, integrity and optimism. They may be meant to write, lecture, compose music, poetry, and dance and when the combination of the Moon and Jupiter is added to their ability to communicate the intangibles they can attract people far and wide. The best of them born into this year can do this. However, there will be some among them who may be extravagant and a little inclined to fabricate the truth.

1977 is a number six and is ruled by Venus. This is a two (Moon) and a four (Earth). The people born into this year love clothes and all things artistic. They may be the people who introduce new hair styles, new art forms, new clothing styles, music, and a new pop star may show up among them when the time is right for his fame. These people are geared to making all things beautiful functional; by that I mean they can make money through some art form and somehow give people the idea they want it. They get inspired with the subtle little nuances thereby making them very creative with music, art, dancing, inspiration, writing, etc. They sense many things around them others do not even imagine to be possible. They can make all these little nuances visible and real to others through creative art or writing.

1978 is a number seven and is ruled by Neptune. This is a two (Moon) and a five (Mercury). These people are psychic and very intuitive. They are very different from the 1960 people. The '60 people are combination of love and the spiritual and are very idealistic. The people born in 1969 and 1978 are a combination of Mercury, meaning they are given to the expression of music, psychic instincts. Their Neptune talent gives them great insight of a more mental expression. With 1960 people it is insight that is more given to love and visual artistic expression. The 1960 people make good critics with music, art, fashion because they have great insight as to what people will like thus profiting from this knowledge. The 1978 people can have karma,or the ability to be sacrificial, in relationship to brothers and sisters. They can also get involved in community affairs to the point of sacrifice if necessary. These 1978 people are very perceptive and can see the close up view of life and things around them, but can also mentally interpret the total view.

1979 is a number eight and is ruled by Saturn. This is a two (Moon) and a six (Venus). The people born in this year are business and public minded with a great instinct for business prospects and outlook. They also have an instinct for making money but can also be excellent at combining love and money and business and pleasure all at the same time. They can be pros at this. This is different from the eight of 1970 for in 1970 the year is a combination of Neptune and Saturn where they can be a fight between the guarantees of life and the nebulous. The year 1979 is a combination that insures public success. In 1979 we began a much different influence where business is concerned and may turn out to be a blessing is disguise but we will know the answer by 1988 and again in 1997. The people born in this year will be able to make money with their business sense.

1980 is a number nine and is ruled by Mars. This is a combination of a one (Sun) and an eight (Saturn). This year can also be business oriented. Mars gears its action toward public success and the public good. These people born in this year are not only active, but leaders in many fields. This year may also produce sports stars and/or many people interested in sports on a non professional basis. Some of them will have a very physical approach to life while others of this year will be very humanitarian in their efforts and outlook on life. Whatever these people do they will have the discipline behind their actions and the self confidence along with it. However, the negative side of this influence may make some of them low on self confidence or at times depressive.

1981 is a number ten and and is ruled by the Sun. This introduces a new ten year period. The new decade will introduce new leaders and there will be those among them who will turn out to be tremendous leaders at the beginning of the 21st century. They will begin many new things for humanity when they come into power. This is a general statement but describing the people born in this year all of them will have the ability to lead no matter how large or small their world. Even those who will not achieve national prominence will achieve prominence in the city, state or neighborhood in which they live. That which they do initiate will more than likely be brought to a successful conclusion. They are not only leaders but leaders who follow through to the finish.

1982 is a number twenty and is ruled by the Moon. This year has a domestic influence. It is a year geared to the mother figure and feminine influence. Those born in this year can be emotional but who also easily pick up on the moods of those around them to a greater or lesser degree. When you have a Moon year the influence is more magnetic, making people born in this year able to pull things and people toward them to their advantage. This also means that they can attract people into their personal orbits who are lucky for them. It can make them more inward than outward with their feelings. Much of what these people are all about will

The Day of Your Birth

not show to others. It is similar to 1928 except with the 1928 people, emotions and family show first and then the public and vocational ambitions. With the 1982 people the reverse will be true. However, with both these years the people born into them have strong family ties and will easily accept the duties and karma for family. In 1928 it is Moon-Saturn; in 1982 it is Saturn-Moon. Even though the total influence of the year is mother influenced for 1982, there exists an underlying influence of the father with discipline and responsibility. We may further interpret that in many ways a 1928 person (male or female) may have to take the role of both the mother and the father for one reason or another. A woman born in this year may have much more responsibility with a career. The 1928 man would perhaps tend to deny his full responsibility toward a career in an attempt to balance his life. Naturally this is a generalization.

1983 is a number three and is ruled by Jupiter. It is a number two(Moon) and a one (Sun) giving the people born in this year an integrated personality. They can be very objective in their thinking and understanding having rather broad minded attitudes and given to philosophical development. As for the year itself foreign affairs will be prominent. It is the beginning of the necessity to have complete honesty and integrity in foreign affairs as well as with people's own private lives. Education may have begun to have problems in many areas. The people born in this year have a great advantage because they will be able to put ego and emotions in proper balance. They will also be excellent in man and woman type of relationships. Above all their optimistic, humorous (yet serious) outlook on life will aid them throughout their lives.

1984 is a number 22 and is ruled by Uranus. This is a cosmic year and the people born in this year will be cosmic in their attitudes. This is the year when a lot of changes should take place in the world scheme of things, sudden and unexpected changes. Those born at this time will be unconventional, yet practical; unpredictable, but realistic. They will be complex and unusual as the year itself will turn out to be unusual. A new invention will have presented itself in 1984 (whether the people learn about it at this time or not). This invention will have a great influence on humanity in the upcoming century. The year is going to tell us something about our cosmic destiny and the positive energy force of the universe. Look to the cosmic years and you will begin to realize what these years are trying to tell us. You will begin to see a pattern which will finally result in us eventually having to face our heritage. No one really can interpret fully what can happen in a Uranian year for it will usually end up being unexpected. One thing is positive and that is a great change is coming and there is really nothing we can do about it but react in the best way we know how. Much of what may have happened in 1984 may remain obscure to most of humanity for it may be just a crack in the door opening where only a few will notice.

1975 through 1980 Uranus and Neptune are semi-sextile. Minor irritations begin. The psychic wave meets every day challenges and the whole concept of the intangible arts and sciences will have been reconsidered by those who previously ignored them or opposed them. Music, creative writing, and all the creative arts begin to be more unique and a lot of unique entertainers will make their appearance on the scene.

1985 is a number five and is ruled by Mercury. This is a number two (Moon) and a three (Jupiter). This is a great year for different methods of communication coming into existence, especially one new form will have presented itself. Little individual communities will begin to look at themselves a little more clearly. People born in this year will be great communicators and one born into this year will become an expert and attain a measure of greatness in the field of communication, writing, lecturing and teaching. Also a person will come on the scene during this year who will be very influential with his words; perhaps a foreign born person. Things will take on a more subjective-objective balance, but with the underlying influence of trying to understand ourselves, our communities, education, religion, foreign affairs. People will try to strike a balance between foreign affairs, the far away and the things near at hand. A new kind of neighborliness may present itself resulting in a beginning awareness that we may indeed be our brothers keeper.

1986 is a number six and is ruled by Venus. This is a two (Moon) and a four (Earth). It is a year of the woman and practical considerations for her welfare in all things. It is beauty in clothing but with practicality. It is love, being loved and loving. It is love with realism and loyalty. It is love with a down to earth caring and attitude. It is money with a practical attitude. There may be a drive during this year of women to be at their finest and adopting a little more femininity without losing their equal rights. The females born in this year may also have this kind of balanced drive. Perhaps a great love story will present itself that will have great international appeal.

1987 is a number seven and is ruled by Neptune. This is a two (Moon) and a give (Mercury). This represents musical expression, poetic idealism and dancing and the people born into this year will be good at all these things. The influence gives psychic talent as the people born in this year seem to be able to tune in on the intangibles of the universe. It is a year where a great inspirational preacher and teacher will show himself. This is a year when we may have to face what we really do believe, putting our money where our mouths are, so to speak. People born in this year can be secretive but they can also be very sacrificial if they care about something or someone. They should also be completely honest in all their affairs. It compares, somewhat to 1978. It is also the year of the entrepreneur, those among us who would take the risk to insure others job chances.

1988 is a number eight and is ruled by Saturn. This is a combination of a two (Moon) and a six (Venus). This Saturn influence is a discipline and responsibility to love, money, emotions and feelings. It will be a year when we may return to the old standards of discipline and responsibility with love and all that pertains to the affections. Perhaps, there will be a return to the old standards of responsibility where finances are concerned. In other words, it may be a year where we as a people will have to make some serious decisions about money and the economy; perhaps getting back to the old time basics. It is a year of business and father (authority figure) influenced, and with values in their proper perspective. Those born in this year will be able to put discipline and responsibility with love and/or the monetary values.

1989 is a number nine and is ruled by Mars. This is a combination of the Moon and Neptune as co-rulers. This will be a very active year with an accent on sports. However, any nine year can lead to war. This doesn't means that there will be war necessarily, maybe only rumors of war. It means that the tendency does exist. Keep in mind that if there is war, it will be a holy (or spiritual) war, fighting over spiritual ideologies. This year of 1989 may be karmic in its influence, filled with either deception or activity toward high ideals for mankind. It is fire so that the fearlessness of Mars may take us forward in positive activity but there is also tolerance and compassion underlying great boldness and aggressiveness. The people born in this year will be like that, bold with tolerance; aggressive with compassion; action based on faith.

1990 is a number ten and is ruled by the Sun. This is a one and a nine and is co-ruled by Mars. The years 1989 and 1990 are years where great force can take place, making it a climate for war; where great leaders will battle for prominence. It can represent a new decade for initiating new positive purposes for mankind and going to the other side of the coin, negative steps for mankind. Either way, to one potential or another, a new leader can come to the fore this year. It is either action toward cosmic destiny where the light can shine on all men or it is action by world leaders satisfying their own vane glory and leading us to defeat. People born in this year are born leaders who possess a lot of energy. On the positive side those born in this year may have a lot of self confidence and determination.

1991 is a number twenty and is ruled by the Moon. This is emotional, domestic, mother influenced (meaning protective and inward). The people born in this year will tend to be protective but with the underlying influence of nine (Mars) they will be very active and perhaps very active in their homes and the domestic sphere of life. The influence has to do with caring, nurturing, family and inner emotional values. Generally speaking it is a year filled with sensitivities, intense moods, public demands and needs. It is the year of the home and a realization of the needs of the home, housing, food, world hunger, and it is this realization where our first real strength is located.

1992 is a number three and is ruled by Jupiter. This is a combination of a one (Sun) and a two (Moon). It is a year that will deal with feminine and masculine values on a more equalized basis and perhaps, we will come to men and women in proper relationship to each other as it should be. This year also can deal with foreign affairs, religion and higher education in a more logical way. It would be higher education as dictated by the 90's rather than the previous 80's. A new system of education may be introduced. It can be a year that will force us to understand a more total view of society (and the world) rather than just the tiny portion of our own space, wherever our space is. The people born in this year will innately have this understanding. They will also have the correct slant of equalized man and woman relationships and not the distortions we have had in the past. These people will be able to touch into the true cosmic purpose of man and woman relationships to each other and to the universe itself the true balance of positive and negative; meaning electric or outgoing, and magnetic or incoming.

1993 is a number twenty two and is ruled by Uranus. Again this year represents a cosmic year. The people born in this year will be very independent as most twenty two people are. They will be inventive, and difficult to really know. Many unexpected things will take place during this year. Perhaps, again some great discovery will be made that will change the pace of society in general. The people born in this year are different, individualistic, but people who will also be trying to make their individualistic or progressive concepts workable in a changing world. The difference between this year of 1993 and 1939 is that in 1993 Mars-Jupiter set the pattern to the Uranian influence. In other words Mars has control over the Jupiter concepts. In 1939 it is Jupiter-Mars where Jupiter had control over the actions and energy. Jupiter is expansion, religion, philosophy, foreign affairs, higher education; Mars is action, energy, masculinity and outward thrust.

1994 is a number five and is ruled by Mercury. This is a two and a three and is co-ruled by the Moon and Jupiter. This is communication as it deals with community endeavors and relatives. However, the people born in this year can be talented at writing and have subjective and objective reasoning in balance. Those born in this year will be much more NOW people but with the ability to also be foresighted concerning the future when need be. They deal with the immediate but yet can think of preparing for the distant tomorrow. This makes them very integrated people and hence very successful. They can be teachers, religious writers, foreign correspondents and world travelers whether actual traveling or just traveling with their imaginations. When you have a Mercury year you can have the influence of the Gemini Mercury or the Virgo Mercury. The influence of the Gemini Mercury is variable, scattered, enthusiastic, accepting most things without question or criticism realizing all have a place in the vast scheme of things. If the influence take on the Virgo Mercury, the people will be precise, critical, but also critical in the sense of deciding whether something can be utilized to the benefit of not only themselves but service to others. This is a criticism that analyzes whether a particular method can last and work ten years from now or just be a flash in the pan.

1995 is a number six and is ruled by Venus. This is a two (Moon) and a four (Earth) and deals with art, clothing, love, money or anything else that is of value to men and women. It sometimes introduces new lines of fashion, but also gives a great appreciation of all things artistic. A new artist, a great singer, can come out of this year. The people born in this year need harmony around them to be at their best. They can be diplomats or counselors. This year can represent diplomacy in foreign affairs at their best. There is also a financial side to this year with practical down to earth approach. This year also represents love and caring as a responsibility and duty.

1996 is a number seven and is ruled by Neptune. This is a two (Moon) and a five (Mercury). When we deal with a seven it can either be idealism or illusion. The people born into this year are difficult to know for they can be either very secretive or talkative, but if they are talkative more than likely they will talk about abstract spiritual things. However if they are negative in their approach to life, may talk about how hard they have it in a self pitying kind of fashion. It all depends upon whether they are responding to the higher vibration of this year or the lower vibration. The people born in this year are also capable of great compassion and tolerance. They can also become involved in drugs and alcohol or high ideals that lead them into prominence with their writings or fine example of teaching. The influence of this year represents the unseen, the nebulous trying to be expressed. It represents the person who either desires to sacrifice for brothers, sisters and relatives or one who is forced to do so by circumstances.

1997 is a number eight and is ruled by Saturn. This is a two (Moon) and a six (Venus) and has to do with business and financial well being. It can be a year of re-establishing business values and the responsibilities and duties of same. This year is father oriented and authority geared. It is a year where we must come to terms with reality. It is factual and the teacher. We may learn something during this year as a people and perhaps may learn lessons the hard way. This may be a time when we have to get down to basics and take a realistic look at where we have been and where we are going, not only with business, but with all things we value such as love and resources. The people born in this year can give great devotion to a loved one and/or they can in addition give great devotion to a business or an ambition.

1998 is a number nine and is ruled by Mars. This is a two (Moon) and a seven (Neptune) and is action, energy and sometimes wars or rumors of wars. It is either positive action or destructive action. This year can be geared to sports and may introduce a new sports super star or during this year a new sports star is born. This year is masculine, passionate, sexual, but with an underlying influence of compassion, tolerance and sensitivity. It represents people born in this year who appear to have an iron glove, but underneath is a velvet fist. A lot of things can be accomplished in a Mars year for when it is used in a positive way, the people can be work-a-holics. However, if it goes the negative way, they can take in too many sexual escapades, drinking and general dissipation. Another positive look is faith in action, having self confidence and faith combined making for great people. It can also give great activity in spiritual matters for people as a whole.

1999 is a number ten and is ruled by the Sun. It is a ten that is composed of a two (Moon) and an eight (Saturn). This year represents disciplined, organized leadership. Ambition will be rightly directed. This influence is emotion and discipline combined well. It is at its best cooperation between the nurturing factors of life and the authority force so that the people born in this year give a new wave of family at-one-ness. It is a ten so it is very much into ego gratification in its true form. By that I mean it is knowing one's purpose and fulfilling it in confidence, and supporting this with discipline in order to get anything wanted out of life. It may be a year when strong destined events take place. It is the door to a new century. A new leader in world affairs shows up about this time. The over-all influence represents people with confidence, discipline and the right mixture of sensitive emotions.

2000 is a number two and is ruled by a positive Moon. The new century will be moon ruled with overtones of Pluto. It may be the century of the woman, when woman comes into her true role in the cosmic scheme of things. The year 2000 will present many fluctuating changes in domesticity and family relations. Emotions and feelings will come into a positive productive era rather than the negative idea we now have with emotions and feelings. It will begin an era of the couple in its true and universal form. This will be the century of relatedness. Emotional attitudes and feelings will finally be understood by humans instead of being abused.

From the year 1989 to the year 2000 will give true illumination and spiritual re-birth for man. Great souls will be born during this period. It is also a time when those born before come into their own as destined spiritual leaders. This period represents a Uranus Neptune conjunction in Capricorn when important changes in our consciousness will take place. It is a time for creating a new world. Perhaps, the intangibles will come into manifestation in a different form than we have been familiar. Technology

The Day of Your Birth

combines the intangibles with concrete form and a union of science and spirituality is born. Science will discover a way to actually see the spirit forces, to see music and sound. These will become visible to the eye through an invented device.

The twenty-first century will be a Pluto century (as well as introducing the Aquarian age) where many upheavals and changes with healing and energy will take place. It will bring us in tune with the cosmic force of healing and we may finally begin to understand what really makes for illness and what it means to be really healthy. Perhaps, we will discover that illness comes from being disconnected from the Universal Force. Those in tune with the true God or Universal Force (call it what you will) will have a certain health not only of body, but mind and spirit. Those out of tune, will have a disturbed (or unhealthy bodily function to one degree or another). The twenty first century will enlighten people to the point where they will begin to understand truly how to heal their own parts. There will be a more holistic view of health, body, mind and spirit.

The Pluto years will be 2009, 2018, 2027, 2036, 2045, 2054, 2063, 2072, 2081, 2090, 2099.

During the twenty-first century we will have a strong destiny for the survival of man. We got off course during the materialistic productive years from 1945 through 1982. We have to get back on balance with the spiritual balance of life. We have to get back to our true sense of worth where our spiritual connections and understanding are concerned. Cutting ourselves off from that source has been an unhealthy era for man.

It was in 1979 when the business influence changed, when different possibilities were to come into focus. We may not have fully realized it but this is when changes began to happen. It would be 1988 before we would realize how to straighten it out. We can really go one step at a time with these influences because a given influence seems to last a decade. This is what we need to be aware of for we either go into that year with a positive look at the experiences of growth for that year or we relate to a negative, more disconnecting influence. It is a question of the different parts of a decade that have to be taken step by step to completion. Ever so often cosmic people are born and of course the people born in 1901 are very unusual and universal people. Healers could have been born in 1901. They are Pluto ruled people regardless of the sign they were born. They didn't have anything in their characters that accepted the impossible. We are going to introduce a year like that again in the year 2009. There were people born in 1901 who were very positive and those who may have been very negative, never in the middle. There are those born in 1901 who would build vast material and financial empires and those who took the other course of trying to understand the true destiny of man.

The people born during the last five days of a given year and the first five days of the next year are transitional people. They are Capricorns capable of possessing the influence of both years. They are the bridge people who fill in the gaps left by everyone else. This is also true of people born at the end of the century and the beginning of the new century. In this case we take three years before the century and three years into the new century.

The twenty first century will not only be a great Pluto century that will introduce new methods of healing, rejuvenation of vital parts of the body, even bringing certain people back to life, but there will be much more accurate psychological knowledge introduced which will be more and more in combination with astrology, numerology and all the other cosmic sciences.

Women will have a greater role to play in the twenty-first century, roles that will have a vital part in the destiny of man. By the end of the twenty first century women may play an even stronger part than men in social roles. This does not mean women will lose their femininity as such, it just means they will take their rightful place in society and world affairs showing and proving a strength they knew they had all along.

Centuries

The centuries starting with the year 1000 represents the Sun which would play its influence out with ego, male status, leaders competing for GLORY and land acquisition.

The century of 1100 is a Pluto century but in this case it may have represented the more destructive side of Pluto like death, illness, and perhaps secret treaties, since Pluto wasn't discovered as yet, its co-ruler Mars would deal with wars and rumors of war. **(called the 12th century)**

The century of 1200 would have a Jupiter influence such as: adventure, gambling at the toss of a hat, religious intrigue, everything bigger and bolder. Perhaps, the extravagance of kings, lords, etc. Longer distant travel in ships would be important and would begin. **(called the 13th century)**

The century of 1300 would be Uranus ruled but since Uranus wasn't discovered yet, it would be influenced by Earth. This was materialistic, practical, realistic. Perhaps some among them were independent and somewhat unconventional for the times. It would play the Uranus part by things happening unpredictably. It would represent castration, mental, spiritual and physical. **(called the 14th century)**

The Day of Your Birth

The century 1400 would be Mercury which would represent writing, communication, relatives, and all things that had to do with community efforts. Greater travel than before with outlying cities would begin. Paying greater attention to neighbors in the immediate environment would be important. It was a subjective year. (called the 15th century)

The century 1500 was a Venus century. This represented art, music, love stores, romance, ornate decorating with a conscious determination to be in harmony not only with loved ones, but neighboring countries as well. However, many times Venus efforts don't end up that way regardless of the well meaning efforts. (called the 16th century)

The century 1600 was a Neptune century dealing with psychic, all the intangibles, delusion, illusion, inspiration, spiritual things, deception, faith, the idealistic and imagination. Perhaps, the whole century had an element of sacrifice to it. Music would be produced that would last forever. (called the 17th century)

The century 1700 was a Saturn century which dealt with patriarchy, the father ruled century, business, discipline, responsibility, conventions, strict adherence to the law. There were also severe disciplines by the authority figures. (called the 18th century)

The century 1800 was a Mars century where there were wars and rumors of wars. It was a masculine, energetic century. There was a pioneering effort, excitement toward new frontiers, sexual emphasis, very male ruled. Mars is the pioneer, and gave the daring to drive forward to untamed lands. (called the 19th century)

The century 1900 is a Sun ruled century and male ruled. It would be the beginning of more sexual openness and freedom. Fearless attitudes, pioneering new forms of entertainment. It would be a new wave of destiny with energy and all things that are associated with movement forward. By the end of the twentieth century we will have tapped the energy of the Sun itself for our heat and energy. (called the 20th century)

I would like to quote from Alan Leo's book Esoteric Astrology.

> *Once in every cycle of twenty-six thousand years, the time taken for the whole of the zodias to revolve around a given point, a superior man is born; to many he is known as the Manu, the divine man, the law giver striking a note of the whole cycle.*
>
> *Every two thousand years a human being is born in whom every human principle is personified and he strikes the note for the sign of the zodiac he represents, for his is a race teacher, striking the note of a new religion to suit the race born under that particular sign (and times).*

Every century a man is born who stands ahead of the race, and again every decade sees a particular man born who is superior in expression to those who follow him.
–Alan Leo

And it is to this last statement I want attention called . . . for every decade a person (man or woman) is born who represents and personifies the influence of that decade, whether he/she is a Political leader, a popular entertainer, film star, athlete, etc., but whatever he/she is he/she becomes a hero to that decade.

And as we go on, every year someone is born that represents the year more than any other person born in that year, and then every day a person is born who is synonymous with that day. Alan Leo seems to have been right for as we research this theory it seems to work.

NUMERICAL RULERSHIPS

Sun is #1
Moon is #2
Mercury is #5
Venus is #6
Mars is #9
Jupiter #3
South Node is 89 or 98

Saturn is #8
Uranus is #22
Neptune is #7
Pluto is #11
Earth is #4
North Node is 36 or 63

These are the numerical evaluations for the Sun, Moon and planets as I have researched them to be.

CONCLUSION

I have long been an advocate of watching all of life for when we do that we also make interesting discoveries about ourselves in the process. Below are some stories with human interest that deals with awareness.

In the course of time pursuing my career in counseling others I have learned to be very observant of mannerisms and movements. The following are stories of those observations.

There are two little girls who live next door to me, one is five years old and the other one is almost three. They come over once in a while to play the piano or I should say I am trying to teach them to play the scales. One day

The Day of Your Birth

they brought their little dog Kippy with them. Monica, the oldest, said to Kippy, "You can listen to us play the scales, but you can't play the piano." Kippy just stood there, moved his head a little like he understood and seemed to listen intently to his little mistresses while they struggled with the scales. Because I always give the girls a little piece of candy after they play the scales, Monica immediately said to Kippy, "You have been a good dog, you can have a piece of candy, too." Needless to say he got the candy when he lined up beside the girls to receive it.

Another story involves a little dog I met on my walks. He saw me coming about a block away. When I got up close to him I said, "What a cute little dog you are." Well, he immediately marked his territory and then followed me. After a block, I turned to him and said, "You better go back home. I don't want you following me." He looked at me and didn't move. I said it again, "Don't follow me." This time stronger. He turned around and went home. The next time I took a walk he turned and walked away from me. I thought he was either hurt or he understood me. So the third time I went by I spoke to him. He responded with a bark, but didn't follow me and now we are friends.

There is a young man about nineteen who does things mostly for my neighbor, little chores. Last winter he was clearing off a very heavy snow from this neighbor's driveway. I usually do my own but I asked him how much he would charge to do mine. His fee was nominal so I let him do my driveway. This young man has a dog, a dog that is devoted to his master and always goes with him everywhere and this day was no exception. His dog was playing with a couple other dogs in the neighborhood while his master was working. His dog saw him come in to my house to get paid. but the dog didn't see him leave. It wasn't long after the young man left, I heard a banging on my front door. I went to the door and it was the dog. I said, "Are you looking for your master?" He barked. I pointed up the street and said, "He went that way." The dog barked again and dashed up the street.

Another day I saw a bird outside my bedroom window on a bush nearby. The bird clearly saw me at the window. The bird chirped. I answered back. This kept up for a good minute or two. It was very clear the bird was trying to communicate and return my comments. It must be the tone of the voice that attracts them to some and makes them fly away from others. They seem to know and have fantastic instincts in this direction.

One morning a little baby bird was trying to learn to fly. There is a red shed in my back yard and the little bird was heading right toward it. The mother bird was racing back and forth in panic. The little bird hit the shed head-on but wasn't hurt for it wasn't going that fast. It fell to the ground and the mother started chirping as if she were bawling it out. The bird shook himself, wiggled around as if to say, "Well, I guess I am all in one piece.

The mother made some sounds and the bird tried again, this time in a different direction than the hard shed. It was a cute little scene for the bird learned the hard way which direction to go, and learned about immovable objects.

A newly born rabbit was near a bush in the back yard. I happened to approach very near the bush. The rabbit was so very small and looked like he was just getting the feel of his legs and beginning to get around. He saw me, this big human being, perhaps, the first one he ever saw. He seemed frightened to death. He stood like a statue. The minute my head and body turned a little, he shot out of that spot like an explosion from a cannon. He probably went home to tell his mother what a big sight he saw coming toward him.

One summer when the monarch butterflies were out and about, I was sitting quietly on my front steps. There is a little fence by some flowers in front of the steps. A butterfly was on the flowers; then it flew onto the fence. I tried to communicate silently to the butterfly to come sit on my hand. I was ever so still. After a few seemingly potent transferences of thought, the butterfly actually did come and sit on my hand to my utter amazement. It was fine for a few seconds until a car went by that seemed to scare the butterfly so it flew back to the fence. I communicated again that the car wouldn't bother it. The butterfly came back and sat on my hand and when another car went by, it fluttered and didn't seem to be exactly at ease but it didn't move. Finally it flew away. This was only a matters of a couple of minutes but it seemed like several minutes at the time.

There was a robin feeding worms to her young baby bird. She began to tire of this so she tried to teach the baby bird to find worms on its own. The baby bird did poorly. The mother seemed discussed so thinking perhaps her baby might starve she pulled a worm out of the ground herself and flung it at the baby bird with her beak. So it seems even birds get out of patience at times.

We make our lives better through a greater appreciation and greater awareness of all the life forms around us.

Also, be more aware of yourself. You may be missing your greatest asset in not doing that which you haven't done before. We cannot separate ourselves from life around us. The degree of awareness affects the quality of our own life.

Bernice Prill Grebner
April 17, 1988

The Day of Your Birth

EPILOGUE

Perhaps a warm combustion
Would have seared us
Had not the relieving wind
Blown our sparks skyward
And concealed us from each other
Amidst the fireflies

David Grebner March 13, 1977

REFERENCES

Poems by Bret Harte

Esoteric Astrology by Alan Leo

Inspiration from writings of:

Alexander Ruperti

Stephen Arroyo